Advance praise for *How the Winds Laughed*

Two ordinary people with extraordinary dreams set sail from Marina del Rey near Los Angeles in *Wa*, a 28-foot Swedish racing boat, for what the young couple believed would be The Great Adventure. After thirty-two months of immersion in foreign cultures, of challenges to their relationship and to their survival, they learned that the seas care nothing for human life. *How the Winds Laughed* is a detailed and deeply honest treasure. Not only do Greene's writing gifts shine, she lays bare her heart.

    Vella Munn, author of more than 50 adventure, historical, and romance novels

How the Winds Laughed is a compelling memoir about two novice ocean sailors embarking on a voyage around the world. En route they suffer enormous mental and physical stress and learn more, perhaps, than they wanted to know about each other. There is much to learn from this well-written book: about the sea, sailing, island cultures, and personal relationships. *How the Winds Laughed* is as much for armchair sailors as it is for experienced mariners.

    Anthony Dalton, *Alone Against the Arctic* and eight other books about the sea

Author Addie Greene has crafted an exciting memoir of circumnavigation, taking readers on an amazing ride as she and her husband Pete, along with their cat Coco, sail around the world in 1971—a time before the Internet and GPS. Greene deftly balances the ordeals of mechanical difficulties and violent ocean storms with the beauty of discovering new lands and friends from cultures around the world. *How the Winds Laughed* is a story of love, adventure, and inspiration for anyone who dreams of life on the high seas.

    Nancy Owens Barnes, *South to Alaska*

How the Winds Laughed

How the Winds Laughed

Sailing Around the World in a 28-Foot Wooden Boat

Addie Greene

JACKSON COUNTY LIBRARY SERVICES
MEDFORD OREGON 97501

McLean, Virginia

Fuze Publishing LLC
www.fuzepublishing.com

 1350 Beverly Road, Suite 115-162
 McLean, Virginia 22101

 P.O. Box 3128
 Ashland, OR 97520

How the Winds Laughed, Sailing Around the World in a 28-Foot Wooden Boat Copyright © 2012 by Addie Greene. All rights reserved. No part of this book may be reproduced, scanned, or distributed in printed or electronic form without permission. Please do not participate in or encourage piracy of copyrighted materials in violation of the author's rights. Purchase only authorized editions.

Book design by Ray Rhamey

ISBN 978-0-9849908-6-3

Library of Congress Control Number: 2012945589

To Pete

Acknowledgments

This book began as a series of ninety articles written for the *Santa Barbara News-Press*. Over a period of fourteen months my editor, Molly Tinsley, helped me craft it into creative nonfiction. As she said, she was "trying to find the statue in that hunk of marble." Her effort was painstaking, deliberate, and sometimes maddening. She put in more time and labor than any New York editor ever would have, even Maxwell Perkins in his day. I cannot thank her enough for believing in me and my work.

I also want to thank my critique partners, Gloria Boyd, Melissa Brown, Mary Brubaker, Delores DeLeon, Sonja Ferrera, Patricia Florin, Ellen Gardner, Marilyn Joy, Kirk Showalter, Deborah Rothschild, and Dorothy Vogel, who suffered through not one but two readings of the entire manuscript five pages at a time and gave me valuable advice on how to improve the book and make it more accessible to non-sailors.

Prologue

It was 1963, and I was the first copygirl at the *Los Angeles Times* since World War II, the only woman in a newsroom of two hundred. Although I wore dresses and business suits, I concentrated on making the men forget my gender by working harder than they did.

A year later I married Pete Eastman, a fellow writer and the first man who ever cared about my mind as well as my body. My homebody self kicked in. I still worked full-time as family breadwinner, but I also believed that a wife should cook, clean, and iron her husband's shirts. Because my mother had been a tyrant whom my father and I both feared, I wanted to right the scales by being a "good" wife.

This tenuous mix of the liberated and the unexamined life exploded when Pete talked me into sailing around the world. "I want a Great Adventure," he said, taking a puff on his cigarette and blowing the smoke to the side as he nailed me with his eyes. The implication: what we had wasn't enough.

Pete and his father had taught me to sail on a 21-foot Victory in Newport Bay, California. I'd gotten hooked on the wind in my face, the rigor of steering the boat so she'd hum through the water, the illusion of freedom. Skimming the water with the pelicans and gulls, I soared with them.

But sailing in Newport Bay wasn't the same as going to sea, and that's what Pete's craving for heroism seemed to demand. A trip around the world. "What about storms?" I asked. "What about navigation? You don't know about those things."

"I'll learn. And I'll teach you. Will you go?" His face was as intense as I'd ever seen it. Would I lose him if I said no? If he stayed, would he forever blame me for sentencing him to the mundane? *No* didn't seem to be an option.

Besides, my job was going nowhere. The *Times* would never make a reporter out of me because I'd have to intern on the police beat swing shift, too dangerous for a five-foot-one female, the managing editor told me. I was delivering coffee and library clips to the reporters and fighting despair. I'd worked hard at Pomona College for *this*?

Wasn't Pete offering me an escape from frustration and boredom, inviting me on a quest too? I thought of Galahad, Frodo. It didn't occur to me that our adventure might be more like Don Quixote's.

I bit my lip hard enough to taste blood; he puffed on that cigarette and stared. And then I agreed. "I want a Great Adventure too," I whispered. "Can we learn enough to do it safely?"

"We won't go until we have," he assured me.

We bought a 22-square-meter, a wooden racing boat shaped like a pencil, and sailed her almost every weekend. I read all the sailing books I could find, learned nautical terms, studied books on weather and astronomy. Pete mastered celestial navigation and how to use a sextant. Later, he taught me to drag the sun to the horizon with the sextant, capture the time, and calculate longitude using trigonometric tables.

Then, in 1966, Pete was swept into the Vietnam War. All through that dreary time, I followed him around the U.S., then to Japan while he served near Saigon and in Tokyo, resolutely keeping the dream alive.

After his discharge, we worked as journalists until we'd saved enough money to buy a P-28, a Swedish racing boat built of mahogany and oak. We named her *Wa,* using the character 和(peace/harmony)—something I'd learned when I lived in Tokyo. Though Pete had begun his first year at Ventura College of Law, the dean gave him a leave of absence.

Pete's parents, both sailors, supported our quest, but my father believed it was a waste of time.

"How long will it take you?" he asked.

"We probably could make it in a year and a half," I blithely replied.

"I hope you're right," he said.

It was January 10, 1971. There were no personal computers, Internet, global positioning systems, or cell phones. Long-distance phone calls were ridiculously expensive. People communicated by writing letters; overseas mail could take weeks to arrive. The Civil Rights Movement was a current event, the Women's Liberation Movement had just begun, birth control pills had been sold in the United States for ten years, abortion was illegal, and the sexual revolution had touched only the hippies.

And Pete and I set sail from Marina del Rey Harbor, Los Angeles, bound for French Polynesia, our first stop in circumnavigating the globe.

Bon Voyage
or
SNAFU

"Help me!" My husband's voice pierced the tumult of wind and water.

Wa lurched and tossed me against her ash ribs. I untangled myself from the bedding and stumbled naked through the cabin, dragged myself up the three steps of the companionway, and grabbed the cabin top. Spray hit me in the face. In the dim light of a new moon, I could barely make out Pete's form on the stern twelve feet away. Above him, the wind vane that steered the boat had disappeared from its bracket.

A wave broke over him, and he staggered. "I've got to get the vane back aboard," he called. Take the tiller." The wind whipped the words from his mouth.

Grabbing the flashlight by the companionway, I scuttled under the boom and unlashed the helm. Foot on the tiller, I pushed *Wa* back on course, held the flashlight for Pete with one hand and hung onto the side of the cockpit with the other. Thank God, he'd taken the time to put on his safety harness. He was wearing nothing else but his glasses.

It was 8:45 p.m., January 24, 1971. We and our chocolate-point Siamese cat Coco were deep in the tropics and more than a thousand miles from land, two weeks out from California, bound for Nuku Hiva, one of the Marquesas Islands.

With the wind blowing nearly thirty knots and kicking up ten-foot seas, Pete struggled with the vane and rudder of the self-steering gear, which flopped back and forth under the stern. Each time a wave hit, I feared he'd be thrown into the sea. The harness, made of three-inch nylon webbing that crisscrossed his chest and belted his waist, was sturdy enough, but if he fell overboard, he might not have the strength to climb back. I wasn't wearing mine and didn't dare leave the cockpit.

It took Pete nearly an hour to drag the vane and its rudder aboard and secure them. Clambering into the cockpit, he shook water from his blond hair and beard and straightened his lithe, lean body. He looked like a golden retriever with a lopsided grin.

My heart beat faster, and I smiled back. Even after being married for nearly seven years, knowing every inch of his body and peering into the dark places of his mind, I still could turn to mush at the sight of him.

When I met him, I believed men wanted nothing from me but sex. He'd swept me off my feet by being the first man to ask for more. He'd burrowed through my shyness and pulled out a violet I didn't know was there.

"This is the pits," he said, "but we're OK."

"Should I take the first watch?" Because we now had no self-steering device, I assumed we were doomed to take turns manually steering, which meant twelve hours apiece a day on the tiller, an arduous proposition.

"Hopefully, you won't have to. I'll rig lines to the tiller to try to make her self-steer. But first I've got to put clothes on. I'm freezing my ass off."

He went below, returned in his yellow nylon jumpsuit, and looked me up and down. "You're shivering," he said. "I'll steer while you get dry."

Although I'd been in the cockpit, I was just as wet from spray as he'd been from breaking waves. I licked the salt from my lips, toweled off, dressed in my red foul-weather jumpsuit, tucked my unruly hair inside the hood, put on my glasses, and buckled on my harness.

He spent a futile hour trying to make the boat self-steer, then made coffee for me, poured it into the stainless steel Thermos, and went to bed. I was to wake him at 12:30.

Wa sliced through the water at six, sometimes seven knots, dashing across waves that broke over the bow, kicking up spray that beat on my jumpsuit. Water cascaded aft along the decks until it ran out the scuppers. My face and hands were wet and cold, but the coffee warmed my insides.

This won't be so bad, I told myself. *An inconvenience. And it will give me a good story for the* News-Press, *if I can take time from steering to write it.* (The *Santa Barbara News-Press,* for which I'd worked before we left, had agreed to buy my stories at ten dollars apiece.) *Pete will fix the self-steering when we get to the Marquesas. I can steer for a few days. Let the winds laugh at us. We're young and strong and will endure.*

At just over twenty-eight feet from bow to stern, twenty and a half feet at the waterline, not quite eight feet wide, and weighing 5955 pounds—hardly bigger than a Ford Expedition—*Wa* was one of the smallest boats ever to attempt a circumnavigation.

Living aboard was like living in a walk-in closet. Pete and I shared the triangular double bunk in the bow with six five-gallon water jugs lashed port and starboard and our clothing shelves above and forward of the jugs. Under the berth a seventeen-gallon water tank was attached to a pump and sink in the galley. Opposite the sink a built-in table served for navigation. Pete had taken the head out of its closet, complaining that having a special room for a toilet was a waste of space. Its replacement was a bucket.

I would learn to envy male anatomy. Pete went to the lee rail and peed over the side. I sat in the cabin on the metal bucket, holding on to the quarterberths as it slithered back and forth during heavy weather, creasing my backside with the rim's ring. Then I had to carry the bucket up the companionway, being careful not to spill its contents, and, holding its handle and attached rope, dump it over the lee rail. This dedicated bucket lived in the lazarette, a locker aft of the cockpit.

Because *Wa* was small, we were often wet. Coco hated it. He wailed with that awful, piercing screech of a Siamese and stomped back and forth in the cabin.

Cooking in heavy weather was a lesson in gymnastics. Feet wide, I braced my knees against the port bunk under the stove and jammed my hip into the corner of the sink. The two-burner kerosene stove, on gimbals to keep it level no matter what the angle of the boat's heel, swung back and forth, sometimes sloshing water or food onto the berth.

I made doughnuts only in calm weather and tried to be very careful with boiling liquids and grease. I baked in a cast iron skillet. After making Scotch shortbread that tasted chalky instead of sweet, I realized I'd used cornstarch instead of powdered sugar. I started labeling containers.

I did the cooking because I enjoyed it and because Pete made almost all sail changes. Seemed like a good trade to me. Although I didn't mind going forward to handle halyards in light winds, I hated it when the foredeck was wet, bouncy, and dangerous.

Having only forty-seven gallons of water, we had to conserve. We used the saltwater pump at the sink for washing our faces and teeth. We washed our clothes and bathed in saltwater, using liquid dish soap, for bar soap wouldn't lather, scooping buckets of water from the sea and dumping them over our naked bodies as we stood braced on the stern holding onto the backstay. My hair got gummy, and clothing rinsed in saltwater never dried. Alone in the tropics, we seldom wore clothes anyway.

Because *Wa* carried only thirteen gallons of gasoline, we rarely ran her engine and thus had no source of electricity. Leaving with a fully charged battery, we seldom used the cabin lights, relying on kerosene lanterns instead. We were out of range of ship-to-shore radio frequencies after the first day.

We didn't have a refrigerator. When the fresh food was gone, we ate canned. Carrots, onions, and potatoes lasted unrefrigerated, if kept dry, for a month or more. Unopened pumpkins survived three months. Eggs fresh from the poultry farm and greased with Vaseline lasted six weeks.

All our choices were dictated by money, or the lack of it. We paid $4500 for *Wa*. For that amount we could buy only a wooden boat—Fiberglass, steel, and ferrocement were out of our price range for anything big enough to be safe at sea. If we'd known then that *Wa's* cockpit and cabin trunk would have to be varnished every three months, not to mention the other endless maintenance she required, we might've worked an extra year and gone with a larger Fiberglass craft.

We spent another $4500 fitting her out, starting with a 44-pound Danforth anchor and two hundred feet of chain. We bought Dacron and made a genoa or genny (the larger foresail) and jib (the smaller foresail). Our only extravagances were diving masks fitted with prescription lenses for both of us. We knew we'd skin dive in most ports, and we wanted to be able to see the marvelous reef creatures of the tropics.

I stocked six months' supply of food, guesstimated on the basis of what we ate every week. I was on a first-name-basis at Smart & Final Iris Company, where I bought caseloads of canned beans, tomatoes, chicken, and ham and gunny sacks of flour and rice. Sailing by the seats of our pants, we could only hope the remaining $1000 of our savings would last until we crossed the Pacific.

The night after we lost the self-steering, the wind still blew nearly thirty knots. It screamed through the rigging and drove walls of water to whack against *Wa*.

When I climbed to the cockpit for my midnight watch, I had to grab a new hand-hold every time I took a step. Spray stung my face, and the boat's violent motion forced me to brace myself, even when sitting.

I'd been straining against the tiller for an hour when I heard something like a chunk of wood whapping against the mainsail. I shone the flashlight on the main but could see nothing. One learns on a boat to be suspicious of strange noises, so I kept searching. Still nothing.

My mind was in a fog. I'd gotten only five hours of sleep the night before, I wasn't used to steering twelve hours a day, and my body felt battered by the rough seas. I stopped looking and let my mind go into autopilot.

Two hours later I called Pete to take over. "I heard something like a block hitting the main," I said, "but I'm not hearing it anymore."

He shone the flashlight where I pointed and peered into the darkness. "It's probably nothing," he said.

Exhaustion made fools of us.

The following afternoon, as I washed dishes, Pete's cry of alarm sounded once more.

When I raced to the cockpit, he jabbed his finger at the jumper stay, a triangular piece of metal used to hold the mast in place. It was swinging free on the starboard side. The steel shrouds attached to the jumper flopped like loose strings. The mast quivered.

At once I realized what that whapping against the mainsail had been. "Oh my God, what're we going to do?" I asked. For at least twelve hours the stay had been broken and the mast in danger of toppling.

Pete thrust the tiller into my hand, scrambled to the halyard, and brought down the mainsail.

"I've got to go up the mast," he said when he returned.

I didn't argue. Shoving down fears of what I would do if he hit the deck and died, I steered *Wa* under the jib alone while Pete fetched his tools. With not enough sail up to keep her steady, she bucked like an ornery horse. It took the power of both my hands to keep her on course.

This new problem was not just an inconvenience: it was potentially dangerous. *Wa's* mast towered thirty feet from the deck with nothing to hold it in place but thin strands of wire. If the mast fell, *Wa* would be crippled. Losing the mast wouldn't kill us, of course, but sailing thirteen hundred miles with only the genoa or jib to power the boat would be a sea of troubles, as it were, and an unknown worthy of dread.

And I couldn't help. I wouldn't climb the mast even at a dock. I was too terrified of heights.

Pete attached the canvas bosun's chair to the halyard and put his tools in a bucket. Then, with a loud grunt, he pulled on the halyard to hoist himself up the mast. He got barely two feet above the boom as the heavy seas smacked him against the mast. He tried another pull, groaning with the effort, and his hands shook.

Twice more he tried; twice more he failed.

Discouraged, he slumped back into the cockpit and lit a cigarette.

"What are we going to do?" I asked.

"The wind'll die. It's not *supposed* to blow Force 6 in the northeast trades."

"I'm dead on my feet. I'm afraid I'll make a mistake and get us into bigger trouble."

He took the helm from me and hove to—pulling the tiller away from the direction of the wind and lashing it in order to keep the boat's forward motion to a minimum.

He put his arm around me and stroked my hair. "I'm sorry, babe. We're going to be OK."

"It's a bad beginning. I'm scared. And I just feel so, I don't know, like I don't want to go for two weeks without screwing."

Pete's voice softened. "Hey, there's no reason we have to keep on sailing. It's not a race. Let's take the night off and cuddle."

I smiled at his touch, my thoughts gladly side-tracked to romance.

The next morning, Pete double-reefed, or shortened, the mainsail and got us under way. He assumed that, with less sail up and lighter winds, *Wa* could handle the stress on the broken jumper stay until we could reach port.

Refreshed after sex and sleep, I washed my hair for the first time in more than two weeks by bracing myself at the top of the companionway and dunking my head in a bucket of saltwater.

I created so much lather from the dish soap that rinsing in

the bucket wouldn't work. So, eyes shut, I backed down the companionway and felt my way to the sink, where I pumped saltwater over my soapy hair until the lather was gone, much of it sloshed onto the floor.

"It's good to see you having so much fun," Pete remarked.

"And cleaning the cabin sole at the same time," I replied.

The next night, I woke to the now familiar call, "Addie, help!" I'd barely gotten to sleep and my body rebelled at the prospect of taking the tiller again. I yanked on my wet foul-weather gear and safety harness. With a sigh I climbed to the cockpit.

"It's the starboard spreader," he said. Shining the flashlight into the rigging, I saw dangling the foot-long piece of wood also used to hold up the mast.

I took the tiller and hove *Wa* to. The mast now had no support on the starboard side.

Pete scrambled about rigging running backstays—taut ropes from high up the mast to cleats aft of the cockpit—to provide extra support to the mast. We retreated below to wait for dawn.

Now there was no question: Pete had to get up that mast. And if he couldn't fix the spreader, what would we do? Could we make it to Nuku Hiva under jury rig? We were more than twelve hundred miles from port.

I sat in the cockpit, chewing on my fingers, while Pete, in protective jeans and a long-sleeved shirt, put his tools in a bucket and prepared a block and tackle. He attached the stationary pulley to his safety harness and threaded the main halyard through the moveable pulley. Then he began to tug on the halyard and slowly, slowly rose.

The mast swayed in a sixty-degree arc. I imagined him falling, hitting the deck, crippling himself. Then I stopped those thoughts. Instead, I stared at his back and whispered, "You can do it," willing him upward.

Every time the mast pivoted, it battered Pete against its metal track. He clung like a spider to its web, buffeted by the wind, and inched upward. If his legs hadn't been strong, he never would've been able to hang on. My fear turned to pride: *this is the man I love, a man of courage and resourcefulness. He will save us.*

When he reached the spreader, he stuck it back in its socket and bound the jumper to it with stainless steel rigging wire.

We were under way again by ten.

On February 9 at 10:30 in the morning, Pete yelled, "Land ho!"

I raced up on deck. A blue clump of volcanic island jutted four thousand feet from the sea off *Wa's* starboard bow. "The Marquesas! We did it!" I shrieked. I was so grateful I could've cried. Instead, I just stared, transfixed.

Coco, awakened by the shouting, ambled up the companionway and stretched. Then he sniffed the air. "Meow!" he said, pointing his nose at the island.

"You're right," I said. "Smart cat. Soon you won't be bouncing around and wet anymore." I didn't tell him his reprieve would last no more than a month.

Suddenly I had many things to do—write a letter to my dad and his wife, Helen, write another story for the *News-Press*, prepare lunch and clean up, then take my turn steering. When I wasn't steering, though, I kept popping back on deck to see how much closer we were to our first landfall.

With a glorious sunset of red, pink, orange, and yellow clouds crowning Ua Pou to the south, we rounded the corner at Hat Island and sailed into the triangle between Ua Huka, Ua Pou, and Nuku Hiva. I broke open the Chivas Regal a friend had thrown to us as we left Marina del Rey thirty days before and toasted the world. We had completed our first passage and thus passed our Great Adventure initiation. *It's all downhill from here,* I thought.

Coco, ears taut, tail arched, paced the cockpit breathing in the land. I breathed it in, too, for the first time in a month smelling fresh earth and grass.

Hundreds of terns and petrels, screeching, circled *Wa*. Coco's tail twitched. I wondered if he was thinking of those birds as dinner and decided to feed him extra that night. I sipped my scotch and stared at the brown and green land just ten miles away. Then I fixed a simple supper of beans that nevertheless seemed special.

Because Pete didn't want to sail into Taio Hae Bay after dark, we hove to and kept watches to make sure *Wa* wasn't close enough to land to run aground. I thought it would be hard to sleep, but once my stomach was full, weariness washed over me.

Pete got *Wa* under way at 2:30 a.m. At 4:30 I took the tiller, with instructions to wake him by seven so he could prepare the anchor and chain.

At mid-morning I sailed *Wa* into Taio Hae Bay, a thumb thrust into the island of Nuku Hiva, taking in great lungfuls of the air—rich earth and a riot of vegetation so fecund it was dank. The gardenia-like perfume of *tiare* Tahiti, the white flower used to make leis, floated from the shore, and the odor of burning coconut husks rode over the top. A rooster crowed, and another answered. A dog barked.

Suddenly there was color—red-painted tin roofs, yellow and orange trim on the houses—after an eternity of the blue, gray, black, and white of the sea and sky.

Taio Hae, a village of about four hundred, strung itself along the margin of the sea like a Christmas toy set. To the left was the yacht anchorage and, just ashore of it, a freshwater shower open to the air. To the right was the wharf. Tucked away in the hills to the right were the buildings of French officialdom—the post office, hospital, and *gendarmerie.*

We have survived the worst together. We can handle anything. Little did I know that I was basking in the bliss of ignorance.

Nuku Hiva
or
From Fish to Nuts

2951 miles and 31 days Los Angeles to Nuku Hiva

The craggy canyons of Nuku Hiva sweep almost straight up four thousand feet from the sea. Most of the Polynesian villagers on this heavily forested island supplemented their subsistence livings by fishing, raising chickens and pigs, and growing vegetables. Their cash crop was coconuts, which they turned into *copra* by hacking out the meat and drying it on wooden racks in the sun. They sold it to a middleman for cosmetics manufacturers, who turned it into soap, shampoo, and body lotion. The villagers used their *copra* money to buy kerosene, coffee, sugar, rice, flour, and clothing. Unlike their First World counterparts, most of them preferred having leisure to having the money to acquire things. Few worked an eight-hour day, and they loved to party.

Searching for someone to mend *Wa's* damaged spreaders, Pete met Venance Ascha, a young man who worked in the government's metal shop. He agreed to weld steel spreader plates for us on his own time if Pete could get the boss's consent for Venance to use government equipment after hours. As payment he wanted.22 or.30-caliber cartridges for hunting the wild goats and cattle that lived in Nuku Hiva's mountains.

We had neither weapons nor shells. Instead, Pete gave him 600 Colonial Pacific Francs (CPF), or $6, for the materials and work. To thank him for the welding and for a chance to get to know him better, Pete invited Venance and his friend Jacques Kio to *Wa* for supper. They brought a stalk of bananas and a *pamplemousse*, or green grapefruit, and settled into corners of the cockpit under the shade of the awning.

Jacques was about five foot ten—a little taller than Pete—and very handsome, with thick, dark lashes and a devilish grin. He wore a *tiare* Tahiti blossom behind his right ear. Because he worked outdoors as a marine mechanic, his skin was much darker than Venance's, the color of creamed coffee. Both men, eighteen years old, had black hair, flashing black eyes, and the rugged build of athletes.

When I served them Chivas Regal, Jacques's eyes gleamed. He sliced the *pamplemousse*, squeezed the juice into his drink, and took a swig. "*Tres bon*," he exclaimed, rolling his eyes.

Then he spotted my guitar. "*S'il vous plait?*" he asked. When I smiled and nodded he began to play, singing everything from American and French pop songs to traditional Marquesan ones. In between songs he finished the Chivas Regal and started on our Marquesan rum. I turned up the flame under the slow-cooking chicken and rice.

The quiet, sober Venance was no match for Jacques, who laughed through the love songs and clowned his way through half a dozen others, the *tiare* Tahiti blossom drooping to a more rakish angle behind his ear.

Pete took Polaroid pictures and brought out our cassette deck, and Jacques and Venance took turns recording. Hearing their own voices delighted them.

Then Jacques pulled a harmonica from his pocket and ran his lips with lightning speed across it while Venance sang. Venance whistled, and Jacques made funny noises into the microphone. When Pete played the tape back, Jacques grinned and preened himself as if he were a young girl in front of a mirror. *Missed his calling as an entertainer*, I thought.

As we finished our dinner, a staccato patter of drums beat across the bay. "We must go," Venance said in French. "It is time to dance the *tamure*."

What is that? I wondered, but didn't ask. They slipped off, leaving us alone in a night of stars.

"I'm really getting into this culture—making friends," Pete said.

"A little booze—or a lotta booze—helps grease the wheels."

"No, seriously. Jacques asked me to go diving with him and his brother, Philippe."

"Wow! Where was I?"

"Cooking." Not realizing I was crestfallen at being left out, Pete went on. "I feel like I've gotten below the surface and been accepted by the community."

"Oi!" shouted the young men of Taio Hae, paddling their *piroques* toward *Wa*, while I sat under the cockpit awning with pretty, blonde American Ingrid Anderson Cruz. Absent Pete and the guys, I'd invited her to spend the morning with me. She was the first woman I'd talked with in more than a month, and I relished her company.

Jacques Kio and Pete in one canoe and Philippe Kio and three boys in the other converged. Chattering with bravado, they lashed the *piroques* to *Wa* and, balancing gracefully on the outriggers, leapt aboard. Philippe, with mahogany-colored skin and just as handsome as his kid brother, Jacques, swaggered into the cockpit and leered at Ingrid. Then he offered us a bucket filled with purple sea urchins, scallops, and silver reef fish.

I scurried below and brought out ham and cheese, pickles, deviled eggs, freshly baked banana bread, sliced mangoes, and *pamplemousse* for the divers. Someone hacked open two green drinking coconuts with a machete and passed them around.

Jacques split the urchins, scooped out a brown, grainy substance, and spooned it onto the scallop shells. Sprinkling one with lemon juice, he offered it to me. The urchin was salty but edible. The scallop was superb—buttery, but without greasiness.

The food disappeared, and the adults relaxed in the cockpit while the boys scampered over *Wa's* foredeck, peered at her rigging, dared each other to go up in the bosun's chair. Then Ingrid spotted an octopus tucked in a bucket in Philippe's *piroque.*

"Oh," she cried, "that's just the right size. Would you like me to cook it?"

Philippe raised his eyebrows. "You don't want to eat *that*," he said.

"Oh, but I do. It's one of my favorites." Then she turned to me. "Do you have scissors?"

He smiled. I don't think he believed her. Before Philippe realized what was happening, Pete and Ingrid had lifted the bucket into the cockpit, and I went below for the scissors.

"This is easier than using a knife," she said, and snipped off the legs of the octopus one by one. The Marquesans stared at her as if she were mentally unbalanced.

"The ones we had in Ecuador were larger," Ingrid explained, "and very tough."

Ingrid, who had golden hair down to her waist, had lived in Ecuador for three years and married an Ecuadorian. Apparently the marriage had gone sour, for Ingrid had escaped South America and sailed west. *He probably was some macho guy,* I thought, *not like Pete, and she couldn't stand being under his thumb.*

"You cook them in very hot oil for about twenty minutes or half an hour," she said. "This one less, maybe fifteen minutes. Even the beak, though it's only used for flavoring. Here it is," she said, reaching her hand into the still living, writhing mass of gray flesh to haul out a white, squishy thing with a brown center.

Pete primed the stove and cooked under Ingrid's direction. She cut up the small reef fish and added them to the skillet.

The adults speared the octopus and fish with skewers. The boys, each with a banana in one hand, dived with the fingers of the other hand into their bowls and smacked their lips.

Coco awoke to the cooking smell, stretched, and meowed like a sultan demanding attention.

Pete, with a dreamy smile, lounged in the cockpit. "Diving in paradise. I'll never forget this day," he said.

He wasn't so happy about the Englishman John, who rowed over the next day from another boat.

He saw my guitar and asked to play, then launched into "The Eddystone Light." I clapped my hands and melded my soprano with his tenor. With blond hair sticking out like hay from a stack and a ruddy face, John wasn't much to look at, but his voice was lyrical and pure. The music took me back to college and the wonderful times I'd had singing folk songs. Pete scowled and went below to make coffee.

John stuck to the neutral at first—"Frog Went A-Courtin'," "They Call the Wind Mariah." I knew them all. Then, his eyes twinkling, he switched to "The Foggy, Foggy Dew." Pete, who came topside with the coffee, glared.

I took the guitar and, thinking to relieve the tension, sang "The Fox Went Out on a Chase One Night." Oblivious of Pete's mood, John joined me. I sang everything I knew that didn't have anything to do with love, unrequited or not. Pete, who didn't know the songs, sat in a corner and pouted.

Finally I said, "That was great, but I have things to do. Will you come back to sing another time?"

Pete coughed. It was clear he didn't want to see John again.

After the Englishman left, Pete spat out, "He was coming on to you! And you led him on."

"We were *singing*, for God's sake. I haven't had so much fun since we got here."

"Yeah? Wondering how big his pecker is?"

If he'd slapped me I wouldn't have been more stunned. Close to tears, I bit my lip.

"You've been having a wonderful time with Jacques and the rest of your drinking and diving buddies, and all I've been doing is cook for them."

"Oh, come on. They're your friends too."

"They can't be my friends. I'm off limits because they're single and I'm married, and that's a no-no in the Marquesan culture. Didn't you see the way Philippe leered at Ingrid? It's all about sex and possession." I paused and stared at him to see if he got it. "Can't I have fun, too?"

"It was pretty clear he turned you on."

Feeling confused by his certainty, I went below and buried myself in a book. *So much for not being under your husband's thumb.*

It seemed so unfair, but I couldn't put a finger on *why*.

The small girl, as brown as the earth under her feet, let water wash over her bare belly from the faucet in her yard. She darted a look at me, then returned to splashing. Three hens fluffed their feathers in the dirt nearby, and a black and white piglet awakened with a snort as water trickled into his nest. He moved to a dry spot under the breadfruit tree, which towered over the house, shading it with many-fingered leaves. The smell of coconuts and mangoes hung in the moist heat.

"*Tamari'i!*" a woman's voice scolded from inside.

"*Bon jour,*" I called, approaching the lime-green wooden house with empty egg cartons in my hand. "*Ça va?*" I asked uncertainly. Maurice McKittrick, Taio Hae's bar and store keeper, had told me to come here for eggs, but he'd told me nothing about Hina Peterano.

The woman came to the porch with a look of surprise, then beamed a smile. "*Ça va.*" Wiping her hands on her skirt, she ambled down the steps. She was a Gauguin woman, round all over, large-breasted, large-bellied, wearing a skirt flowered with red and yellow hibiscus and a halter that looked like a postage stamp on a bowling ball. As brown as the girl under the faucet, she loomed over me.

"*Mme Hina Peterano, n'est c'est pas?*"

She nodded.

"*Je suis Addie Eastman. Avez-vous les oeufs? Deux douzaine, trois douzaine?*" Clutching my three egg cartons, I didn't know whether or not to stick out my hand for her to shake. Pete and I had been in the Marquesas for two weeks, and planned to stay for another two, but I still was fumbling my way through the island's customs.

A little boy peeked out from underneath the house. Hina spouted a torrent of Marquesan at him, and he scrambled back out of sight.

"I speak some English. Please come." She flung her arms wide in the welcoming gesture of Polynesia. I followed her up the steps.

There was no glass in the windows; a breeze whispered through the house, cooling it from the tropic heat. A baby lay snuggled in a quilt on a double bed in the far room. A toddler played on the floor.

"Where did you learn English?" No one in the village except Maurice spoke it.

"From the boats. I go today." She waved her arm toward the bay. "Boat from *Nouvelle Caledonie*. Please." She smiled and pointed for me to sit on the day bed, which was covered with a brightly colored print. A yellow grass skirt had been flung across it.

"*Le bateau de Nouvelle Caledonie?*" I asked. *What is she talking about?* There were only fishing boats and three yachts in Taio Hae Bay. I was sure we weren't communicating.

The boy, carrying a basket of brown eggs smudged with chicken droppings, sauntered into the house. "Aach," Hina said in disgust. "There should be three dozen." She pointed at the girl beside the faucet. "Tamari'i go . . ." Hina cupped her hands over her head and brought them down with a splatting motion. "*Une douzaine.*" Apparently the little girl had broken a dozen eggs by cracking them over her head.

I laughed. She helped me put the eggs in my cartons, and I gave her 200 CPF for the two dozen eggs.

"*Vous jouez le guitar,*" Hina said. "Maurice go your boat. *Vous jouez tres jolie pour Maurice.*"

I chuckled. Word had gotten around. Pete and I had invited Maurice and his grandchildren to dinner on *Wa* several nights before. The four children had gotten seasick as the boat rocked in the surge, so I'd played the guitar and sung, hoping to get their minds off their stomachs.

"*Vous jouez le guitar pour moi?*" asked Hina, smiling. A battered guitar appeared from the darkened room next to us, brought by a girl of about fourteen. She'd lost the angularity of childhood but was still slender. She smiled shyly, exposing gleaming teeth, and handed me the guitar. I played one song and gave the guitar to Hina.

Her fingers flicked over the strings like sparks. "*Tamure, tamure, mure rure ra,*" she sang as the beat quickened. "You know *tamure?*" I shook my head. She pointed to the grass skirt beside me. "*Pour tamure.* I go boat *Nouvelle Caledonie. Tamure.*" She pointed to her daughter and wiggled.

"Ah," I said, not understanding. "*Vous tamure?*" Hina laughed, waved her hands in protest, and pointed to her sizable figure.

"*Vous tamure?*" I asked the girl, thinking it a polite question, not a request. She giggled and looked at her mother. Hina spoke in Marquesan, and the girl disappeared into the far room. In moments she reappeared dressed in a grass skirt with brown and white speckled cowrie shells around the belt, a straw brassiere spangled in cowrie shells, and a grass pillbox hat.

Hina began to play and the girl danced, twisting her belly around and around, wiggling her hips. Her feet rocked back and forth on the floor as she swayed to the music. My jaw dropped, and I felt my face flush. So that was what Venance Ascha meant about dancing the *tamure.* It was one of the most erotic things I'd ever seen. I guessed the Marquesas's low-key colonizers had drawn the line at cannibalism but turned a blind eye to the natives' sexuality. *So like the French.*

"*C'est bon, c'est tres jolie,*" I cried, clapping my hands in time to the beat.

"You also?" Hina asked. Smiling, she beckoned to me.

Hina wanted me to *tamure?* Though introverted, I never had been shy about making a fool of myself for the sake of a laugh. "OK," I agreed, sucking in my breath. Maybe I could learn it well enough to dance it for Pete.

Hina's daughter fastened the skirt around me with grass ties. It reached to the floor, and the bodice of my pink flowered dress bloused out over it. Then she set a grass hat on my head. My glasses slipped to the end of my nose in the heat.

Hina began to play the *tamure,* and the girl and I faced each other, she gesturing to show me the movements and I watching her from waist to feet. Her belly made circles one way and her hips the other. Her knees went in and out, barely visible beneath the skirt. All these movements must have come from some hidden source, for the girl appeared to be putting out no effort at all.

I wriggled and strained, attempting to do the thing with my stomach muscles. I wound up doing something like the twist à la Chubby Checker. We went faster and faster, and my glasses slid to the floor. Hina laughed, and her daughter laughed, and I collapsed.

"I am too old," I panted.

"Mais non," Hina scoffed. *"Quel age?"*

"Vingt-neuf." Twenty-nine and counting.

"Ah," she said, pooh poohing me. *"Je suis trente-quatre."* She held up all ten fingers three times and then four fingers.

I felt a twinge of regret. *Five years older and she has six children.*

Hina reached under the day bed and offered me a box of cowries.

I thanked her warmly as she put a dozen shells in my one empty egg carton. *What a lovely gift.* With a rush of gratitude I felt as if I now belonged, just as Pete had.

As I left the house, skirting pigs and chickens in the yard, and reached the road, I glanced at the bay, where a gray ocean liner had indeed appeared: the *Nouvelle Caledonie.*

Before I could return to *Wa* with the eggs, the sleepy village had become a bustling port. Anything that floated and could be fitted with a motor was zeroing in on the *Nouvelle Caledonie.* Speedboats turned the bay's placid waters choppy. The runabouts took their turns at the ship's gangway, bucking in the surge, waiting to take the two hundred and forty passengers ashore for 20 CPF apiece.

"Time to ogle the tourists," I told Pete.

They were a mixed lot, young and old, of many nationalities. The *Nouvelle Caledonie* and her sister ship the *Tahitien* stopped twice at Taio Hae during their four-month round trips from Marseilles to Brisbane and back, so the Marquesans were inundated with tourists once a month.

We stopped by the open-air meeting hall to say hello to Philippe Kio, who was decorating the support posts with woven palm fronds and stringing yellow *hoa* flowers in between. The tables were bright with red and yellow hibiscus, and a crown of *tiare* Tahiti circled each guest's place. The white flowers' heavy scent hung in the air. Farther down the road at the open-air curio shop, the craftsmen of Taio Hae hawked their wares—wood carvings, shell jewelry, grass skirts.

Maurice McKittrick wore his false teeth and a clean shirt with his shorts. His bar was packed. He served three people speaking Marquesan, two speaking French, and three Danes and a Swede, who conversed in a kind of *lingua* Scandinavia. When we sat with them, they switched to English. *Wow!* I thought, *this is like being in Europe.* Then I looked at the green, dirt-smudged walls, the windows with their broken and missing louvers, the dogs wandering in and out. *No, not Europe.*

We drifted away and came upon a Canadian woman, blonde hair graying at the temples, tanned face lined, wearing a red flowered sundress and sturdy brown walking shoes. "This is so exciting!" she exclaimed. "They promised us a big festival if we'd pay $8 for the meal. The ship had to sign up a hundred passengers."

Eight dollars apiece for dinner was beyond our budget, so we rowed back to *Wa* to eat and then returned ashore for the festivities. By the time we reached the meeting hall, the crowd was rambunctious, for part of the $8 package was unlimited drink. I looked with envy as a girl passed out ice cubes, created in Maurice's store with a generator.

Hina had assembled her band, which was playing background music. When the music stopped, young Marquesan men and women wearing woven palm fronds trotted into the middle of the cement floor and began swaying back and forth to the beat of drums, all the while making grunting noises. Their leader, an older man, threaded his way amongst them, exhorting them. They had trouble keeping in step with each other.

"Too much Johnnie Walker?" I whispered to Pete.

The men raised their right arms in a kind of black power salute and slapped their left hands at the bicep. They thrust their fists at the tourists and cried "Ugh!"

"You've got to be kidding," I said. The tourists watched seriously. Didn't they know they were being made fun of?

Pete grinned. "Is old Marquesan dance from 1965," he said.

Later I asked the locals about the dance. "Oh yes," they replied without a smile, "it is an ancient war dance from the days of fighting with the Taipis."

I never did find out whether they were having me on.

One of Pete's last tasks was to make whisker poles, which we would use to hold matching foresails, or twins, in front of the boat. We would need them for our next passage—to Tongareva in the Cook Islands—due west and downwind.

We hiked into the mountains above Taio Hae to look for wood and found some two-inch saplings that Pete cut with his rusty machete. Up rode a scrawny, hunched Marquesan man and his son on two horses whose bones stuck up from their hindquarters like wings.

Oh, oh, I thought. *We're in trouble—stealing this man's wood.*

Pete introduced himself and explained that the wood was for the boat.

"*Mais non,*" Yvon, the Marquesan, replied. "That wood is brittle. It will break. You must use *hoa,*" he said in French. He indicated another sapling and, looking askance at the rust on Pete's cutting tool, handed over his sharp machete.

With four hard blows, the first tree fell, then the second. Pete wiped the blade on his shorts and handed back the machete. "*Merci beaucoup. Voulez vous retournez á le bateau pour kaikai maintenant?*" Pete improvised the dinner invitation, throwing in what he presumed were cognates, sprinkling his speech with Marquesan when he didn't know the French.

"Thank you, no. I must cut and dry my *copra*," Yvon replied in French.

We waved goodbye and started down the mountain with our future whisker poles. Then Pete turned back. "*Voulez vous moi travailler avec vous pour le copra?*" On the spur of the moment, Pete was asking to cut *copra* with a man he'd just met.

Yvon was speechless. His jaw dropped, and he began to laugh as if it were the craziest suggestion he'd ever heard. Then he got suspicious. "Why?" he asked.

"For the experience," Pete said in French, "and for money if I work well."

With a shake of his head and a smile, Yvon agreed to let Pete cut *copra* with him "for the experience." He explained where he lived and told Pete to be there at eight o'clock the next morning.

The next day, while Pete was gone, I made a chocolate cake. It was Hina Peterano's thirty-fifth birthday, and she'd invited us to a family celebration. When he returned, he stank of rotting coconut. Keeping my distance, I sat in the starboard berth and asked, "So what was it like, cutting *copra*?"

"The worst part was the bareback ride. The horses are scrawny. My butt's not used to that."

"What about the work?"

"My job was to gather fallen nuts. I hacked them open with an ax, and Yvon scraped out the meat and stuck it in gunny sacks."

"Why do you stink?"

He grinned. "Some of the nuts were full of maggots."

I made a face.

"Yvon's back at his house now setting the wet meat on racks to dry. When the schooner comes, he'll get about a hundred and thirty-five dollars a ton for the *copra*."

"Can he make a living at that?"

Pete shrugged. "He works six days a week, always cutting two sacks of *copra*. He has twelve kids and another one on the way and seems to be OK financially, what with his herd of pigs and as much fruit as the family and the pigs can eat."

I shook my head in wonder. Pete had never studied French. "How could he possibly have told you all that?"

"We used a lot of gestures." He began to pantomime, and I laughed. He always won at charades. "The Marquesans say Yvon is too old for that work, but his grown sons will have nothing to do with his coconut plantation. They've gone off to work in Tahiti. It's kinda sad."

"Well, there's nothing you can do about it, unless you want to stay here and cut *copra* the rest of your life." I smiled, but only on the surface, knowing Pete probably could've been happy gathering coconuts and skin-diving for a living, with plenty of time to laze about and dream. I sniffed him again. "Remember about Hina's birthday party?"

"Oh, yeah."

I handed him a towel, shooed him out of the cabin, and waited for him to row ashore to the shower.

The sky turned from pink to the gray softness of silk as we passed the elementary school and rounded the corner at the First Chinaman's grocery store. There we met Philippe Kio, who'd played in Hina's band.

Under a huge breadfruit tree laden with grapefruit-sized green orbs, around the Second Chinaman's storehouse, and across a grassy lot we strolled. The sounds of clattering pans and the grunting of pigs came from the next yard, and I smelled the stench of the family's outhouse as we passed. A kerosene lantern sputtered at Hina's door.

"*Kaoha, kaoha. Kanehau pour votre naissance*," I called, wishing her a happy birthday.

Etienne came out to greet us, and his and Hina's six children, ranging in age from the girl who'd taught me to *tamure* to the infant Joel, clustered on the day bed in the open-air living room. Red printed curtains fluttered at the windows, and the red linoleum floor glistened. Hina served us rum punch, and we sat in a circle in chairs and listened to a recording Philippe had made on our cassette. He, Pete, and I were the only guests.

Then Hina, Philippe, and Etienne, alternating on two guitars and a ukulele, played and sang for more than an hour in Marquesan, Tahitian, and French. During one old "French" song, "Pistol Packin' Mama," Hina sat back with her legs wide apart, braced both hands in front of her guitar like six-guns, and gave us a big wink, all the while singing lustily. Although I was willing to dare the sea in a 28-foot boat, caution usually took over when I was with people, but her zest for life stirred something deep inside me.

The buffet table was jammed with *poisson crux*—raw tuna marinated in lime juice, onion, and spices—smoked bonito, roast chicken, rice, breadfruit, baked bananas, French bread, coconut pudding, and cake. In a corner of the table was that old "Marquesan" dish, potato salad, ringed with sliced tomatoes. I could have kissed Hina at the sight of it, not because I craved potato salad but for the effort she'd made to please her American friends. The guest of honor at her own birthday party was the cook for eleven. I thought of all the cooking I'd done for the Marquesans and felt a new kinship with her, who must've labored all day for this party.

Would we ever again meet people who were as warm and giving, and as full of the joy of life, as the Marquesans?

Leaving Taio Hae was almost as hard for me as it was for Pete.

Tongareva
or
Déjà Vu All Over Again

*1109 miles and 11 days Nuku Hiva to Tongareva
under way 2 1/2 months*

The gennies, held stiff by *Wa's* new whisker poles, billowed in front of her like two giant kites. Pete set the repaired self-steering gear, and the boat swept across the sea like a princess, slipping through cobalt-blue water as the wind whispered in her sails. It felt like flying. The beauty of her motion, the shush of water against her hull, the touch of wind against my cheek seemed to confirm this was my Great Adventure, too.

We were headed for Tongareva, or Penrhyn, northernmost of the Cook Islands and our first atoll. No more than ten feet above sea level, it was shaped like a pearl necklace of twelve islets tossed upon the sea, surrounding a lagoon where we'd anchor. Between the islets were reefs, and along the atoll's western edge there was a break in the reefs, or pass, into the lagoon.

At midnight Pete awakened me. "Come and see, babe. It's beautiful."

Sleepy and naked, I uncurled from the bedding and followed him up the companionway. The waning moon gleamed like an orange slice. When he turned on the spreader lights, the genoas became gauzy wings that seemed to lift *Wa* and carry her toward

Never Never Land.

Pete slipped behind me and put his hands on my breasts. "Let's go below," he murmured.

It was times like that, when romance trumped reality, that I believed we were living in happily ever after.

The next morning we hooked a 28-inch yellow-fin tuna. Coco was right there to help Pete bring it aboard. Pete cut a plate of fillets, enough to last us and Coco for four meals, and tossed the rest of the fish overboard. I felt my gut wrench at wasting good food, but we had no refrigerator, and I couldn't risk getting sick from spoiled fish.

Sailing under the twin genoas was so effortless I had time to write. And both of us relaxed completely—something we hadn't done for months. This is what I'd envisioned cruising would be all about—unending days of tranquil repose.

Pete studied his trig book and drew diagrams of curved triangles, trying to work out the formula for getting both longitude and latitude from a single (longitudinal) sun sight. If he could do it, navigation would be easier, for we'd know where we were from dawn to dusk. But the formula eluded him.

As it was, one of us had to train the sextant's darkened lens on the sun, drag its lower rim to the horizon using the sextant's arc, capture the time on a stop watch, compare the stop watch's time with the chronometer's time, and correct the chronometer by listening to WWV, the National Institute of Standards radio station. A few seconds of inaccuracy meant miles of difference at sea. I took three of these sun sights between eight and nine in the morning. The first time I calculated our longitude using trigonometric tables and the *Nautical Almanac*, it took me four hours. When I became adept, taking the sights and plotting them on the chart took fifteen minutes.

Eight days later, I was lounging on the starboard berth with my notebook, and Pete lay on the forward berth reading. The peace was broken by a loud crack. We raced up on deck.

My heart sank. The port spreader dangled from its loose shrouds like a marionette. The mainsail sagged against the starboard spreader, which was broken, too.

The idyll was over.

"Head straight downwind," Pete yelled. "I'll get the sails down."

I scrambled to the tiller.

The main dropped with a thump, then the jib. The shrouds flopped and the mast swayed back and forth; I was afraid we'd lose it for sure this time. Only the undamaged forestay and backstay and the shrouds from the masthead held it up.

And what would we do if the mast fell? Tongareva wouldn't have any facilities for replacing it, and we were two thousand miles from Tarawa, the nearest port of any size. Once again I choked down my fear. We had to save the mast.

It was five o'clock in the afternoon; we were an estimated twenty-eight miles from Tongareva—much closer than we wanted to be since the force of the wind and current could carry *Wa* crashing into Tongareva's reef in the dark.

We took turns steering straight downwind—twenty knots coming from the east—to keep the pressure off the mast. Pete figured we were making one knot just from the force of the wind, which would put us sixteen miles from the island at first light.

I cooked and we ate. Pete took star sights to verify our position. At ten we began regular watches, and neither of us got more than two and a half hours of sleep.

What a terrible night! I quivered with the tension, and my hands on the tiller were stiff. What if a two-knot current were carrying us straight for the atoll? Would I be able to see it in the dark, with the waxing moon long since set? Would I be able to hear surf on the reef in a twenty-knot breeze, with the wind whistling in the rigging and the halyards clanking against the mast? If *Wa* ran aground on a reef, the pounding surf could kill us.

Slack water—the change of tide—was at eleven o'clock, we knew from checking *Brown's Nautical Almanac*. Otherwise, the book warned, we'd face currents up to eight knots in a shoal-studded pass. Pete would have to get the engine running early to get us to the island, and through the pass, before noon. In addition, we had no chart of Tongareva, so we had to allow extra time to find the pass.

Thinking it would take Pete an hour to start the engine, and allowing two hours to find the pass, I got him up at four. He hadn't run the engine in two weeks. Water has a habit, in the tropics, of condensing in the bottom of partially filled gasoline tanks. The fuel line, of course, also was at the bottom. The engine wouldn't start.

A stream of curses came from below, then abject silence. I felt his pain.

He drained water from the engine and cleaned the carburetor three times, removing encrusted salt and dirt. We both took sun sights to give us a longitudinal line of position. Mine went straight through Tongareva and put us northwest of the island. Pete's were incomprehensible because of a time error.

Frustrated to the point of rage, he decided to trust my sights, gave up temporarily on the engine, and set the jib tacking east and south. Then he saw it—as brown as a chunk of Hershey bar cast upon the sea. As we drew closer, Tongareva looked like a toothbrush on its back, with palm tree bristles.

His spirits renewed, Pete got the engine running at 10:30, and we headed straight for the atoll. Tongareva looked to be about fifteen miles away. Our hope now was to make it by second slack water, at five, so that we wouldn't have to sit out another night with *Wa's* vulnerable mast at the mercy of wind and sea.

The two-inch diagram of Tongareva in the *Sailing Directions* recommended using West Pass into the lagoon but didn't show where it was.

As we came closer, I saw thin green lines, breakers on the reef, and a large white building. Then a man and woman in a blue skiff with an outboard appeared from behind the swell and hailed us.

"Which way to West Pass?" Pete shouted. The man pointed and began to lead the way. He stopped briefly to haul in a tuna, then motored alongside *Wa*.

"Are you in trouble?" he asked. He was fortyish, stocky, and very brown, with a shock of black hair and eyes like black onyx.

"Both spreaders are broken. I don't dare sail," Pete replied.

"Let me help you." He hoisted himself aboard, then turned to his wife and spoke in *Tagnata*, the Maori dialect of Tongareva. She sped away toward the nearby islet.

Saved! I was so grateful I could've hugged him.

He held out his hand to Pete and smiled. "I am Saua Taruia."

Pete gave the tiller to Saua, who guided *Wa* into a lagoon that lightened from deep blue to turquoise to green as we reached the village of Omoka. His wife, who'd picked up two men on the nearby islet, or *motu*, followed in the skiff.

Pete anchored fifty yards from shore in roiling water, and Saua went ashore with his wife and the two men. Because Omoka, a village of about three hundred people, was on the leeward side of the island, it faced the trade winds blowing relentlessly across the 16-mile diameter of the lagoon. Waves slapped against *Wa's* stern, and a five-foot surf broke with a crash of foam on the white coral beach.

A row of houses stuccoed with bleached coral, austere compared with the brightly painted homes of the Marquesans, dotted the shoreline. The warm somnolence of Taio Hae was gone. These people, though also Polynesians, were poorer, their clothes more ragged, their skins more weathered. In the flat sameness of the village as it curved around the lip of the lagoon, in the squatness of its houses and palm trees, there was little to please the eye.

Saua and his wife returned with the two men. Mrs. Saua, a woman of about thirty, would've been beautiful if she hadn't lost several front teeth, but that didn't keep her from smiling. She had long, black hair held in a clip.

The two young men introduced themselves as Tien Akatapuria and Rakoroa Taia. Handsome Tien, slender and rugged, looked as if he'd just gotten into mischief. Darker-skinned Rakoroa seemed to take life more seriously.

"We haven't cleared," said Pete, pointing to the yellow quarantine flag whipping from *Wa's* backstay. Because we'd come from a different country (French Polynesia), international law required us to check in with immigration, customs, and the health authorities before entertaining visitors. When the officials saw the yellow quarantine flag, they would board us, check our passports and documents proving *Wa* was ours, and fill out the required paperwork.

"The resident administrator will be along," Saua assured him. He smiled at Pete's raised eyebrows. "The R.A. is a good man—the first Tongarevan to have the job." He sounded proud—the Cook Islands were a New Zealand colony, and government jobs normally went to New Zealanders, he said.

Soon the villagers, mostly men, began to arrive in their skiffs.

"We haven't cleared," Pete told them, and glanced ashore nervously, but they climbed aboard anyway.

"It's all right," Saua said.

The children swam out and swarmed aboard. When Pete pointed to the quarantine flag, they paid no attention.

"It's all right," Saua said again.

Pete stroked his beard. Too late now to worry about an irate customs officer.

Although I still worried, I prepared quarts of the powdered soft drink called Funny Face, a Kool-Aid wannabe, washing cups and glasses as quickly as the villagers emptied them. As each new man arrived, Pete scanned his face, hoping it was the administrator. "Are we in big trouble with the R.A.?" he asked.

"No problem." Saua smiled.

Pretty soon the R.A. arrived in his launch. I shook his hand and gave him a soft drink. "You should've cleared in Rarotonga," he said, "but I see you have trouble with your mast. You can stay as long as you need. I'll cable Rarotonga, tell them you're here."

That was the last we heard of customs and immigration. Saua later told us most yachts that stopped at Tongareva did so without clearing, got permission to land "for water," and stayed for weeks.

The party continued all afternoon. Although I had a sore throat, I struggled on as best I could knowing the men were going to help us. They came both to be sociable and out of curiosity about the small boat. They were sailors and had a keen eye for *Wa*'s rig. Many had ideas about how she should be repaired.

By the time the villagers left at dusk, I was ready to collapse. I was opening a can of cheese—our first meal that day—when Tien returned. "Saua is expecting you for supper," he said.

I groaned. "Could you tell him we're tired and want to sleep?" I should have told him I had a sore throat.

"Oh, no," he said firmly. "Everything is ready." He took us ashore in his skiff.

Tien led us under palms and breadfruit trees and past some concrete bunkers. "What are those?" I asked. They seemed totally alien to the simplicity of the island.

"Those are left over from the war, when the Americans had a base here," Tien replied. From Tongareva on, all across the Pacific, the ghost of World War II would follow us.

Tien took us into a yard of coral gravel that hurt my bare feet. In the kitchen, open to the air and floored in concrete, a table was set for Tien, Pete, and me under a kerosene lantern. I was acutely embarrassed—they'd expected us to eat with them, had waited, then sent Tien to fetch us.

After supper everyone gathered in the yard between the kitchen and the main house. Saua and his wife said they'd been married only a short time; his three children were her step-children. Saua's mother lived with them and took care of the children while the Taruias fished and cut *copra*. Thus they subsisted, as the Marquesans did, on fish and what they could grow, but the coral soil had to be coaxed into producing anything but sand. *No wonder they seem poorer than the people of Nuku Hiva*, I thought. The Marquesans could grow almost anything in Taio Hae's rich volcanic loam.

Saua wore a *lava-lava*, a single piece of cloth wrapped from waist to knees. Pete presented him with a half bottle of rum, which brought a broad grin to his face. Soon we said goodnight and promised that we'd meet the next morning. Saua, Mrs. Saua,

Tien, Rakoroa, Pete, and I would cut *copra* together, and in the afternoon we'd take down *Wa*'s mast. I was thrilled to be included in what had been men's work in the Marquesas.

Although these people weren't as carefree as the Marquesans, there was no doubt in my mind that they were Polynesians. The generosity and openness of spirit that had caused Pete to fall in love with Taio Hae pervaded the village of Omoka, too.

The next morning a skiff came by, and the five men in it hailed us. Pete invited them aboard. The men were weather-beaten, their faces and hands deeply wrinkled, their teeth scraggly or missing. If they'd been Americans, I would have guessed them to be well past sixty. Only their bodies were young and fit—darkly browned, muscled heavily across the chest and stomach, with arms and legs as hard as coral. They were dressed in shorts, with plastic goggles around their necks.

"Are you going for a swim?" asked Pete.

"We don't cut *copra* for a living, we dive," said John in a pronounced New Zealand accent. "We are on our way to one of the reefs in the middle of the lagoon." He swept his arm across the emerald water, which sparkled in the morning light. Waves lapped at *Wa*'s stern, and the scent of coconut wafted from the land.

"What do you dive for?" Pete asked.

"Pearls and pearl shell," John replied.

"Do you have time for a cup of coffee?" Pete asked.

The men glanced at each other. "Of course," said an older man. "There is always time for a cup of coffee." I lit the stove, put on a pot of water, and waited, listening, in the companionway.

"You speak very good English," Pete said to John, who preened.

"I lived in New Zealand for many years," he said, as if this made him better than his companions.

"But he is the youngest of us," another man said. "I have been diving for more than twenty years."

"And how many more years can you dive?" asked Pete, probably trying to figure out how old the men were.

"A few more. No one dives after fifty. The work is too hard." So these men who appeared to be close to seventy were in their thirties and forties. Pete hunched forward. He was fascinated.

"Do you dive every day?"

"Except Sunday. No one works on Sunday. We go only in the middle of the day—from ten till three—because of the light."

"I dive only for pearl shell," said another man, "because it makes more money. But I wouldn't throw away a pearl if I found one." He grinned. I served the men their coffee and joined them in the cockpit.

"How deep do you go?" Pete asked.

"Twenty fathoms."

Pete took off his glasses, wiped his face with a towel, put his glasses back on, and stared. "Twenty fathoms? That's a hundred and twenty feet."

These men not only had no air tanks, they didn't wear flippers. They dived to more than a hundred feet carrying gunny sacks. Only a handful of people—the Japanese women pearl divers in the Coral Sea and the sponge divers in the Mediterranean—free-dive that deep. Jacques Cousteau describes the sponge divers as being burnt out by the time they are forty. The pressures on the human body day after day at depths over a hundred feet are immense.

Pete sipped his coffee and gestured as if he were an acolyte seeking the word. "How many minutes can you stay down?"

"Oh, three or four, not much more than that."

Pete sucked in his breath. "Will you take me diving some day?"

"Of course." The leader smiled indulgently, as if he were dealing with a child. "Some day."

As the men finished their coffee, one of them pulled from his pocket a handful of pearls and five shells with the pearls still attached. "These are yours," he said, thrusting them at Pete.

"Oh, no, I couldn't take them. They are your livelihood."

"There are plenty more. Please take them."

They waved goodbye and sped off across the lagoon.

"Polynesians are incredible people," I said.
There were tears in Pete's eyes.

Although I hadn't been in a church since the day we were married, Pete convinced me to set aside my agnosticism for just one day and "go with the flow."

Dawn rose slowly, pulling up her various window shades, tinting the lagoon gray. As the sun broke with a splendor of orange over green water, we hurried along the coral path to the big white church, for the last bell had rung, and it was six o'clock.

Strident voices boomed the opening hymn as Tien, Pete, and I scurried to find seats. A jangle of dissonants, the song sounded as if it'd been scored by Igor Stravinsky, yet it was joyous. It was Maori music, Tien told us. As it ended, the sun broke golden over the coconut trees and through the church's open door, spattering light against the white-washed walls. I felt a sudden connection to these people through our common language of music.

Saua and another man gave prayers. Saua's was for rain, which had been scarce.

It was Palm Sunday. The Reverend Uzziah Taruia's message compared Peter's denial of Jesus to a Maori legend of sacrifice in the face of an enemy assault. Tien, sitting between Pete and me, translated from *Tagnata* to English.

All at once came a *plink* against the corrugated iron roof. *Plink plonk.* The minister's voice droned on. *Plink plonk plink.* The congregation began to murmur, and I glanced at Pete, who mouthed, "The power of God."

The congregation began another anthem, which the beating against the roof drowned out, as if a dozen percussionists were striking kettledrums. Rain streamed down the church's stained-glass windows.

At Saua's house afterwards, we had more prayers. Rain or no rain, I stared at my hands in my lap and wished I were on the boat in bed.

Tien took off his suit jacket, tie, and black shoes, and we chatted over home-made scones and coffee. At eight o'clock the first bell rang again. Tien donned his shoes, tie, and jacket, and we walked to the squat, gray building that served as a parish house.

Even with the windows open, the heat was suffocating. Sweat trickled down my cheeks and along the crevice in my back. Again I wondered why I was there rather than in one of *Wa's* comfortable bunks drinking coffee. Dabbing my face with a handkerchief, I sank onto a bench next to Tien. The Sunday School teacher taught us three 18th Century Presbyterian hymns in Maori for the following service.

Shortly before 9:30 we lined up outside the parish hall like so many schoolboys and marched to the church, which was now packed with the same villagers as before plus the late risers—men in white shirts and slacks and women in brightly colored dresses and straw hats decorated with shells. They wore their long, black hair in single plaits.

Tien translated as the Reverend Taruia continued his Palm Sunday lesson, then used as the text for his sermon the story of Jonah. He compared Jonah's troubles with those of the *Tagnata* fishermen, warning them not to waver in their belief in God, and finally praising God for delivering Tongareva safely through another hurricane season.

A woman cantor began another dissonant, Maori hymn in a booming alto. The congregation broke into passionate, four-part harmony, a cappella, on key.

After the service, dinner at Saua's consisted of three different kinds of fish, rice, breadfruit, bread, biscuits, *poke* (po keh)—coconut pudding thickened with manioc, and *floua*—coconut cake. Pete took Polaroid pictures, and we went back to *Wa* for a nap. When the first bell rang again at 1:30, we hurried ashore for Sunday School and more choir practice, then attended the three o'clock service, much the same as their morning counterparts.

I felt as if I were in a time warp that had carried me back to Puritan America—except that the *Tagnata* dwelt not on the wrath of God but on the love of Jesus. Still, I couldn't manage any more church services for a while.

For five days Pete and I had turned the Taruias' household upside down while *Wa's* mast languished on their front porch and half the village of Omoka dropped by to watch us remove the spreaders and repair them. Saua, fiercely protective of us, chased the other villagers away when he thought they were interfering. Mrs. Saua fed us every night except the one when they came to eat on the boat.

We spent all our waking hours with them. I wasn't used to constant verbal and emotional contact, especially with people whose language I didn't know and whom I was afraid of offending with some *faux pas*. At the same time, naturally reserved, I felt guilty for not embracing them as they had embraced us.

Pete, on the other hand, thrived in this emotional hothouse. He had long conversations about village life with Tien and Rakoroa, who were former teachers and whose English was excellent. Saua, Pete's mentor, worked with us on the mast, offered advice, and shared his wisdom.

I asked Tien how I could say thank you for all they'd done for us.

"Have you any yeast?" he replied. "The store's all out."

The next morning I brought the Taruias all the yeast we had—six packets of Fleischmann's "quick acting." Saua asked, "You will make bread now?"

Finally my chance to say thank you. Pete returned to the boat to fetch my *Joy of Cooking*, and I picked an easy recipe for white bread. But that was the only simple part of the process. Mrs. Saua's English was marginal, and I knew only a few words in *Tagnata*, so we communicated mostly with gestures. Saua, helping Pete with the mast, flitted in and out.

The recipe called for ingredients to make two loaves in standard loaf-sized pans. Mrs. Saua, for her family of six plus Tien, Pete, and me, pulled out two pans the size of baby bathtubs.

"Do you have measuring cups?" I asked, wondering how to modify the recipe to fit those pans.

She shrugged and called to Saua, who answered, "No."

"How do you prepare the dough?" I asked.

He translated and she demonstrated: she scooped flour from its tin container onto a strainer made of window screening, then sifted the flour through the screening into a large bowl. I'd never had the courage to bake without measuring. I decided to use an over-sized coffee cup and hoped that would work.

Then came the matter of shortening. "Do you have butter?" I asked, thinking she might have a tin from New Zealand.

Again she called Saua for help. He produced a packet of Hellaby's beef drippings.

Next, the leavening. "You must make the yeast come alive," I told her, pouring warm water on three packets of Fleischmann's, which bubbled out of the bowl.

Her eyes grew round. "Why do you do that?"

"To make the yeast grow. What do you do?"

"I put it in the sun." No wonder it took her all day to make bread.

The last hurdle was water. I decided to experiment with *nimata*, or drinking coconut, not only because water was scarce on Tongareva but also to give the bread the drinking nut's subtle flavor.

After two laborious kneadings, Mrs. Saua shaped neat loaves, and Saua started a fire in the outdoor oven using coconut shells to heat the rocks.

Despite the lack of equipment and ingredients, the bread was delicious.

"Thank you for teaching me I don't need to 'cook by the book' to succeed," I said to Mrs. Saua.

When Saua translated, she grinned, unself-conscious about her missing teeth, and thanked me.

I handed her my *Joy of Cooking*. "This is for you," I said. "Saua will translate the recipes for you."

It was my favorite cookbook and a gift from my heart, for she had invited me into her kitchen and her life, just as Hina Peterano had.

"I think I need some space." I was brushing my hair as we got ready for bed.

Pete stopped scrubbing his teeth and stared. "Whaddya mean?"

"I sort of feel like some creature in a zoo that everyone fawns over."

"They've adopted us. Aren't you honored?"

Unwilling to say "no" to *honored*, I shrugged. "Smothered is more like it." We'd come from the quiet spaces of the ocean, where we sometimes went for hours without speaking to each other, where solitude allowed me time to think and dream. It was hard work being a good guest to those who had given their friendship to us without reservation.

He shook his head in wonder. "I feel like a son, or a younger brother, to Saua. He's opened up my world in a way no one ever has before."

"Because he's kind, and not overbearing like your father?"

Tears came to his eyes. "Yes. Because he's shown me the true meaning of love."

I tossed aside the hairbrush and put my arms around him. "Don't *we* know the true meaning of love?"

"That's sexual love. I mean brotherhood."

"We have brotherhood, too—aren't we best friends as well as lovers?"

"It's not the same." He ran his finger down the bridge of my nose. "Sometimes I think sex gets in the way."

Alarmed, I pulled away. "In the way of what?"

"Saua's brotherhood is Godliness. He's like St. Francis."

"Gimme a break! Saua's a very nice man, but he's *not* St. Francis."

Pete wouldn't give up. "He humbles me. I want to bask in his light and learn."

I sat on the starboard berth and clutched the cushion. "We went to church and prayed with them six times on Palm Sunday. Easter is in three days, which will mean six more trips to church. I've got to get away—I feel as if I'm losing myself."

"Hang in there, babe."

"I have barely one cycle's supply of Enovid." It was my birth control pill.

That got his attention. "Why didn't you say?"

"I didn't think staying would be an issue."

"Why must you leave?" Saua asked the next day. "Easter is in two days."

"Well, the mast is fixed," I stammered.

He beamed a smile. "That means now you have time to enjoy Omoka."

I glanced at Pete for help, but he seemed to be enjoying my discomfort. "We never intended to stop here," I mumbled.

"But now you're here. Don't you like our village?" asked Saua, looking hurt.

I'd backed myself into a corner and didn't know how to get out. I hesitated. "I'm running out of birth control pills," I finally blurted.

Saua looked at me in astonishment. "You take pills to keep from having a baby?"

Miserable, I nodded.

"You should make a baby, not take pills to keep from having one," he said firmly.

I agreed with him on that one and threw Pete a look that said so.

Pete nodded toward *Wa*. "The sailing is too hard," he said. "I couldn't handle the boat without Addie, especially if I had to take care of her, too."

Saua grunted. "I think the hospital has some of those pills," he said. It was my turn to be astonished. Given Saua's attitude, which probably was typical of the *Tagnata*, why would the hospital carry birth control pills? "I will see."

Half an hour later he returned with birth control pills. "Now you can stay for Easter?" he asked hopefully.

I held my breath, not daring to look at Pete.

"No one knows we're here," he said. "My parents, and Addie's father, will worry." Saua grunted again and let it go.

The next morning, as Saua and Tien guided *Wa* out the pass, Pete wept. I wanted to comfort him but knew I was the cause of his distress.

∿∿∿∿∿∿∿∿∿∿∿∿∿∿∿∿

Tarawa
or
Around the World in 365 More Days

*1896 miles and 22 days Tongareva to Tarawa
under way 3 1/2 months*

Pete had run out of cigarettes and was going through nicotine withdrawal. He spent most of his time reading and holding his breath to cut the tobacco craving. It was as if he'd disappeared into some alternate reality, leaving only the husk of himself behind.

Because the varnish in the cockpit was weathering, I sanded it in preparation for applying three new coats. While I worked, my anger festered at his sloth. Finally, when I'd finished writing two stories for the *News-Press*, I confronted him.

"I wish you'd do something useful," I said. "I can't do it all myself."

He looked up from Caroline Mytinger's *Headhunting in the Solomon Islands*. Sunlight glinted off his glasses, so I couldn't see his eyes. The only other thing he was wearing was his safety harness.

"Who makes sail changes in the middle of the night? I haven't seen you up on the foredeck lately." He hunched his knees next to his chest, as if to protect himself, took off his glasses, and wiped sweat from his face with a towel.

I sucked in my breath. "I'm sorry. That's fair. But I guess I want a companion, not a zombie."

Because I seldom criticized him about personal issues, he

looked at me as if I'd hit him over the head with a frying pan. "A zombie?" He put down his book, climbed the companionway, hooked his safety harness to the lifeline, and disappeared forward. Hanging on to the forestay, he stared at the horizon for hours. Although he was less than twenty feet from me, he might as well have been on the moon. Even the husk of him had disappeared, and I felt completely alone.

The first thing I did upon approaching the islet of Betio, capital of Britain's Gilbert and Ellice Islands Colony (GEIC), was run the boat aground. We were at Tarawa, another atoll, in the southwestern corner of the lagoon.

As Pete jumped overboard to shove us off, a young guy in a power boat hailed us. "Why don't you go into the small-boat harbor?" he shouted. He leapt aboard *Wa*, leaving his buddy to man the power boat. He was of medium height and wiry, with a shock of unruly blond hair and skin as brown as a Polynesian's. "I'm Mike Thurston from Rabaul, New Guinea." He thrust his hand at Pete, shook mine, and sailed *Wa* around a corner into a small basin.

We anchored only feet from Mike's blue 30-foot sloop, *Destiny*. He'd gotten permission from the immigration and customs officials before boarding us, but they were right on his heels in a bright yellow tug.

Coconuts were the colony's sole commercial crop, the officials told us, just as they had been at Nuku Hiva and Tongareva, but the islet of Betio was only two miles long and seven hundred yards wide and had a population of eight thousand people in 1970. What the officials didn't tell us was that coconuts alone couldn't feed that many people, nor could government jobs.

Still, Micronesians migrated to Betio from the outer islands looking for work. They were eager for the goodies of modern civilization—new clothes, radios, tape recorders, and motorcycles and were lured by the excitement of movies every night, dances more nights than not, bars and cafés.

Because of this population pressure, the British had established a family planning clinic in Betio and exported some Gilbertese to the less populated islands in the British Solomon Islands Protectorate.

After the Micronesian officials left, we accepted Mike's invitation for coffee, for we hadn't put up our awning, and the sun was blazing hot. As we boarded *Destiny*, he offered Pete a cigarette. I glared at Pete, and he glared back. He'd been without cigarettes for three weeks. What better time to kick the habit?

"He quit smoking," I explained.

"It's his choice, not yours," Mike said.

"It wasn't really a choice," Pete said. "I ran out, and the store in Omoka didn't have any."

"This will taste *very* good, then," said Mike, smiling.

Mike tossed his head, flicking his hair back into place. There was something impish and yet steely about him. Pete took the cigarette, lit it, and glanced at me out of the corner of his eye. Was I going to make this an issue? Either way, I felt left out.

Most of the three weeks at sea from Tongareva to Tarawa had been idyllic, just as most of the passage from Nuku Hiva to Tongareva had been. Pete and I had become as close as we ever had been. Now that was over. Gone. Pete again was doing a male bonding thing, and I was nowhere.

Mike boiled water for coffee and chatted with Pete while I sat in *Destiny's* cockpit and sulked. Then Mike pulled out two green apples. They were the first I'd seen in four months. My discomfort ebbed as I crushed the apple with my teeth and sucked its sweet tartness until there was nothing left, not even seeds or stem.

"You can get fresh fruit here?" I asked. My mouth watered at the thought.

"Tomatoes, cabbage, carrots, celery, lettuce—while they last. You have to get to the Nano Lelei early. The women see the ship come in and head for the market. They don't leave much."

Mike loved to tell stories. After high school he'd become a barge captain and carted supplies all over New Guinea, which was a colony of thousands of islands whose inhabitants spoke hundreds of languages. He'd sailed from village to village delivering kerosene, rice, flour, and other staples and taking away *copra* for processing in Rabaul. He worked for his father, Australian-born Jack Thurston, who owned businesses and land on the island of New Britain. Then wanderlust struck Mike. Although his father was furious at him for leaving, he had set out *east* across the Pacific, against the wind, to explore the world.

We talked in *Destiny's* cockpit until late afternoon, when the sun cut across the top of the breakwater and under the awning like a laser beam.

"Why don't you come round with me to the place where I take my shower," Mike said. "I'll introduce you to Eilaoa and his family. I don't think they'll mind if you use their shower too, but turn off the tap while you're soaping. Water is scarce here."

With that invitation, he chased away the rest of my anger. I hadn't showered in more than six weeks.

Mike led us ashore at low tide. The breakwater, terraced at a 45-degree angle, was slippery and difficult to climb. I grasped the dry concrete blocks above the high tide mark and clung to the wet ones with bare toes.

Dusk gathered itself into pockets of stars as we climbed to a causeway, which led downtown. The smell of coconuts hung on the air, and motorbikes buzzed on the main street, which swarmed with people.

We turned a corner under palm trees and followed the dirt road along the lagoon. Concrete bunkers and the shell of a plane, upended like some grotesque monster bug, seemed to be fighting to escape the undergrowth. The Battle of Tarawa: 1696 U.S. Marines and sailors lost their lives.

We walked to the last house, Eilaoa's, a large, white building with a thatch roof.

"*Talofa*," said Mike, heading for the bathroom after small talk.

"Thank you for letting us use your shower," I said.

"It is Polynesian to be hospitable," Eilaoa replied. He was tall and slender, with cheekbones that looked as if they'd been chiseled.

"I thought the Gilbert Islands were Micronesian," Pete said.

"They are." Eilaoa seemed to look down his long, aquiline nose as he said this. "I am Ellice, from the island of Nanumanga," he said proudly. "My family has lived there for centuries, but I couldn't make a living there."

His tone of voice hinted at tensions between Polynesians and Micronesians in the colony.

"Mike says you used to be a teacher," Pete said.

"I was. But Ellice and Gilbertese teachers here make only $26 a month. I make $120 a month as a *copra* inspector."

Mike returned, shaking drops from his hair. "Next," he said.

"I'm sorry, the water may have a little salt in it," Eilaoa apologized as I left to take my shower. But as it washed away weeks of sticky seawater, it tasted sweet to me.

Pete once again removed *Wa*'s jumpers and spreaders and took them to the cooperative for re-welding. Although they hadn't broken again, he didn't trust the welding job done in Taio Hae and his own work at Tongareva. I put three coats of varnish on the rails and one on the cabin trunk and caulked the deck.

It seemed all we did was work on the boat. In the evenings, when we had a chance to explore Betio, I discovered that a town with a population density as great as that of Philadelphia was just as noisy and grimy. Disenchanted, I would have liked to leave.

"*Wa* hasn't been out of the water in ten months," Pete reminded me. "The paint's chipping, and I'm worried about teredos." These were worms that burrowed into the hulls of wooden boats and turned them to a pulp like soggy Swiss cheese.

"So I guess we haul," I said.

"I asked about that." He sounded weary. "It would cost a hundred dollars."

I was alarmed. We didn't have a hundred dollars to spend on Betio's marine railway; the little money we had would have to go for food. "What'll we do?"

"We'll go 'on the hard,'" he said, explaining how we would intentionally ground *Wa* at high spring tide, then work until high tide returned. We would have to do this twice, once for the port side and once for starboard.

"The next spring tide is a week from now." I paused and stared at him. "That means we're not going to make it across the Indian Ocean this year, doesn't it?"

Pete shook his head. "Not even close."

Feeling I had somehow failed, I didn't consider that making the trip in a year and a half had been a fantasy. After all, some cruisers took ten years to circumnavigate. I was relieved of the pressure to be constantly on the move, but chagrined that motherhood had been shoved farther into the future.

I wrote to my father telling him the trip would take at least *two* and a half years because of cyclone season in the Indian Ocean. He tried to be understanding in his reply, but his disappointment came through.

Given a whole extra year of travel, Pete wrote to his 62-year-old mother, Susan, chair of the Biology Department at Marymount College in Rancho Palos Verdes, inviting her to spend her summer vacation with us.

Despite the hard work during the days, our evenings were filled with camaraderie, sometimes on *Wa* and sometimes at Pong's, a Chinese café that served sweet and sour dishes and curries for sixty cents a meal and steak for a dollar. Mike always ate with us, and we felt a growing kinship with him. For me it was tinged with sexual attraction.

Mike, like the other bachelor sailors we'd met, had a girl in every port, and I wasn't about to risk my marriage for a fling. Nevertheless, I couldn't help comparing his skillfulness with Pete's ineptitude at all things mechanical. Bachelor's degrees in English literature had left both Pete and me woefully unprepared for this life we'd chosen.

The day Mike sailed from Betio Harbor, I felt as if I'd lost a friend. Ever cheerful, he promised we'd meet again in Rabaul, New Guinea, for he was finally on his way home.

Abaiang
or
It Takes Two to Toddy

under way 4 1/2 months

Wa danced northward along Tarawa's western edge under a twenty-knot trade wind and crossed the five-mile channel to Abaiang, another of the sixteen islands forming the Gilbert Islands group. Eight-foot waves sluiced between the two atolls, which acted like a funnel, driving thousands of miles of ocean through the passage at more than three knots.

Inside Abaiang lagoon, we searched in vain for the "white church" listed as a landmark in the *Sailing Directions*. Instead, we anchored three hundred yards from two pandanus and thatch houses on platforms—*kainnakotari*, or community outhouses, hanging over the water.

The lagoon's white sand bottom sloped up imperceptibly, and the green water shimmered like milk jade. The only sounds were the lapping of water on *Wa's* hull, the rushing of wind in coconut trees, and the faint roar of surf on the windward reef. Coming from the village were the sounds of children's voices, like the tinkling of bells.

As Pete and I stowed the sails and cleaned the decks and cockpit, three little black heads popped up beside the boat, and three pairs of skinny arms grabbed for *Wa's* rail.

I held out my hand to help one of the boys aboard, and the other two hoisted themselves onto the fantail. Five more swarmed right behind them. The little boys, fascinated by the shrouds and anchor chain, pattered up and down the decks. I served them glasses of Funny Face.

Will my children be as full of joy as these boys are? I couldn't help wondering.

Meanwhile, more boys came swimming, the little ones with red balloons wrapped around their arms to keep them afloat. Then a man arrived in a canoe. Twenty of us crammed aboard *Wa*, and I served more glasses of Funny Face. I was glad I'd filled the water tank and jugs before we left Betio.

The newly arrived man was worried about his seven-year-old son, who didn't swim well and had come the three hundred yards across the lagoon on another boy's back. He found his son on *Wa*'s cabin top. Relieved, he scolded the boy, then joined us in the cockpit. The father, Noere, was a handsome man of about thirty with a shock of black, curly hair haloing a brown face. Although his mouth smiled, his brown eyes were solemn.

Noere was a teacher in the mission primary school. His village was Tuarabu, with a population of three or four hundred people.

This whole windward coast of Abaiang was dotted with such villages. So different from Betio: four hundred people instead of eight thousand.

Pete spread out our chart to show him how we'd found Tuarabu without knowing its name. Actually, we'd been looking for Tebwiroa, site of the supposedly prominent "white church," where we'd been told to meet Australian Father Barry Fletcher, "a good bloke." Noere was pleased that we'd found Tuarabu instead.

We adults switched to coffee, and Noere rolled cigarettes using tobacco that looked like licorice. I served seconds of Funny Face to the children.

It turned out *Wa* was the first yacht to anchor at this village. There had been a handful of others to visit the island, but Abaiang had been left mostly to the Gilbertese since World War II. The island took delivery from one ship a month, Noere told us, whereas

Tarawa had several ships a month and a plane once a week from Fiji.

As the sun sank red and gold into the lagoon, we arranged to meet him on shore the following day, Saturday; he promised to show us around.

No sooner had Noere and the children left than a man, with three little girls stacked in front of him like peas in a pod, approached in a canoe. Pete hadn't the heart to turn them away. Tired as I was, I joined them in the cockpit. Then a canoe with two men and two boys arrived. I served more Funny Face. All eight went below to look at our home. They stared with wonder at the water pumps, the radio and radio-telephone, the books, our blue-eyed cat. They had never seen a Siamese—didn't know such cats existed.

When the sky turned a sheet of gray over black water, they left. Pete and I relaxed in the cockpit listening to children's voices drift across the lagoon. Palm trees swayed in the wind. Cooking fires winked like matches amongst the trees, making the houses' thatched roofs glow.

Pete puffed on his cigarette. "I told the villagers if we were flying the yellow quarantine flag, we didn't want company."

"Thanks. You've finally figured this cruising thing out!"

Next morning, after we rowed to Tuarabu, Noere took us to his house, which was fifty feet from the shore. Its walls were built of three-foot pandanus stakes, with the area above open to the air. Its roof, made of woven pandanus leaves, was supported by the massive trunks of pandanus trees. All houses in the village were made entirely of island materials. No iron, no steel, no glass. Tuarabu's culture, by and large, remained in the Stone Age.

Nearby were *papai* pits, holes dug eight feet into the ground for raising the starchy staple, which was a kind of taro. The elephant-ear leaves reached to the tops of the pits.

Bananas and a yellow squash also grew there. The soil was

the richest on the island because the villagers composted it with breadfruit leaves, and it was always moist, Noere said.

His sitting room was bare except for his teacher's certificate on one wall. The floor, coral gravel, was covered with two layers of mats, the bottom layer coarsely woven from coconut leaves and the top of the more finely woven pandanus. The bedroom was almost entirely taken up by a board platform. The "kitchen" was a fire pit between the house and the lagoon, and the family used the *kainnakotari*—community outhouses stretching over the lagoon—where they also bathed.

As we talked, Noere's neighbor and fellow teacher, Tekitonga, arrived. Tekitonga was hardly taller than I, with black hair as curly as Noere's and a smile that lit his whole face. His nose seemed like a clump of dough pasted on as an afterthought.

Noere brought out his tobacco tin, black stick tobacco, and dried pandanus leaf, which looked like thick rolling paper. He rolled himself a cigarette and offered the tin to us. The heavy smell of the burning stick and leaf filled the room.

Pete later said the smoke made him feel light-headed and relaxed. In further experiments with stick tobacco rolled in cigarette paper, he decided the pandanus must be narcotic. Practically every adult on Abaiang smoked pandanus cigarettes.

Talk turned to education and the fact that the colony, with 25,000 Gilbertese and Ellice under the age of nineteen, had only four high schools.

"Why aren't all the children being educated?" I asked. "And why aren't there any high schools in the Ellice Islands?"

Noere and Tekitonga glanced at each other, and Noere cleared his throat. "The British believe it's unnecessary," he said. "They want to educate only enough people to fill the civil service."

I thought of the schools in Taio Hae and Tongareva, which Pete and I had visited, and wondered why the French and New Zealanders educated kids and the British didn't.

Tekitonga shrugged. "If you make your living fishing and raising coconuts and *papai*, you don't need to know how to read and write."

"But you're teachers," I persisted. "You must object to that policy.

If the GEIC is to become independent and a democracy, its citizens must be literate."

Noere's wife, Tokanimanga (called Toka), brought in tin dishes heaped with food, which ended our conversation about education. I suspected the Gilbertese were just as happy to get off that subject.

A big woman, Toka swayed as she walked, and her bare toes seemed to grip the ground like suction cups. The five of us sat cross-legged in a circle on pandanus mats around the food. Noere said grace. Then Toka passed platters filled with three different kinds of fish, a chicken boiled especially for the guests, which the others didn't touch, rice, and *papai*, which tasted like potato-squash. Sweeping away flies with one hand and eating with the other, sometimes using my fingers and sometimes a spoon, I gorged.

I was embarrassed that Toka had gone to the trouble and expense of preparing a chicken just for Pete and me. Although Toka sat with us, she didn't eat. After our experience with Saua's family on Tongareva and Eilaoa's family on Tarawa, I was used to being the only woman eating but still wasn't comfortable with it.

We washed the fish and *papai* down with "toddy," a drink of coconut sap mixed with water. It tasted yeasty, as if it were alcoholic, but Noere told us, "I must set an example for my students and do not drink sour toddy."

As we completed our tour of Tuarabu late that afternoon, a man carrying four coconut shells on strings emerged from his house and began to climb a tree in his yard.

"Why don't you watch us cut toddy," Tekitonga said. "It's a ritual. It has to be done right or the tree will grow sulky and dry up," he explained. He showed us the notches hewn in the trunk, to make climbing easier, and the four branches cut to within two feet of the trunk and bound with twine. "Toddy trees don't bear coconuts," he said.

Pete followed Tekitonga up the trunk while I stood at the foot of Noere's tree. (After several months in island cultures, I was used to being considered, as a woman, a second-class citizen.) When a boy, at about ten, was deemed responsible enough to cut toddy, it was said he'd come of age.

Noere climbed with four empty bottles in one hand and held on with the other.

"*Kao ka ta kea ta ka,*" keened another man from branches nearby. The lament seemed to be placating someone and wasn't unhappy.

The branches above me rustled as Noere started his work, and he began to whistle something tuneless and wandering. "Some men sing and some whistle," he explained to me later. "It doesn't matter which we do, but we must do it from the heart."

Noere moved around the crown to the other side to tap his last stalk, taking away the full bottle of coconut sap and replacing it with an empty one. It was like tapping a sugar maple, except that toddy trees delivered all year long.

Noere climbed down with his bottles, walked to the kitchen fire pit, and poured some of the sap into the teakettle, which he then filled with again as much water. It was ready to drink. The villagers drank toddy the way Americans guzzled sodas.

The remaining toddy, boiled, turned into a reddish-brown, sweet liquid called *kamaimai*, which the Gilbertese also drank and used in cooking.

Unwatered and saved overnight, toddy fermented. In twenty-four hours it reached an alcohol content of eight percent. By then it bubbled so fiercely that a cork couldn't be kept on the bottle. It tasted, I found later, like a combination of apple cider and champagne. In three days sour toddy reached full maturity and "went off"—turned acidic—and was undrinkable. *What a wonderful tree is the coconut, that it should produce booze all of its own accord for only the labor of fetching it!*

As darkness crept out from behind clouds, Pete and I hurried back to *Wa* to get ready for our dinner guests. Just as they arrived, the sky broke with rain. When they scrambled aboard, I realized with dismay that there were three more people than I'd counted on—

Tekitonga's wife Teresa and four children instead of two. Braving the downpour, Noere and Tekitonga hunched into their raincoats like turtles, and Pete took meager shelter beneath his Float Coat, while the women and children fled below.

Toka and Teresa spread their ample bulks across the entire port and starboard bunks while Noere's baby and three boys, one Noere's and two Tekitonga's, huddled on the cabin floor. I hunkered in the forepeak waiting for the rain to stop. With all those people in the way, I couldn't cook.

When the squall ended and the children moved into the cockpit, I groped in the darkness past a forest of female shins for the rice, enough of one kind of canned meat for ten, and canned string beans. Unfortunately, almost all our food was stowed beneath Toka and Teresa. It would have been much easier to lift the cushions and search for cans from the top than to kneel and play "Go Fish" for one can at a time, but I had no choice. If I'd asked the women to get up, they had nowhere to go.

I'd never cooked for ten. I couldn't find the corned beef and so was reduced to choosing mackerel, the lowest form of edible protein we had aboard.

Three one-pound cans of mackerel and a lot of curry and flour went into one pot, three cans of beans into another pot, and six cups of dry rice into a third. The kerosene lantern sputtered. The stove spat alcohol as I primed it, then flared with the match. The women, who spoke no English, stared in fascination. I don't think they'd ever seen a foreigner cook.

Then I heard the squawk and a furious flapping of feathers. They had brought us a gift. *Oh no, they wouldn't have, they couldn't have,* I wished silently. I glanced out the companionway at the chicken, feet bound, struggling in Tekitonga's arms.

Coco sniffed the air, though the rooster was to lee of him. His eyes burned blue. Just as the cat pounced, Pete grabbed him by the tail—and held him that way for most of the evening. Coco strained on his tail, the tip of it flicking back and forth, his whiskers twitching. The rooster gurgled.

I prayed the rice, beans, and mackerel would be ready soon.

Because we had only four plates and two bowls, I got out the pie tin, cake tin, and bread pan, which I gave to Pete because it was the most undishlike. Rather than share with him, I decided I would wait until later. That was the custom in the islands anyway, right—everyone eats except the woman who fixed the food?

When they had finished, out came the guitar, which Tekitonga played, and we all crowded into *Wa's* cockpit to sing the songs of Abaiang. Toka and Teresa sang with zest, harmonizing and improvising, while Tekitonga stopped them and lectured with mock severity when they hit wrong notes. After a practice session, they recorded on the cassette. When I played it back, their eyes danced.

After they left, I glared at the rooster. "What are we going to do with *him*?" I asked Pete.

He shrugged. "Eat him, I guess."

"I wish they'd brought a bottle of wine instead." No sooner were those words out of my mouth than I felt guilty. These people couldn't afford to buy wine. They had given us something scarce and precious to them, a chicken dinner, and I was disparaging it instead of being grateful for their warmth and hospitality. Still, entertaining people in close quarters, serving unpalatable canned food, and singing what seemed to be the same songs—it was all old hat.

Was I jaded after less than five months of traveling, or did the malaise cut deeper? At every island so far I'd felt estranged from Pete, who plunged into the culture and ignored me. And the closest I'd come to his kind of bonding was with Hina at Nuku Hiva and Mrs. Saua, who didn't speak English, at Tongareva. I tagged along with the men and felt, sometimes, more like Pete's dog than his wife. Another wave of guilt washed over me. Why didn't I get with the Great Adventure instead of wanting more?

The next Saturday, we rowed ashore at eight, prepared to walk four miles to the village of Tani Maiaki, but it was not long before a young man on a motorbike stopped and offered us a ride. He drove me at breathtaking speed, dropped me off at the *maneaba*, or open-air meeting hall, where we were to be guests at a wedding, and returned for Pete.

The *maneaba* had a high thatched roof supported by coconut trunk columns around its edges. A breeze blew through, but the morning was still hot and humid enough that sweat trickled from my hairline and down my back.

There must have been fifty people there. All were dressed in *lava-lavas*. Apparently they were expecting us. One of the groom's uncles, a man with gray hair and a bent back, put down a pandanus mat for me. He spoke English. When I answered in Gilbertese, he was pleased.

A girl walked to the empty acetylene tank in front of the *maneaba* and pounded on it with a piece of iron. As the sound boomed through the village, the people rose from their mats and gathered outside.

All in white she came, in white lace with a veil and silver slippers. Her groom, wearing a white wreath, a tight gray suit, and black shoes, led her by the arm. They headed the procession through Tani Maiaki to the church. Everyone sang.

Bride and groom walked arm in arm into the small, thatch-roofed church and along the *lava-lavas* laid down for an aisle to the altar. Relatives and friends jammed in and knelt on the pandanus mats to hear the vows, and Pete and I were swept into the church with the rest. When Father Mea joined them as man and wife, the congregation burst into joyous song.

After the ceremony the groom's uncles took turns carrying the bride through the village on their shoulders. A hefty young woman weighing more than two hundred pounds, she bounced as she rode, and one of her new uncles was a very slight man. Sweat poured down his cheeks.

The groom's mother, drunk on sour toddy, ran alongside, her gray hair flying, doing a will-o'-the-wisp dance. The village children followed, singing.

How different from my own wedding, I thought, where the only children were Pete's cousins, and most of the guests were middle-aged or elderly. It was my mother's wedding, really—the wedding she hadn't had because she was married in a courthouse during the depths of the Depression. All her friends were at my wedding as witness; only three of mine attended. My body had gone through the motions, but I wasn't there. I'd agreed to the ceremony because to do anything else would have caused a permanent rift with my parents.

The uncles carried the bride three times around the outside of the *maneaba*, then set her down to walk in her high heels across their backs into the building for the feast. I winced as those spike heels driven by her two hundred pounds dug into the men.

For a while the bride, looking drained, sat next to Father Mea, whose quiet presence shielded her. Then she moved to the left side of the building opposite her husband. He looked tired and uncomfortable in the tight-fitting suit. His flower wreath drooped in the heat, and sweat trickled from his hairline. He still had on his tie and shoes. I wondered whether the suit belonged to the community and if that was why it was too small. I hadn't seen a man dressed so formally in nearly six months.

The singing began. The bride's relatives, sitting behind the groom, and the groom's relatives, sitting behind the bride, took turns, singing lustily in four-part voices on key. They clapped in time to the music. I longed to join them but contented myself with nodding my head to the rhythm.

The groom's father, a thin, ascetic-looking man in a black *lava-lava* and white shirt, joined Pete and me. In fine English he said we were the guests of honor, which embarrassed me, for I didn't want to upstage the bride and groom. We protested, but to no avail. Pete promised that he would have color pictures of the wedding printed and bring them back to Abaiang. This thrilled the groom's father, for family pictures were treasured, and I'd previously seen only black and white ones.

There came a rumbling: with a shout all the children leapt up and ran from the *maneaba*. A gray, two-ton truck labeled Abaiang Co-op drove up. This was the only four-wheeled vehicle in running order on the island. A man unloaded a 12-volt battery to power the electric guitar, and then as many children as would fit climbed into the truck for a ride to the next village to pick up the band instruments.

The women gathered outside with the food. Four of them hefted the coconut basket of rice, which was four feet in diameter. Just as they brought it inside, rain began.

They set before us dishes of pork carved from a roast pig, canned corned beef, rice, *papai*, and *papai* pudding. We ate with our fingers and drank *kamaimai* from glass mugs. The people behind us sang.

As the people in the back rows were served, the uncles did ceremonial dances. One was performed by a man who was a hundred years old. He wrapped a mat around his waist *lava-lava* style, tying it with a rope of human hair, and swayed feebly to the singing while the uncles behind him danced in support.

Then the band came, snare drum after snare drum. Bride's and groom's relatives asked their opposites to dance with a sweeping motion of their arms. Girls dusted the dancers' necks with talcum powder and perfume.

When the band started to play, I looked at Pete with amazement. "That's Chubby Checker's 'The Twist.' How in the world?"

He grinned. "They've got radios. They're just eleven years behind the times."

The people shouted with glee as he and I were pushed onto the dance floor.

I'll show 'em. My country invented the twist. I winked at Pete, wiggled my hips, and ground my bare feet into the mat. My dress flopped about my knees as I moved faster and faster with the music. Was the band speeding up? The Gilbertese pulled away from Pete and me, leaving us alone in a circle of brown bodies. They clapped and shouted, and I moved faster, until I was panting so hard I had to sit down.

Pete told the groom's father we had to leave.

"Oh, no." He looked offended. "You must stay for the feast."

Pete and I exchanged glances. "That wasn't the feast?" I asked.

"That was just a snack," he said sternly.

Two hours after the first meal, more food arrived.

Determined not to offend our hosts, I took one or two spoonsful from each of the dozen dishes and pieces of two different wedding cakes, one of which was an uniced white sheet cake with the bride's and groom's initials carved in the top. The hefty Gilbertese next to me was putting away a whole plate of *papai*.

I was curious about a dark red meat that smelled of iodine and salt. When I'd cleaned my plate, I pointed to the serving dishes and asked, "What was that?"

"Did you like it?" the groom's father asked with a smile.

"Yes, it was good; it tasted like meat."

"That was a whale washed up on the reef."

I blanched, wondering what had killed the whale, and decided I didn't want to know.

The groom's father asked Pete to make a speech.

"May love and happiness, good health and good luck be with you all your lives," he began. "Thank you for allowing us to attend your wedding. We're honored." The groom's father translated.

I knew Pete meant those words from the bottom of his heart. I felt only gratitude that these people—strangers just hours before—had shared one of life's most important rituals with us. For better or worse, their celebration of the bond of marriage had refreshed my faith in my own.

Three's Company
or
The Sailor Virus

under way 5 months

Sun burned the coral runway to a white heat. Bare, bleached, bone-dry, it seemed to steam dust. Even the palm trees drooped. Pete and I retreated into the shade at Bonriki International Airport on Tarawa. Three customs officers lounged nearby on benches.

Meanwhile, cars were crawling off the road and under the fringe of palms so their drivers could watch the two-engine plane land. When it circled, children ran to the chain link fence enclosing the runway and climbed its rungs to get a closer look.

We were there to meet Susan Eastman, Pete's mother, to whom I felt closer than I ever had to my own. I'd spent every weekend with her during the spring of my senior year in college, while Pete was working swing shift, and had seen her through a nasty divorce.

She'd been a Phi Beta Kappa on her way to getting a PhD in microbiology when she'd met Pete's father, who was doing his surgical residency. At that time she was known as Gertrude; today we'd call her a nerd. She was physically awkward and didn't have a clue about sex.

Dr. Eastman, who was in a hard bounce off a love affair, promptly discarded the name "Gertrude" for the less nerdy "Susan" and swept her off her feet. Five years older than he, she gave up a promising career in microbial genetics.

When Pete was born, his father was serving in the U.S. Navy off the coast of Italy. Susan and her mother doted on the little boy, whose needs were met before he asked. Then Dad returned to find a two-year-old stranger as kingpin of his household. That changed immediately. Susan went on to raise four children, entertain her husband's colleagues, and iron endless dresses and shirts. Dr. Eastman, a serial philanderer, eventually found a woman he preferred to Susan and moved out.

She'd been devastated and had not coped well, trying to juggle her job and three out-of-control teenage daughters, who thought nothing of inviting fifty people over for beer and music. (I fled during these parties and sat under a tree in the vacant land above the house waiting for the kids to go home.)

During quieter times, Susan and I drank together and cried together, and I shared confidences with her that I hadn't with anyone else. She listened to me, valued my advice, and treated me as a friend, something my own mother had never done. I never told her, but I believed she lived too much in her head, unaware of the visceral, and that's what had killed her marriage. I also believed that was the difference between us, and therefore my marriage would survive.

While we waited, Sir John and Lady Margaret Field, the resident commissioner and his wife, arrived in a limo flying the British flag. It was the only limo on the island, of course, and sported the license plate FIELD. Their driver hopped out of the car and opened the back doors for them, and the portly Lady Field stepped into the dust.

"Good afternoon," Pete said. He'd gone to private school and was adept at hobnobbing with anyone.

"Good afternoon," she replied, scowling at Pete's and my bare feet. "You must be Americans." Her tone suggested that she'd just met two slugs.

"We are," said Pete, ignoring her tone. "We sailed here on a small boat."

By this time the balding Sir John had finished conferring with his driver and joined us.

"Look, dear, these people are American sailors," his wife said, placing her hand on his arm. "I didn't catch your names."

We introduced ourselves.

"Why are you at the airport?" Sir John asked.

"To meet my mother," Pete said. "She's chair of the Biology Department at Marymount College and has the entire summer off."

"Oh," Lady Field said. I felt as if I were a virus under a microscope and that she had just discovered something very interesting about me. "We're here to meet our niece, Ginny, who's flying in from England."

"That's nice," Pete said. "You must be pleased she's come."

"Oh, yes, she's a lovely girl. So talented. And an excellent sailor."

Ah, I thought. *I'm a sailor virus, redeemable because my mother-in-law is respectable and we have a boat.*

Just then, Susan, in a dazzle of lemon-orange sundress, got off the plane. Blinking in the harsh sunlight, probably confused after her two-day journey from Los Angeles to Hawaii to Fiji to Tarawa, she didn't see us at the fence.

"Mom!" Pete screamed.

"Susan!" I shouted.

She turned, her face lit, and she rushed to give us a hug through the wire. Her red hair was a scramble, her face and arms freckled. Warmth poured through me as we touched.

We watched between cracks in the pandanus walls of the terminal while she went through customs.

"She's got tomatoes—four of them," Pete whispered, excited. Then, disappointed, "They're confiscating them." The lettuce, which had met its tropical demise anyway, also was confiscated. Six oranges, however, and a four-pound Chateaubriand that had left Los Angeles frozen brick-hard, got through customs.

As we turned to leave, a raven-haired, bubbly young woman stopped us. "Are you the American sailors?" she asked in a clipped, British accent, sticking out her hand to Pete. She was almost as tall as he was and slender. "I'm Ginny Field."

When the elder Fields came up behind her, Pete introduced them to his mother.

"Ginny and I would like to sail with you," Lady Field announced. "I'll leave a message at the Betio post office telling you a convenient time."

"We'll look forward to it," Pete said, and waved goodbye as they got in the limo.

Susan chuckled. "You didn't tell me you were friends with the head honchos."

"We just met them a few minutes ago," I said. "And we wouldn't have if Pete hadn't spoken first."

"Oh?"

"Lady Field didn't think much of our bare feet. But you saved the day. You made us respectable."

She laughed. And the three of us promptly forgot the encounter.

With Susan in the middle, arm-in-arm, jabbering and giggling, we sauntered through the dust of South Tarawa, Pete carrying one suitcase with his right hand and I the other with my left.

We boarded a bus to take us back to the Bairiki ferry stop but climbed off at the Otintai Hotel, where Pete and I had our first iced drinks in months.

"This is positively civilized," I said. Susan, not realizing I hadn't met an ice cube in nearly six months, looked at me strangely.

Lady Field's message was brought to us by an office boy on a bicycle: she and Ginny would meet us the following morning at 10 o'clock.

Oh my God, I thought, *they actually meant it!* Then I thought of the grungy deck, daubed with caulking. Lady Field's first impression of the ill-bred Americans would be confirmed. *And what if she finds out I pee in a bucket?*

There was nothing to do but scrub *Wa* as best I could. And worry about being patronized.

The next morning promptly at ten, a power boat flying the British flag chugged into Betio Harbor and pulled up to *Wa*. Pete threw fenders over the side to keep the two boats from rubbing against each other. Then he reached a hand out to Lady Field, who looked like a teapot in a skirted, leopard-print bathing suit and a broad-brimmed straw hat. Her skin was almost as white as *Wa's* topsides.

"Stand on the cockpit cushion and grab my hand," he said. "I won't let you fall. Hold the shrouds," he said, patting one to show her where, "with your other hand."

She teetered, but Ginny gave her a boost from behind, and she landed with a thump on deck. Ginny grasped the shrouds, stretched one long, tanned leg across the gap, and stepped aboard onto her toes, like a dancer. Her cutoffs and a red and blue-striped T shirt accentuated her lithe body. She was at least a head taller than her aunt.

"Oh my," Lady Field said, "did you *really* sail across the ocean in this thing?"

"They did," Susan said. "I watched them leave Los Angeles."

"I'd be scared to death of falling overboard."

"That's why they have these lifelines," said Susan, running her hand along one, "and they have safety harnesses that they wear when they're on deck."

At the mention of "deck," Lady Field looked down and noticed the caulking. It looked like a bad case of the chickenpox the size of horse turds. Then she stared at us with raised eyebrows. I felt as if I were back under that microscope and was sure she was wishing she hadn't come.

"Let's get you into the cockpit," Pete said, "so we can go for our sail." He gave her his hand again, and she clung to the cabin top with the other as she shuffled the few steps to the cockpit.

Susan patted the cockpit cushion next to her and said, "It's so good to see you again. I've thought a lot about how isolated you are on this remote island." She smiled broadly as Lady Field plunked herself down. "Don't you miss England?"

Lady Field sighed. "Of course I do, but we manage. Sir John says I do much better than just muddling through."

Ginny, her face radiant, handled the sheets while Pete sailed *Wa* out of Betio Harbor. I went below to make tea.

"I loved England," Susan said. "My mother, sister, and I spent several weeks there at Canterbury, Royal Tunbridge Wells, Oxford, and Stratford. And of course London—what a marvelous city."

"I'm from Kent, and I *do* love Canterbury."

"So much history. I was in awe after visiting the cathedral. And then I reread the *Canterbury Tales*."

They went on and on, pausing only to say thank you when I served their tea.

When we got to the pass, we stopped to swim. Lady Field, as game as her niece, took off her hat and dived like a leviathan in ruffles into the green water. She was graceful once there, in her element, as if she had been a champion swimmer in her youth.

Getting her back aboard was a different matter, for we had no Jacob's ladder. Pete grabbed one hand and I the other and tried to haul her bulk onto the deck. Her hands were slippery, though, and she felt like dead weight as she slipped back into the water.

Ginny dived in, popped to the surface behind her aunt, and said, "I'll push. Auntie, I'm going to be a bench for you to stand on," she said, and dived again. Lady Field rose magically in the water.

"Elbows," Pete said, "one, two, three." We grabbed her elbows and hauled, and a dripping Lady Field landed on the fantail with a grunt.

Returning to Betio, we anchored under sail, with an excited Ginny on the tiller and Pete shouting directions.

"That was *so* much fun," Ginny said. "I like your boat. She's lively and sails well, but she's solid, too. I hope you enjoyed yourself, Auntie."

"I believe I'm too old for this sort of thing, but I enjoyed your company," Lady Field said, nodding at Susan. "Would you come to the Residency for supper?"

Susan glanced at Pete and then me. We all were wondering whether she meant just Susan or the three of us.

"That settles it," Lady Field decided, this time directing her attention at me and then Pete. "You must all three come Friday at six o'clock. I'll send the launch for you." She shuffled from *Wa* onto the waiting power boat, the driver and Ginny acting as tugboats to her barge. They waved goodbye and sped from the harbor.

~~~~~~~~~~~~~~~~~~~~

"We'll have to wear shoes," I told Pete. "Do you have any?"

He stuck out his tongue at me. "Of course I do." He hunted for them for ten minutes and, when he dragged out the black dress shoes, they were moldy.

"Oops," I said. "Can you get rid of that with shoe polish?"

"At least cover it up," Susan said. "The question is, are your slacks moldy?"

Fortunately, they weren't.

On Friday afternoon, Pete dressed in white shirt, black slacks, and the re-blacked dress shoes. I found a pair of white sandals to go with a green print dress. Susan wore the same lemon-orange sundress she'd worn on the plane. Then we waited for the launch Lady Field had promised to send.

It didn't come.

Finally, after a puzzled half-hour, we went ashore and called. "Oh yes, I sent Teiho some time ago," Lady Field said. "But he seems to have developed a drinking problem. He may have disappeared into one of Betio's bars. You'd better take the ferry."

The interior of the Residency was awash in light. Two crystal chandeliers hanging over the white tablecloth made the silver and glasses sparkle. A Chopin nocturne murmured from the living room. I smelled roast beef.

A Gilbertese servant in red and blue livery seated us at the table. I tried not to dwell upon what Noere and Tekitonga would think if they saw us there. The disconnect was too great.

"That was a lovely sail," Lady Field said graciously, as a servant filled our glasses with champagne. "And their boat is so small, John, I was surprised." She rose and lifted her glass in a toast. "To all of us here, to the British Foreign Service, and to our friendship with the people of the United States of America."

Two servants brought the first course, a cream of mushroom soup. The second course was white asparagus. Susan, Pete, and Ginny carried the conversation. My introversion had come on like a fever.

"It must be difficult here," I finally said to Sir John, echoing what Susan had said to Lady Field, "with no symphony orchestra, art museums, or libraries."

"So true," he said, "but my task is to prepare the natives for independence. That's an important job, and it *must* be done."

"Is there a timetable?"

"Within ten years. I'll rotate out before it happens, but I have to get them ready."

I thought of how widely dispersed and tiny the thirty-three Gilbert and Ellice Islands were and how simply the people of Abaiang lived. Were they ready to join the community of nations? I didn't think so.

Another servant poured Sauvignon Blanc.

The third course was salmon poached in wine. It was followed by the roast beef with slivers of fresh carrots and green beans. I had to restrain myself from inhaling the food.

"Thank you, Lady and Lord Field," I said, "for this wonderful supper." I was sure they had no idea how grateful I was. The servants hovered in the background waiting to fill our glasses with Merlot.

Then, as we prepared to toast the Queen, protocol for the meal's finale, Lady Field announced it was time for dessert. With great ceremony, a servant brought a domed platter and lifted the lid. Underneath was a strange-looking mound.

"What's this, Mary?" Lady Field asked.

"The fish cake, ma'am."

I studied Lady Field to see if the servant had brought it by mistake.

"How lovely!" Susan said.

I raised my eyebrows, and Pete and I exchanged glances. He put his hand over his mouth to cover a smile.

Sir John frowned at the servant, who was oblivious, and opened his mouth, but Lady Field shook her head. She lifted her fork with dignity, and we ate the savory cake.

When Susan had acclimated to the tropics, we took her to Abaiang to meet Noere and Tekitonga. The next day, which Pete dubbed Susan's Sunday, the first boatload of boys arrived at 9:30 and swarmed over the railing into the cockpit.

"We have to work," Pete told them, as he searched the cockpit locker for his waxed thread and needle. "Can you come tomorrow?" He was feeling pressured to get last-minute jobs done before we left the Gilberts.

"Don't turn them away," Susan protested.

"Mom, they'll keep coming."

"Don't be silly. There are just four boys."

"OK." Pete shrugged. "But only for a little while." Loath to argue with his mother, he hauled the mainsail off its boom track into the cockpit to stitch a hole along the foot. The four boys and Susan scrunched into one corner.

After serving them Funny Face, Susan took their pictures. Because the soft drinks had run *Wa's* water tank dry, Pete asked the boys if they would get us more water. While two of them hauled five-gallon gerry jugs to shore in their canoe, the other two boys sang for the cassette deck while Susan clapped her hands.

I sanded the forehatch, and Pete stitched by hand through five-ounce Dacron, a stiff material more impenetrable than denim.

By the time the boys had returned with the water, six adults had arrived to pay their respects. The boys left, the new visitors crammed into the far end of the cockpit, and Pete stitched on.

When it began to rain, our guests, Susan, and Pete hunched together in the main cabin. I escaped through the forehatch into the forepeak. Our visitors departed.

But as Susan and I waved them goodbye, I spotted a whole gang on their way, swimming and paddling canoes, until nearly two dozen kids were aboard. Again, as some left, others arrived, so that there was a constant exchange, like a tidal pool. Susan, with a smile that lit her entire face, offered soft drinks, lollipops, balloons, and Polaroid pictures. The children, who felt her joy, gave her the most beautiful shells I'd ever seen.

Pete retreated forward and sat on the cabin trunk while I sanded. "She'll have to learn the hard way," he said, but I could see she was having the time of her life.

Throughout the day the children, and a sprinkling of adults, came and went. All the children in Noere's class and, I swear, half the rest of the school besides, boarded *Wa* and scurried up and down her decks. They sang in raucous voices for the cassette player. Susan looked frazzled but happy. I wondered how she'd managed to go for six hours without peeing. (Pete and I just jumped overboard when the need arose.)

Two hours later, Susan was still going strong, leading the kids in a boisterous song. "This will teach her a lesson," Pete said with a scowl.

It was sundown when Pete finally shooed the last kids away. "I got a little tired," Susan confessed, "but wasn't that wonderful!"

"You'll listen to me next time," Pete said.

"About what? I had a glorious time."

Nauru
or
Coco Bites Hickety; Hickety Bites the Dust

*395 miles and 5 days Abaiang to Nauru
under way 6 1/2 months*

We were a strange crew—Pete and I, Coco the Siamese cat, Hickety, a second gift chicken of uncertain gender, plus Pete's mother and the middle-aged priest, Father Barry Fletcher, whom we'd finally met at Abaiang.

Wa had only three living areas—the forepeak, the main cabin, and the cockpit. The farthest anyone could get from the others was ten feet. *Wa's* facilities were primitive: no head and no private place to use the toilet bucket and dress unless one latched the "head" door to the galley sink and hunkered behind it.

This will be a no sex passage, I told myself. *I hope it's a fast one.* For while our journey persisted in sending Pete and me in different directions, our physical intimacy seemed to affirm our bond.

What prompted us to make this trip? Father Fletcher. As much an adventurer as a man of God, he was a lean fellow, about forty, and more often than not wore only shorts and flip-flops. His skin, almost as brown as Noere's, stretched tautly over high cheekbones and wrinkled at the corners of his eyes. He'd talked up the island nation of Nauru, telling us how his brother had worked there as an engineer and promising that the people would embrace us with their hospitality.

Intrigued, Pete and I had agreed to sail there as a foursome, then head on to the Solomon Islands, while Susan and Father Fletcher flew from Nauru back to Tarawa after our stay. From Tarawa Susan would fly back to the States.

For Pete, having Susan and Father Fletcher aboard eased the pain of leaving Abaiang. His kinship with Noere and Tekitonga had come close to the brotherhood Pete craved, but at least we were taking a bit of the island with us in the person of the priest.

We sailed against a small breeze from the southwest, but by the time we'd beaten our way to the entrance of Abaiang lagoon, the incoming tide was setting a current of two knots against us. We couldn't make way in the three-knot wind. When we began drifting backwards, Pete anchored in the pass.

By late afternoon the tide had changed, but there still was no wind. *Wa* bobbed in place like a hobbyhorse all night. We had no choice but to sit there: her Albin gasoline engine had died two weeks before, the victim of water-laced fuel, slipshod maintenance, and spare parts a quarter of a world away.

We took turns on the tiller, each of us on for an hour and a half, the women on watch while the men slept. There was no need for two to be on deck, but we hadn't enough bunks. The port quarterberth was eaten up on one end by the stove and at the other by suitcases, the *Sailing Directions*, notebooks, and the typewriter. The forepeak, roomy as it was, was suitable as a double berth only for the most compatible people in a calm sea, for if there were any motion the sleepers would be thrown against each other.

All that windless night and the following morning we made only thirty miles, averaging little better than a knot and a half in nineteen hours, mostly from current. "I'd rather have a gale," I complained to Susan.

"You're joking." She looked alarmed.

"Remember 'The Rime of the Ancient Mariner'? '*Day after day, day after day, We stuck, nor breath nor motion; As idle as a painted ship Upon a painted ocean.*'"

"That's just a poem. Besides, Coleridge was an opium addict."

"Mom, you'd better stick to mitochondria," Pete said.

"Coleridge was one of the greatest poets of all time. Opium did wonderful things for his imagination."

To cheer us up, I baked brownies.

Forty-eight hours off the anchor at Tuarabu, we were only sixty miles closer to Nauru. Father Fletcher, watching his vacation dribble into an ornery ocean, went forward to pray. That afternoon, an hour after someone had thrown overboard a blue and yellow cheese can, it still floated fifty yards from us.

Late that afternoon, as I gazed over the undulating blue Jell-O of the sea, I saw crinkly patches, like crushed voile. Wind was ruffling the water. Soon the patches joined together and turned the blue Jell-O into ripples.

A smile broke over Susan's face as she clutched the tiller and filled *Wa's* sails. "It's like being pulled into the infinite," she said. I could've hugged her. She understood what I felt but hadn't been able to put into words.

Meanwhile, Father Fletcher had moved Hickety from the cockpit to the fantail, where the fowl clucked and pecked at coconuts and the crusts of brownies Susan gave it. I hoped we'd run out of fresh fish, which would make Hickety the logical choice for supper.

Coco was going mad. Because he was not allowed out of the cockpit, he took his battle station by the tiller and watched hungrily. Father shifted Hickety aft to the coil of anchor line, then to the counterweight on the wind vane, where the bird perched like some foolish weather cock.

"I'm tired of running a barnyard," I said. "Let's throw the thing overboard and put it out of its misery, or eat it."

"You can't kill Hickety," Susan said. "Hickety, pickety, my black hen. She lays eggs for gentlemen."

"This is a rooster," Father said.

"Besides that, Hickety's brown," Pete added.

"She's a hen," I countered, "because of her cluck and lack of comb." Having grown up on a ranch and raised chickens for 4-H, I felt sure of myself.

"The bright green tail spells rooster," Father said.

Just then, Hickety crowed. He looked so proud of himself that he crowed again, and again.

"Guess I'm going to eat crow," I grumbled.

Father Fletcher diplomatically said nothing.

"But he's such a nice chicken," Susan piped up. "I don't want to eat him."

"Do you want to give him to someone at Nauru who *will* eat him?" Father asked.

"Why would they eat him? Why couldn't they just make him a pet?"

"Because fresh protein is hard to come by on a small island," Father said. "They have a choice of pigs, chickens, and fish."

"Let's go below and let Pete take care of it," I said. She looked stricken but followed me down the companionway. I shut the main hatch, then made coffee. "How about a game of gin rummy?" I asked. She played, but her heart wasn't in it.

Pete dispatched and plucked Hickety. Father Fletcher made a fishing lure out of the feathers. No one enjoyed the fried chicken more than Coco.

Five days from Abaiang, at three in the morning on July 28, Father saw the lights of Nauru—the glow of the phosphate works on the windward side of the eight-square-mile chunk of land. With a good wind now behind us, we came up on the island by the time I'd fixed breakfast.

Father Fletcher cast his lure of Hickety feathers over the stern and hooked a tuna, which nearly pulled him overboard. He braced his bare feet against the railing and his body against the backstay and began reeling it in—a flash of silver that sparkled in the sunlight. Its powerful head and snub nose reminded me of Muhammad Ali.

"God, it's huge!" Pete cried. "Can you do it? Here, let me help. The boat's forward motion is favoring the fish, not you."

Knowing what Pete meant, I leapt to tend the sails while Pete turned *Wa* toward the wind and the fish.

Father Fletcher lifted his rod and sank it, lifted it and sank it, each time pulling in the slack, never taking his eyes off the tuna. I wished I had a movie camera. I'd never seen anyone work a fish so expertly. I forgot he was a priest.

With Pete's help on the tiller and later with the gaff, Father Fletcher reeled in a tuna that was more than four feet long. It had taken him the better part of an hour.

"That will make a fine gift for our hosts," he said as he mopped the sweat from his face with his T shirt.

"Thank you, Hickety," I said.

With an elevation of two hundred thirteen feet, Nauru was a high island compared with the atolls we'd been visiting. The greenness of its hills reminded me of the lemon orchards outside Santa Barbara when I was a child.

We came up on its lee side, tied to a sixty-foot barrel buoy that dwarfed *Wa,* and waited for the immigration launch which, we'd been told by marine radio, wouldn't arrive until two o'clock. Grateful for the extra time to cool off and relax, Pete and I dived over the side.

No sooner were we in the water than the launch roared out. It had been sent by one of Father's friends, Joseph Detsimea Audoa, Nauru's minister for justice, who had to be in Parliament by two o'clock. With that sort of help, we got through customs and immigration in record time and were whisked ashore.

Joseph himself, a large, dark-skinned, heavily built man, met us. He was wearing a black suit, long-sleeved white shirt, black tie, and black shoes. I hoped he didn't notice my bare feet. Joseph gave Father the keys to his car and house, where Susan, Pete, and I were invited to take showers later in the afternoon. Another friend brought around a carton of cigarettes and cold beers. I began to understand Father's enthusiasm for Nauru. He immediately moved into Joseph's house.

Joseph, a widower, lived alone. His living room was filled with mementos from all over the world—a quart decanter from the Coty perfume family, a mynah bird, an electric organ. We sat in a circle on wicker furniture. A chicken strolled across the ceramic tile floor, checking for crumbs, and left by way of the open kitchen door.

Father Fletcher mixed drinks at the bar.

I excused myself to take a shower. Suddenly I was in a real bathroom—my first in more than six months—with green tile, yellow towels and bath mats, and a shower curtain printed with ferns. As I felt the water stream down on me, I said to myself, "Here I am in the house of the minister for justice, who isn't even here and doesn't know me, and I'm taking my first hot shower in seven months." It blew my mind.

A new nation born January 31, 1968, Nauru was and still is the smallest republic in the world and the smallest island nation. In 1971 the population consisted of three thousand Nauruans—Micronesians similar to the Gilbertese—along with three thousand foreigners.

Tricalcium phosphate, deposited originally as dead marine organisms, made Nauru unique—and wealthy. In 1971 the country enjoyed the highest per-capita income in the world because it produced five percent of the world's phosphate.

To mine this white gold, Nauru imported Gilbertese, Ellice, and Hong Kong laborers. In their spare time the Gilbertese and Ellice fished and sold their catch to the Nauruans and Chinese. The Chinese in their spare time ran a proliferation of cafés and shops, all franchised by Nauruans.

The last of the foreigners were the "Europeans"—mostly Australians, who ran the Nauru Phosphate Corporation and worked in professional positions. Few Nauruans were qualified to hold these jobs; the country boasted only two university graduates.

The island was shaped like a Stetson. Its coastal rim was similar to the barrier reefs of many other islands. The top of the hat—Topside—however, was a different world. Where the phosphate was mined out, jagged coral pinnacles scarred the landscape like a forest of stalagmites five to ten feet apart and fifteen to twenty feet high. As wind and rain weathered them, they turned gray—a plateau barren and desolate as the moon.

Only a scant fifty years before, the Nauruans had lived largely in the Stone Age, as their Gilbertese cousins on Abaiang still did in 1971. Such a staggering leap in two generations had a profound effect upon the way modern Nauruans viewed themselves and the world.

On Nauru, electric power had replaced kerosene lanterns, indoor plumbing the outhouse and a bucket at the well, washing machines the tub, hand power, and elbow grease. But the old and the new dwelt uneasily side by side. The people often had expensive furniture but just as often preferred to sit on the floor. Sometimes they slept outside, for their new concrete houses with shuttered windows were hotter than the old native dwellings of pandanus and thatch.

Three years after becoming a republic, Nauru still was fiercely independent. Its eighteen MPs, five ministers, and president took their jobs seriously. They met three days a week—Mondays, Wednesdays, and Fridays. During the session Susan and I attended, they discussed the budget.

As the finance minister, a bantam of a man with more tail feathers than hair, read through the budget item by item, the MPs called for clarification.

"What's that four thousand dollars for furniture?" one MP asked him.

"It's for the new office building," the finance minister replied.

"Would you explain the contingency-emergency fund?" asked another.

"It's for pencils, phone calls, miscellaneous expenses."

"Why do we need so much money for emergencies—we never have any emergencies," another MP commented.

"Because if we *do* have an emergency, we must be able to pay for it." The finance minister raised his voice and glared. He'd been under fire all morning.

These were niggling questions, but the MPs had reason to be

suspicious of administrators and their figures after having been bilked by the Germans, the British, and the Australians. They knew that Nauru's seemingly abundant wealth had to be kept safe for the time when the phosphate would be gone (which happened in the 1980s).

I wondered why our legislators in Washington, D.C. couldn't be as prudent.

Although Joseph Detsimea Audoa wore a suit to Parliament, at other times he dressed in a short-sleeved white shirt, shorts, and knee socks—the uniform of the British in the tropics. I used to think, in Betio, that the British looked absurd in the thick, knitted socks, but the uniform on Joseph seemed natural—and imposing. When he walked into a room, people stopped talking, turned to him in deference, and waited for him to take charge. He wore his natural leadership with grace and dignity.

Before becoming minister for justice, he trained as an X-ray technician in Australia, he told me. He'd learned most of the material but hadn't memorized the bones. When the examiner summoned Joseph to identify the parts of the human skeleton, Joseph had a clever excuse: "If I touch those bones I will die. There is a curse on them." He chuckled at my look of surprise. "The man believed I was that superstitious. He gave me a low pass, but I did well on the rest of the test."

He had barely survived World War II, when he was interned with twelve hundred other Nauruans on Truk, the forward anchorage of the Japanese Imperial Fleet. Their Japanese captors allowed them a rice ration about the size of a golf ball, and they subsisted on coconuts, pandanus, and fish. More than a third of them died on Truk between 1944 and 1945.

One evening Joseph joined us for dinner on *Wa*, and we four went through part of a bottle of scotch, four bottles of wine, and most of a bottle of Benedictine. The conversation ranged from the Vietnam War to the American Civil Rights Movement to Micronesia's place in the community of nations to Nauruan fishing techniques to sailing strategies in crossing the Pacific. He seemed starved for talk. And unlike so many other islanders, he treated Susan and me with the same respect for our intellects as he did Pete.

"What was Nauru like before World War II," I asked, "when the British Phosphate Company was in control?"

Joseph cleared his throat and sipped his wine. "It was very bad," he said. "We were required to remain in our own districts after ten o'clock at night. The Chinese, Gilbertese, and Ellice, too. The British didn't want trouble. Beer was doled out one can a day to the 'Europeans' and Chinese. Liquor was available only for 'medicinal' purposes."

"Didn't you resent that?" Pete asked. "After all, it's your country."

"There were many strikes, and conflict was constant."

"Nauru should be grateful it had you and Hammer DeRoburt to fight for independence," I said, referring to the country's first president.

"And the help of the United Nations," he added.

Joseph stayed until we ran out of booze, at three, and even then he wanted to continue the party at his home. I wondered how hard it was for him, living in a close-knit tribal society, to face his empty house.

Pete and I left him under the fluorescent light upon the harbor wall surrounded by darkness. His head down, he shuffled away, as if reluctant to leave our company.

I felt a deep bond with this thoughtful man, ahead of his culture. His loneliness lit up my own.

The hardest thing about cruising was saying goodbye. It was doubly hard at Nauru because both Father Fletcher and Susan were leaving us. She and I had spent most of our time ashore. We'd toured the phosphate mines, gone to Parliament, visited in people's homes. Wherever we went, her graciousness and spunk had won over our hosts.

The morning she left, more than a dozen Australians, Chinese, and Nauruans joined us at the airport at six-thirty. There'd been a big party the night before, and one of the women was more than a little shaky behind her dark glasses. It was a tribute to Susan that the woman had forced herself out of bed.

I stood on one foot, then another, not knowing what to say, for I had no idea when we'd see her again. I realized how much I loved her, but I could say it only with my eyes.

Pete clutched her arm, not wanting to let go, and sniffed back tears. Susan boarded the eight-seat jet for the hour's trip to Tarawa, where she was to transfer to the same Fiji Airways plane she'd arrived on six weeks before.

The plane wheeled to the end of the runway, turned, and, with a whir of dust, raced the runway's entire length, taking off with a sputter and roar into a gray sky.

I remembered Susan's face—lit with an inner light as she steered on her way to Nauru, and smiling with joy as she entertained the children of Abaiang—and I wept.

As a small way of saying thank you to our hosts, Pete and I invited eleven people to Star Twinkles for a farewell Chinese dinner. I looked around the table at Nauru's polyglot culture—Nauruans, Gilbertese, Ellice, Chinese, and Australians all sharing food together—and realized this was the way the world should be.

We had cocktails, ate our fill, and drank twelve bottles of champagne. Someone tried to pick up the check, but Pete grabbed it. It was for forty dollars. I tried not to think about the money, which we could ill afford, but these people had entertained us in their homes and at restaurants for more than a month. We had to say thank you.

The next morning Pete and I crawled out of bed at ten-thirty. We were to be at Joseph's at eleven-thirty for beer and oysters.

The real reason for the party was to admire Joseph's new videotape machine, which had arrived on the plane with the oysters. In 1971, Pete and I had never seen one. An Australian doctor assembled it for Joseph and began filming us. Pete stuck his thumbs in his ears and waggled his fingers at the camera. Joseph hooted.

"You're silly," I said, and waved at the camera.

"Lighten up," he said, stepping behind me and grabbing me by the shoulders. He stuck out his right foot and sang, "You put your right foot in, you put your right foot out, you put your right foot in and you shake it all about."

I took the plunge and joined him. As the camera followed us, we hokey pokeyed around the wicker chairs and behind the bar, almost knocking over a bottle of whisky. "You put your head in!" I sang as we rounded the corner behind the couch. Two chickens, which had been hiding there, squawked and flew out the open kitchen door.

The Australian doctor, short and paunchy, chortled so hard he was having trouble keeping the camera steady. I craned my neck to see the screen, which showed a grainy couple bouncing around doing something that looked like senior calisthenics.

I remembered how much fun I'd had doing the *tamure* with Hina Peterano's daughter in Taio Hae. I resolved to "lighten up," as Pete said. Little did I realize that, as I was deciding to "lighten up," the world around me would darken. Soon, in Melanesia, I would be looking only through the eyes of shallow white people, whose lenses were opaque. Gone would be the easy camaraderie, warmth, and generosity of the Polynesians and Micronesians. In their place would be the darkness of racial discrimination and fear.

Honiara
or
Two Near Misses

801 miles and 9 days Nauru to Honiara
under way 8 months

Sea fever swept *Wa* with its fire—a wind averaging twenty knots and a one and two-thirds knot current setting to the west. We hardened up to 195º, that is, sailed closer to the wind, and made 154 miles southwest one noon to noon—no small feat for a boat whose theoretical maximum speed was six knots. That was to be our best run in 104 days crossing the Pacific, during which we averaged a hundred miles a day.

Five days later, we were in the British Solomon Islands Protectorate, province of the southeast monsoon. The big island of Malaita-Marmasike loomed huge in front of us, blue as stormy water, filling the whole southwestern horizon, obscuring sea and sky.

It was abeam by noon. Pete jibed *Wa* round the corner to run her north of west through Indispensable Strait between Malaita and the island of Guadalcanal. We had a hundred miles to go to Honiara, the largest city on Guadalcanal and the colony's capital.

I couldn't take my eyes from the now green land. Vegetation more dense than I'd ever seen swept down the folds of the mountains like satin in sunlight and, in shadows, like velvet going the wrong way. Pete and I sat all afternoon in the cockpit watching the colors change with the sun as the panorama slipped by like a travelogue in slow motion.

The next morning, we crossed Sealark Channel and by early afternoon sailed into Iron Bottom Sound and the thumbprint of bay that marks Honiara. At its western edge lay a ship at anchor. Pete steered for it.

The ship was a passenger vessel onloading perhaps a thousand people from a nearby jetty. At my suggestion, we anchored between it and the shore. Barges and skiffs buzzed by, rocking us in their wakes, and the tourists waved and shouted greetings.

No other small vessels were anchored there, and between *Wa* and the shore a beacon stuck out of the water warning of submarine cables close to the surface. A choppy surf bounced us around, and the wind blew twenty to twenty-five knots. Surely this couldn't be the anchorage of a major port and the capital of the Solomon Islands. The *Sailing Directions* gave no clue as to the anchorage, and our small-scale chart didn't even have Honiara on it. The longer we waited for customs and immigration, the more uneasy I became.

Then a man strode onto the jetty and yelled to us to go around the edge of the bay to the yacht club, where there was sheltered water. We gratefully prepared to up anchor and sail off. But to do so, we'd have to tack upwind to get out of the bay.

We decided we'd come off the anchor on the starboard tack in order to stay as close to the ship and as far from the lee shore and jetty as possible. Pete raised the mainsail and the anchor, and I took the tiller. But when I tried to follow the plan, like a stubborn child *Wa* pointed her bow toward shore and let the sail fill from the port side. Pete rushed to raise the jib.

Meanwhile, the jetty was looming closer, and I tried again to bring *Wa* onto the starboard tack. The self-steering gear jammed. There wasn't room enough to jibe, that is, bring the boat around the long way. Fear seized me; my hands shook. I clutched the tiller to steady them. I had to sail *Wa* where she preferred, however close to the jetty that might bring us.

I gritted my teeth and sailed *Wa* hard on the wind. Tourists crowded to the edge of the jetty to watch.

"It looks like they want us to crash," Pete yelled. "Do they think this is the Indianapolis 500?"

I heard them hollering, "Go, go, go!" Out of the corner of my eye I saw them jumping up and down and punching the air with their fists.

Wa missed the jetty by five feet, but the jagged rocks onshore kept coming at me, getting bigger. I missed those, too, by less than ten feet, and sailed *Wa* through the churning surf that was trying to carry her to her doom.

Shaking with relief, I brought *Wa* around Point Cruz into the yacht club harbor. A lean young man with dark hair and a dark brown beard—the man who'd shouted to us from the jetty—waited in his dinghy. He led us to an open spot and helped Pete tie a sternline to a sunken barge.

When it was all over, Pete and I collapsed in heaps of shattered nerves in *Wa's* cockpit. I desperately wanted a stiff drink. It was past five o'clock and too late to clear customs, so we couldn't go ashore until the next morning.

"Never mind," said our fellow yachtsman, who introduced himself as Jacques Sapir. "I'll go ashore and ask the police if I can bring you to them. I'm sure they won't mind, and you can do the paperwork tomorrow morning. I'll get Robyn to put on some *kai*—I know you don't want to cook tonight—and I'll bring some beer back."

What a wonderful welcome! I hoped he knew how grateful I was.

After he left, Pete said, "If we're going to do things like that, we ought to have an engine."

"Or good charts," I said, blaming myself for getting us into trouble in the first place. If we'd had a large-scale chart of Guadalcanal, with Honiara on it, it would have shown us the yacht club anchorage, and we would have known where to go.

I remembered the three equipment failures we'd had on the way to Nuku Hiva, the broken spreaders on the way to Tongareva, running aground at Tarawa. This was worse: we came within five feet of smashing *Wa* to splinters and ourselves with her.

With a reliable engine, we agreed, we could afford to take risks as we just had—and get away with them. Lacking an engine, we'd been just plain lucky. We couldn't count on luck another time.

After going to immigration and customs the next morning, we stopped at the post office. I mailed my latest batch of stories to the *News-Press* and was sorting through our letters from home, some of which had been sitting in General Delivery for two months, when I heard Pete yell, "Outrageous!"

"What?" I asked. He was holding a parcel.

He pointed to the customs declaration, which listed total COD charges, including airfreight, of $136. "That carburetor should be less than forty bucks."

"Is there something else in there?"

"Spark plugs and a head gasket," he snorted. "Total rip off." So much for our engine. He bought postage and returned the package to the dealer.

We thought about it over the weekend, but I suppose our decision was inevitable. Jacques had mentioned, over dinner, that he'd acquired the dealership for Yanmar diesel engines. A one-cylinder would cost about six hundred dollars Australian, without the shaft and propeller. In other words, a whole new diesel engine for about five times the cost of a new carburetor and some parts for an eleven-year-old gasoline engine.

On Monday Pete told Jacques we'd like to buy the Yanmar PMX6 and sent to the States for our last nine hundred dollars. Although it seemed like an extravagant sum, money had been coming in, both from my writing and Pete's occasional stories for the *Tustin News*. But what would we do when that nine hundred dollars was gone?

Because we planned to be in Honiara for some time, we decided to do another job that had been nagging at us since we'd left California—take off the rails and Fiberglass the deck. Everything we'd tried, from waterproof putty to caulking compound, had failed to stop the leaks that soaked the forepeak and main cabin in heavy weather.

So the work began in the anchorage on a sometimes rocking boat. We didn't realize how much we'd bitten off until our mouths were full of wood shavings, Fiberglass dust, Resorcinol glue, and engine grease.

Pete and I stopped work at sunset. With a towel under one arm, he strolled to the yacht club's men's restroom and I to the women's, where we washed away the day's toil in cold, fresh-water showers. The yacht club invited cruisers to use the showers without charge. Our contribution was to frequent the bar.

Dutifully, we gathered with Jacques and willowy Robyn Sapir and Ralph and Bertha Martin in the *haus wind*, a thatch roof over concrete, furnished with tables and wicker chairs. The Martins had sailed from San Francisco on the trimaran *Seeker*. Grizzled Ralph, who had the muscles of Pop Eye the sailor, had made his career in the Merchant Marine. Bertha, whose blue eyes sparkled beneath gray hair, had been a stay-at-home mom. I envied her having a lifelong sailor as her captain. Occasionally we were joined by Margo, an English woman who'd grown up in Peronist Argentina, and Jim, an Aussie-British journalist.

Although Pete and I had met other yachtsmen in Taio Hae, our social lives had revolved instead around the local people. In Honiara we associated only with our fellow sailors because the local people kept to themselves. Thus I felt as if I were stuck in a vacuum and never did "absorb" the island and its people. Pete said we had no choice: our task was to complete the work on *Wa*.

Social activity consisted of "grogging on," a ritual of "shouting rounds," or paying for one round of drinks for everyone. To the person who left after the first round, the others called out, "Come on, whadareya?" in derision. Pete and I learned to shout our round early so that we weren't compelled to down seven or eight drinks. The Australians deemed it a mortal sin to accept two or three free drinks and leave. After four Victoria Bitters I was high; the able groggers were just beginning.

One evening after several beers, we began discussing racial problems in Honiara, where most Melanesians were uneducated, acted as servants to the whites, and were not allowed to patronize the yacht club or hotels.

"It's much worse in the States," said Margo, a brittle, slender blonde, with a wave of her hand. "Just read John Howard Griffin. That will tell you how racist the States are." She was daring me to respond.

Griffin, a white man, had blackened his skin because he wanted to learn about racial discrimination first hand. "Griffin traveled through Louisiana, Mississippi, Alabama, and Georgia, and he was appalled at how he was treated," I said, swinging my eyes around our circle. "So Margo was right: he was discriminated against. But that was in the deep South. It's different in the rest of the United States."

"Are you trying to say that Louisiana, Mississippi, Alabama, and Georgia aren't part of the States?" she said. "You have only forty-six states now instead of fifty?"

If the beer bottle had been made of Styrofoam, I would have beaned her. "We're trying. People now can sit anywhere they want to on buses and at lunch counters. We passed the Voting Rights Act in 1965. And Martin Luther King became a symbol of hope for all of us."

"That's why you assassinated him?"

"We're trying to create a country in which equality of opportunity is a reality. I don't see that here." I stood, drained my beer, and stalked into the night.

Early on a Saturday morning, Robyn and I rowed ashore and headed for the Melanesian market. Taller than I by six inches, she walked fast, and her blonde ponytail bounced on her back with every step she took. I had to hustle to keep up.

The sky, a brilliant blue, was laden with moisture, and we sought the shade of the flame trees. Passing the bookstore, the movie theater, the cooperative, and numerous Chinese shops, I commented, "I don't see any Melanesians running these stores." Robyn nodded, as if what I'd said was too obvious to mention.

We reached the market, a thatch roof supported by wooden pillars over a dirt floor, about a mile from town. Tables ran the length of the building. Cucumbers, tomatoes, bunches of watercress, lettuce, and parsley, all grown on Guadalcanal, seemed to sprout from them. For ten cents I could buy three avocados, half a dozen mangoes, a large pawpaw, or a bunch of bananas. For a dollar I filled my *panier* with enough fruit and vegetables to last a week. All the sellers were Melanesian.

Besides the produce I knew, there were a number of plants I'd never seen. The strangest was a mottled green and white tube eighteen inches long and an inch in diameter. "What's that?" I asked Robyn.

"Snake bean. It's quite good." Something caught her eye, and she strolled on.

I decided to try out my Pidgin, the universal language throughout the Solomon Islands and New Guinea, whose tribes speak nearly nine hundred separate tongues among themselves.

"How yu kukim despela?" I asked her—how do you cook the bean.

The old woman turned away from the friend with whom she'd been speaking and stared at me. Her eyes sparkled in the pockets of her shiny black face, and her skin was like well-worn leather over bony elbows and hands. She wore a blouse and a *lava-lava* of faded green cotton. She'd been watching me out of the corner of her eye and didn't smile.

"Yu bolim despela?" I asked, hoping the bean could be boiled. She stared blankly.

"Kukim despela long wara?" I added. *"How long? Longtaim?"*

"Yu kukim longtaim."

"Long ten minutes, fifteen minutes?" I was getting exasperated.

"Long ten minutes, fifteen minutes."

"Tenku tumas," I said, thanking her, and hurried off to catch up with Robyn.

~~~~~~~~~~~~~~~~~~~~~~~~~~~~~~~~

The sellers crowded together on benches beside the tables. Some slumped with heavy-lidded eyes, as if asleep. Naked children slept on coconut mats under the tables amid the baskets, bundles of food, and cooking utensils. Babies snuggled in their mothers' arms, and a few nursed. An occasional old woman, too, was bare-breasted.

They had none of the plumpness of the Polynesian and Micronesian women. The young women were slender; the old women's cheekbones protruded from drawn, wrinkled faces. Their feet seemed like rough-hewn chunks of wood.

The men were lean as well. Most were barefooted, as were the women, and most wore only *lava-lavas*, or *lap-laps*, from waist to knees. Their hair was closely cropped or Afro. Their skin ranged from black to white coffee brown. The men tattooed themselves from forehead to waist with purple dye; on their arms they wore name tattoos. I wondered about these marks—whether they were signs of manhood or militance. The people had been cannibals just a hundred years before.

Even the smallest children chewed betel nut. By the time they reached adulthood, their mouths were stained bright red; by old age their teeth were the color of dried blood or black. Branches of betel nuts were on sale, and many of the saleswomen chewed the green and yellow nuts and spat out streams of red saliva.

I sensed people avoiding eye contact. I felt a barrier I couldn't penetrate, which was bewildering after my experience with the Polynesians and Micronesians. Smiling didn't help, nor did saying hello. Even those who spoke back didn't give of themselves. *Is this the way the people behave with strangers, or have they learned distance after many years of British rule?* I was still wondering when Robyn came to fetch me.

"Come on, let's get an ice cream," she said, and led me across the dirt lot behind the market to the Dairy Queen.

"Aha! an outpost of civilization," I exclaimed.

The young fellow behind the counter grinned. "He's a Yank," Australian Robyn explained, as if introducing one member of a rare and eccentric species to another.

"You know, I don't think I ever would've guessed. *Giddie mite*," I said to him, using the standard Australian greeting, and ordered two vanilla ice cream cones.

As days stretched into weeks and Pete and I labored full-time on the boat, our detachment from Melanesians continued. Those few we met worked either as bar boys at the yacht club, sales personnel in the local stores, or housewives selling their produce at the market. The bar boys dressed in regulation navy, brown, or black *lap-laps*. They went bare-chested and wore no shoes.

The male patrons of these places, on the other hand, wore shorts and shirts with flip-flops or, in the evenings, shoes and knee socks. Thus the color barrier was reinforced by a dress barrier, which seemed to build higher the invisible wall preventing social contact.

One morning I broke through the barrier as I trekked outside town to pick up our alien registration certificates. The heat at nine o'clock sent sweat down my back. When a pickup truck pulled up, I stepped toward the cab. The driver, a man alone, was burly with a round, dark face. Remembering the motorcyclist who'd picked me up at Abaiang before the wedding, I opened the door and got in. I was determined to treat this guy as my equal; if nothing else, I would spite Margo.

He greeted me in perfect English, not Pidgin, so I knew he was educated. This was a chance to make friends with a Melanesian.

"Thank you for the ride," I said. "You have a beautiful island."

"You're the first 'European' woman who's ever gotten into a car with me."

Something in his tone made me uneasy. "Oh? I guess not too many English and Australian women walk."

"Where are you from?"

"America."

He smiled as if I'd said the magic word. "My uncle was proud to help the Americans during World War II. They gave him many medals." He churned up dust as he ground to a halt in front of the immigration office. "I'll wait for you."

"That's not necessary. Don't trouble yourself."

He just nodded. "My name is David."

"I'm Addie."

After I picked up the certificates, he was still there. He asked if I'd like to see a Melanesian village on the outskirts of town.

Suppressing my earlier uneasiness, I said, "Yes, I'd like that very much." All the while Pete and I had been on the island of Guadalcanal, we'd not once stuck our noses out of Honiara. Maybe, with David's help, I could meet some islanders.

The village was in a clearing under coconut palms. The "leaf houses," as the whites called them, made of coconut and pandanus thatch, sprouted from the ground as if growing there. Some were on stilts as a protection against Guadalcanal's heavy rains. A few women, washing clothes, waved at David. So did the children, playing on the hard-packed red clay outside their houses.

But instead of stopping at the village or returning to Honiara, he drove on, explaining, "I just wanted to show you a little more." Again I quelled my anxiety and smiled, thinking, *I can't show this man I'm uneasy.* "You're the first white woman who's ever gotten into a car with me," he said again. "The English women would never do that."

Fear crawled around my spine. "Perhaps that's the difference between the English and Americans," I said, "a different attitude."

"Yes." He sounded bitter.

"Maybe you're prejudiced in favor of Americans because of your uncle's experience during the war."

"His picture is hanging in the lobby of the immigration office. Did you see it?"

The imposing portrait was of a man with a bush of gray-white hair over a lean, proud face. His features were fine. He wore the dress blue uniform of the U.S. Marine Corps, and his chest was lined with medals.

"That man's your uncle? It's an impressive picture." I studied David, appraising him anew. His family was among the Guadalcanal elite. "He's a distinguished looking gentleman. I'd like to meet him."

"I'll take you to him. He lives with me and my wife."

"My husband would like to meet him too," I said, hoping to dispel any idea that I might be interested in David as more than a friend.

He hung his head, puzzled by my attitude and trying to figure me out. I was certain he'd gotten the wrong idea. *Fool*, I told myself. *Don't blow your cool. You got yourself into this; now get yourself out.*

"My husband would like very much to meet your uncle," I repeated. "He served in the U.S. Army, in Vietnam. Perhaps we can visit you some Sunday."

He turned off the highway onto a dirt road winding toward the beach. We'd just crossed a river into a wilderness area of dense shrubs and coconut groves, miles from the nearest house. David stopped the truck in a clearing a few yards from the beach. I began to tremble. I sucked in my breath, willed myself to calmness.

"We'd better go back to town. It's getting late. I have some marketing to do before the shops close at noon."

"I thought you might like to look at the beach." He slid across the seat and tried to put his arm around me.

I opened the passenger door and jumped out. "Only a quick look." I slammed the door and stared at him through the open window. "Then we've got to get back. My husband will wonder where I am." I was hoping the thought of a vengeful white man would be enough to stop him.

David got out and studied the sand. *Cautious*, I told myself. *Cautious. Don't make him mad or belittle him.* My heart pounded. I kept my eyes away from him and pretended to be interested in the shells as I walked along the beach. *Don't run. You'll be prey.*

He followed me but made no attempt to catch up. When I saw, out of the corner of my eye, the sag in his shoulders, I returned to the truck. Although the crisis—the conflict of wills—was over, he tried once more to put his arm around me and kiss me. "No, David," I said and pushed him away.

He started the truck, and we returned to Honiara in silence.

If he'd been white, I would've had nothing but contempt for

him. But he was black. Remembering two hundred years of American slavery I felt, in some sense, personally responsible for his combination of arrogance and abjectness. I wanted to atone, to make amends. My encounter with David left me as puzzled as I probably had left him. I invited him and his wife to visit us on the boat the following evening after work.

The next evening at dusk David, dressed just like the British, and a young woman called Roslynn met us at the yacht club beach. Smartly attired and the first Melanesian woman I'd seen with straightened hair, she was married to a German businessman. I wondered what David's wife would think about his spending the evening with another woman, and I guessed she'd keep her thoughts to herself if she was a traditional housewife, unlike the emancipated Roslynn. Did David fancy himself a man about town? Roslynn's husband was in Fiji on business.

We went to the Hotel Mendana for cocktails and then to Sum's Kitchen, where Jacques and Robyn joined us. After several beers, Pete invited David and Roslynn to *Wa*, where the three of them talked until the early hours of the morning. I sat and listened. Remembering Pete's jealousy over a guitar-playing Englishman in Taio Hae, I hadn't dared tell him about my previous morning's escape.

David invited us to his house the following Sunday, but he didn't come to pick us up, and we never saw him again.

As our days in Honiara lengthened into weeks, I felt the pressure on our pocketbook. The engine had been expensive, and we'd spent more than a hundred dollars on Dynel cloth, resin, and other materials for the deck. Life at the yacht club was costly. The ten dollars per story I made, and Pete's occasional writing income from the *Tustin News*, weren't covering our expenses.

"We don't have the money to buy enough food to get us to Rabaul," I said one day after shopping.

Pete stopped tinkering on the engine and stared at me. "How could that be?"

"We've burned through that nine hundred dollars—the end of our bank account. I don't know when the *News-Press* will pay me again, or how much is coming." I paused. "I could ask Dad to borrow a thousand dollars."

Pete set his jaw. "I'll get a job."

Fortunately for us, the *Teledex IV* arrived in Honiara. An 120-foot vessel owned by the Teledyne Corporation, it searched for oil below the seabed, and it needed crew.

Pete committed to work one month—until six weeks before the beginning of cyclone season—as junior satellite navigator. The senior navigator, Larry, had to teach him about computers. In 1971, satellite navigation was in its infancy.

The *Teledex* stayed out five to seven days. Pete and I hadn't spent a night apart since he'd gotten back from Vietnam, and I missed him terribly. I curled in the forepeak, hugging Coco, and listened to water suck at *Wa's* hull with a lapping, feeding noise just inches from my ears. The boat rocked gently in the land breeze, which whished through the forehatch. *Where is he?* I wondered. *Is he on shift?* I dabbed sweat from my face and envied him working in an air-conditioned room.

During those lonely nights I remembered all the good times we'd had—the beauty of sailing under twins, the freedom of the sea, and how close we'd been during more than a hundred days of sailing. I forgot about the equipment failures and how I often felt left out when we were in port. I wanted desperately to idealize the Great Adventure, to make it my own fairy tale come true.

Days were better. To fill the hours I worked on *Wa*, sanding the interior paint and varnish, then repainting in white and revarnishing the mahogany until she glistened. Caring for her, making her more beautiful, was an act of love. I ran my hands over the finished work, feeling the smoothness of her skin. Sometimes I talked to her. "Well, old girl, you've brought us safely across the Pacific. Can you make it the rest of the way?"

I talked to Coco, too, and was sure he missed Pete. Every evening he took up his post on *Wa's* stern and meowed for an hour. During the night he stuck close to me.

Then Coco got a job.

The next time Pete was home, we heard a thumping on deck, a thrashing, and then a bump, bump, bump down the companionway in the middle of the night.

"What's going on?" Pete groaned and rolled over.

"I don't want to know," I replied. The noise stopped. Out of the silence came a crunching of teeth, a gnawing, a smacking of lips.

Pete switched on the main cabin light, and we peered out from the forepeak to the cabin floor, where a startled Coco pinned down a gray, pulsating mass with both front paws. His back paws were braced against the planking. The squid thrashed. Coco munched. The battle must've been a fierce one, for the squid was half Coco's size and full of ink. The cat looked as if he'd just come from a coal scuttle, but he didn't care as he gnawed off tentacles.

The next morning there was nothing left of the corpse. Coco was bloated and sluggish all that day and the next. I found the black splotch on deck where the unlucky squid had jumped aboard. I never could get the paint clean.

When this tale became common knowledge among the yachtsmen, the skipper of *Chiome*, a converted Thursday Island pearl lugger, asked if I would lend Coco to him to track down a rat. "I've tried to catch it for days," he said. "The thing makes a racket at night and eats my stores. And it freaks out the girls in my crew." I wondered why he had an all-girl crew but didn't ask.

He came for Coco at dusk. I reminded him not to feed the cat, or Coco would curl up and sleep. When I went to fetch him the next morning, the creature was relaxing on someone's pillow. I suspect *Chiome's* crew had slipped him something to eat. Serene and well rested, he hadn't caught the rat.

More and more yachts were stopping, then hurrying on their way, for it was late October, and the favorable southeast monsoon was about to switch to the unfavorable northwest monsoon—cyclone season. I yearned to follow those other boats out of Honiara.

Late one Sunday afternoon as I was watching yet another yacht approach, I saw a blue hull. What boats did I know with blue hulls? As it came closer, I could see that the mast was an odd color—dark green. "It's Mike!" I cried out to Coco. All the good times that Mike Thurston, Pete, and I had had in Betio came back to me.

I yelled, "Greetings, Captain Thurston," and waited until he'd gotten his hook planted before stepping into the dinghy with Coco. I was unkempt and covered with paint splotches, but I didn't care. Of all the people I'd met in more than nine months of cruising, Mike was my number one friend.

As I rowed closer, he straightened from coiling ropes on the deck and grinned with a smile of white teeth that lit his whole, clean-shaven face. His cheeks seemed a little thinner, but impish humor sparkled in his blue eyes.

Coco jumped aboard *Destiny* as if he owned the place. "Ah, Coco, you remember the chicken you almost got away with." Mike laughed. He'd briefly left a chicken, ready for the frying pan, next to the stove. By the time he'd returned, Coco had dragged the chicken across *Destiny's* cabin and was carrying it up the companionway. Pete would've whacked Coco, and I would've yelled at him. Mike had just laughed and called for us to see what our clever cat had done.

I glanced around the deck at the stowed sails and neatly coiled ropes. Then I stared full on at Mike. It felt as if nothing had changed, except here we were, in a different port, and I was as drawn to him as I was in Betio. He shook a strand of blond hair from his face and went below to put on coffee water. Coco and I followed him.

Destiny's main cabin was as tidy as if she'd been in port a week. I thought about the endless mess on *Wa* and wondered how Mike did it. His boat was in better shape than ours had ever been, and he seemed to put no effort into it.

While Coco explored the forepeak, I sat on one of the berths in the main cabin. Mike handed me my coffee, clinked mugs, and sat opposite me. Our knees touched.

"So where'd you come from?" I asked.

"Nggela Sule Island—just across the way."

"Thirty miles with the wind blowing twenty knots on the beam?" I raised my eyebrows. "You must be exhausted."

"It's a bit of all right." He shifted positions, increasing the contact with my knees. I thought of how scroungy I looked and didn't care. He sipped his coffee. "Where's Pete?"

"He took a job on the *Teledex IV*, an oil exploration ship."

"Oh, really. So he's gone?"

"Out for a week at a time, usually."

"You must be lonely."

"I try hard to stay busy," I said, and pointed to the paint splotches on my arms and legs. "Some of it even manages to make it onto the interior of the cabin."

Mike's eyes narrowed. "He's a lucky man." He paused and searched my eyes. "He doesn't know how lucky he is."

I felt my face flush. I put down my coffee and took his hand. "I think he knows." Although I wasn't willing to admit it to anyone, I wasn't sure.

He set aside his coffee and lifted me to standing. "If I weren't an honorable man . . ."

Just then, Coco leapt from the forepeak onto our bare feet. We both laughed. "You are the most ornery of all possible cats," I said.

The spell broken, I was able to look Mike in the face. "How about sharing my steak and salad at the yacht club's Sunday barbeque?" I asked.

"I'll bring the wine," he said.

Just after the barbeque Pete returned. Instead of going to bed early, as we had every other time he'd come back, we stayed until past midnight with Mike on *Destiny* catching up on our travels for the last four months. *He's as glad to see Mike as he is to see me,* I thought. The familiar sense of being left out returned. But since I'd been a little too glad to see Mike myself, I felt I didn't have the right to be annoyed.

We made plans to cruise together through the Solomons to the island of New Britain and to leave as soon as possible. We now had enough money to get us to Rabaul.

Most of all, I wanted to get out of Honiara. The British and Australian suppression of the Melanesians made me sick to my stomach, and there was nothing I could do about it.

Gunkholing Through the Solomons
or
Mike to the Rescue, Again

638 miles and 17 days Honiara to Rabaul
under way 11 months

The night was silver and gold, with great black lumps of land sticking from the sea. There wasn't a whisper of wind, but *Wa* created her own, which brushed my face like gauze as I sat at the tiller and her new engine chugged its one-cylinder song, "puk puk puk." We were gunkholing with Mike from anchorage to anchorage, day by day, never losing sight of land.

This new adventure didn't prevent me from worrying. We'd been gone nearly a year and were only a quarter of the way around the world. At that rate the entire trip would take four years—too long—I'd be in my mid-thirties. *When will I have a baby?* I shoved the thought from my mind and worried, instead, about money. *Will we be able to get jobs in Rabaul? By the time we get there we'll be broke; we'll have no choice.*

Live in the now, I kept telling myself, *you'll never have this experience again.*

At the village of Batuna, site of a lumber mill, the three of us went ashore, watched some girls play a game with coconut shells and berries, looked at the Seventh-day Adventist (SDA) school and church, and visited the mission. As a bell called the faithful to evening service, Mike, Pete, and I headed back to *Wa* for rum punch with fresh pineapple.

No sooner had I poured the drinks and started dinner than men selling carvings began to arrive. Pete bought three. Mike tried to get the men to buy the carvings given to us in the Marquesas. They didn't appreciate his joke.

The carvers kept coming until we turned out the lights.

Batuna's kids, chattering on the wharf, woke me at first light. I hunkered on the bucket and wondered how I could empty it unobtrusively over *Wa's* stern. As soon as I stepped on deck, they asked to come aboard.

I dug out what remained of our ten-pound can of hard candy, making the mistake of bringing out the whole thing rather than transferring part of its contents to a dish. Before I realized what was happening, the kids had passed the can from *Wa* to *Destiny* to the wharf and back. Four dozen fists dipped greedily in and stuffed mouths and pockets. The can returned empty, and the kids wandered away. *Why are these people so pushy?* I wondered. *No boundaries—got to set boundaries.*

Later the village men came around, this time with fruit, probably because they'd heard about the five pounds of candy I'd dispensed. The fruits were not gifts. They wanted food in exchange, and the pick of our canned goods at that. They wheedled, seeking one can for four coconuts, one bunch of bananas, or one pawpaw. I'd paid twenty to forty cents apiece for the cans, and their fruit would've brought ten cents per item in the Honiara market. Nevertheless, I traded as they asked, while Mike called me a sucker.

"I'm giving them sheep's tongue because we hate it," I said. "These forced vegetarian SDAs will be happy to have it. Besides, they're poor and we aren't."

Mike wasn't convinced. The men, their eyes sparkling, watched as I pulled out cans. I felt anger rise in me because I was being taken, but I couldn't change course. They found me a fool. Mike was right.

Our first encounter with Melanesian villagers was not so much a social exchange as some strange game of one-upmanship. I didn't like the way I was feeling about these people and wanted to get away.

We cleared customs at Kieta, Bougainville Island, New Guinea, and sailed on to Arovo Island. There we joined Mike on *Destiny* for drinks with Harry West, a government official from Port Moresby, the capital of Papua-New Guinea. West, who slicked his brown hair and wore horn-rimmed glasses, had been district commissioner in Rabaul, where he'd gotten to know Mike.

I listened as Harry and Mike, two men who'd shaped Papua-New Guinea, talked about the running of a country as if they were discussing the price of eggs. This was a Mike new to me. He was quiet and thoughtful, yet there was power in his words.

He wanted an update on the recent assassination of Jack Emanuel, Rabaul's last district commissioner. Allegedly, Emanuel, in an effort to resolve a tribal conflict, had begun negotiations with two warring factions and had left his police escort behind, even though some of the tribesmen were wearing war paint. Fourteen Melanesian members of the Tolai tribe had been arrested and charged with stabbing Emanuel.

"Why'd they go after Emanuel?" Mike asked. "He wasn't such a bad bloke."

"Would you go out into the bush alone with fourteen Tolais?" West responded. "It was a foolish thing to do. He knew better."

Mike shrugged. "Has the pot boiled over," he asked, "or is it simmering?"

"Rabaul is quiet—too quiet. One small thing—a careless brushing of someone's arm—could blow the lid off," West said.

Mike rubbed his chin. "What about the trial?"

"It's been delayed. The Matungans are bitter and angry."

"Who are they," I asked, "and why are they angry?"

"Politically active Tolais." West paused to sip his drink. "They want the trial held now. The Matungans believe the trial will stir up the other Tolais. They think this will help them gain leverage in the elections, which will be held in mid-February."

"Isn't that a good thing—that they're depending on due process?" I asked.

He studied me. "If the trial and the elections don't go the way the Matungans want, there'll be a bloodbath."

Wonderful, I thought. *And we're going to be stuck in Rabaul until the end of cyclone season.*

Five days and two overnight stops later, Mike banged on *Wa's* cabin top. The sky was barely gray. We crawled out of bed and were under way by 5:20, heading for Madehas.

"Jock and Louise Lee will show you real New Guinea hospitality," Mike had told us. "They're the only whites on their 800-acre island, so they love company."

We docked at a pier next to a lawn flanked by hibiscus bushes and a big white screen. "That's for the movies the Lees show three times a week," Mike said. "The people from the labor quarters," he said, flinging his arm to the right, "come to watch."

"It must be their only entertainment," I said.

Mike grinned. "It is, except for the trouble they get into."

Pete glanced sidelong at Mike. "What kind of trouble?"

"Whatever you do when you've had too much to drink."

"There're no stores here," I protested. "They're on an island."

"The natives are *very* inventive. And they've got canoes to take them to the store in Sohano, an hour away." He waved to a man and woman emerging from the house.

Jock was a fiftyish, stocky, fair-skinned Australian troubled with skin cancers. Louise was a graceful woman with an abundance of red-brown hair and energy. Two German shepherds and a Danish poodle barked a welcome.

The Lees had been at Madehas for eighteen years. They'd converted the island from jungle and swampland into a *copra* and cocoa plantation that produced eighty tons of cocoa a year.

Jock's mornings began early. He was at the workers' quarters by six to inspect the labor line of more than fifty men and direct his foremen as to which areas to clear, improve, or harvest. After a leisurely breakfast, he started the engine of his workboat, the *Caroline Louise*, and saw his wife off to Buka Island, where she worked as a warehouse manager to supplement their plantation income. Louise hated the trip across Buka Passage, she told me, because she was afraid the workboat would tip over, but she gritted her teeth and made the trip each weekday.

Jock also made sure the children from the labor quarters were aboard the workboat, for they had to attend school in Sohano. Jock then checked the plantation again to see that the labor line was doing its job.

Besides stacks of old *Newsweeks, Times,* and yachting magazines, Jock and Louise owned an extensive collection of books on the American Civil War as well as biographies, novels, and medical textbooks. And Jock loved to talk. Each morning at tea time Mike, Pete, and I wandered ashore and chatted until noon. A servant served lunch, and Jock took a nap. After the hot part of the day had passed, Jock donned his floppy white hat and strolled out to check the plantation. Then there was time for more talk, a game of tennis in late afternoon on the grass court behind the house, and more talk over drinks. When Louise arrived home from work, she joined the discussions, often siding with me, women against men. I drank in her support and sisterhood like a thirsty plant sucking up water.

One evening, as I helped her with dinner, I asked, "What do you think is going to happen in Rabaul?"

"I don't know." Her eyes narrowed. "I'm glad I'm here. Are you having second thoughts about going there?"

"No. Mike seems to think it will be all right."

"The Tolais are fierce warriors. In the nineteenth century they attacked the lowlands of New Britain and chased the non-aggressive indigenous tribesmen into the mountains. Their reward was some of the richest land in New Guinea." Louise, shredding lettuce, paused and studied me. "They've been swaggering ever since, and some of them are hotheaded enough to put the rest over the edge."

"Wow! So you think the Tolais deliberately set out to murder Jack Emanuel?"

"No. He was foolish and paid a heavy price for it. He thought they would be reasonable. They probably saw that as weakness on his part and believed he wouldn't be fair—that he would favor one tribe over the other in the conflict."

She sighed and put her arm around me. "You'll do just fine in Rabaul. You and Pete seem to be lacking the Aussie dumb gene that so many people bring up here from Sydney."

I laughed and hugged her back. Louise was the first woman I'd met cruising with whom I felt completely comfortable.

The week passed uneventfully until Sunday afternoon, when a woman with pain in her face came saying there was fever in the labor quarters.

"*Wonem despela?*" asked Louise, questioning the woman as to the nature of the illness. The patient's urine was black, and she was pale and nauseated. These were symptoms of blackwater fever, or cerebral malaria. It had killed dozens of New Guinea settlers by cooking their brains.

Louise boiled water to sterilize her equipment, then took syringes and medicine in a sterile tub to the labor quarters. I wanted very much to go with her but was afraid to ask. She was bent on saving life. I wasn't sure I could be of any help.

"I got there in time," Louise told me when she returned. "The woman will be all right." She put away her equipment, wearily, and sat.

"How did you know what to do?"

"Books. Then a lot of practice."

"Don't you mind giving injections?" I asked. The thought of sticking a needle in anyone made me squeamish.

"No, not to people," Louise said. "The animals object when I give them shots, though. And I have to use such a dirty great needle. And of course sometimes it won't go in, and I have to keep puncturing the hide."

The picture of Louise approaching the aft end of a sick and irritable cow with a syringe nearly a foot long and jabbing it repeatedly into the animal's hindquarters didn't square with the picture of Louise, in a dress, sitting on a bamboo lounge chair and looking every bit the lady of the house.

After eleven days at Madehas, we said a reluctant goodbye to our new friends. Cyclone season was almost upon us, and we had to get to Rabaul.

The first day an inhospitable sky rained barrels upon *Wa*, and squalls marched all around the compass, giving us either too much wind or too little. Like a man possessed, Pete rushed to the foredeck and back, raising sails, lowering sails, while I steered. He turned the engine on and off, on and off. The third time around, the Yanmar jammed with a thud. Pete radioed Mike, ahead of us, who said it might be the connecting rod. Unless Pete could fix the engine, we'd have to sail to Rabaul.

The following day the wind freshened to gale-force gusts; *Wa's* pitching ripped four feet of seam low in the mainsail. She limped on under the genny, then the jib. I gritted my teeth and steered as saltwater beat its way inside my foul-weather gear. Off watch, going below, I had to hang on with every step.

By day three, my left knee had become infected and throbbed; all I wanted to do was rest. But the self-steering gear wouldn't work with the wind jumping about, and Pete needed relief on the helm. The rain soaked me, the throbbing in my knee traveled to my groin, and I flushed with heat. The infection had gone systemic. My mouth went dry, my eyes burned, and my body ached all over. I began taking double doses of penicillin from our medicine kit and hoped I could hang in until we got to the island of New Ireland, a little more than a hundred miles away.

We fought the wind for every inch, and every inch *Wa* gained, the seas knocked her back. It was a struggle of desperation. I caved in exhaustion and took it out on Pete as I fell apart.

"Why are you such a slob?" I screamed. He'd left navigation equipment, books, clothes, and engine parts strewn over both quarterberths.

"I had to fix the engine." He sounded wounded and self-righteous.

Trying to regain my temper, I lowered my voice. "But you didn't fix the engine. It's brand new and broken. Why?"

"I don't know why."

"We spent our last six hundred dollars on something that turns out to be a piece of shit, and you can't fix it, and you don't even know what's wrong with it. So you just made a huge mess and gave up."

"OK, smartass, you fix the engine."

Of course, I couldn't fix the engine. "Don't tell me what to do," I screamed as I hurled the *Sailing Directions* onto the cabin floor. On top of them I threw books, clothes, and engine parts. I stomped across the mess, not caring what I broke. I climbed the companionway and grabbed the tiller. "I'll steer. You clean it up. It's your mess."

His eyes narrowed, and his lips pursed into a dried-apple knot. He turned his back on me, went below, and began putting things away.

As I steered, I regretted my outburst. Pete *had* tried to fix the engine. Never mind that he couldn't. He was no mechanic—I knew that, as much as it frustrated me. The point was, he'd tried. I knew the Yanmar was a good engine—that Pete had done something to make it jam, and someone in Rabaul could fix it. We just had to get there.

It took us sixty-three hours to claw our way a hundred and ten miles to windward in everything from calms to gale-force gusts. When *Wa* reached Kambotorosch Harbor on the island of New Ireland a little before midnight, the wind died, leaving us becalmed and drifting south with the tide. On the ship-to-shore radio Pete called Mike, who'd been in the harbor for hours. Mike upped anchor, turned on his engine, and came out to tow us in.

The next morning, as he prepared to leave New Ireland for Rabaul, on the island of New Britain, he asked if we'd go with him. "I'm sure you don't want two shabby Americans tagging after you," I said. He'd been cruising for more than a year and would be the pride of his hometown Rabaul Yacht Club.

"Later, then," he called. "I'm not looking forward to seeing my father, who was angry when I left sixteen months ago."

We watched him set sail across the St. George's Channel.

That day Pete and I made up and cuddled in the forepeak for hours. My fever vanished. I was grateful that I was young and strong and healed quickly. And I realized all that anger—all that negative emotion—probably had made me sicker.

"I'm well enough," I said at the end of the day. "Let's head for Rabaul."

Next morning, we sailed out of the harbor while bells on shore chimed "Hark, the Herald Angeles Sing." Watching black islanders in *lap-laps* walking under coconuts and pawpaws to the grass and mud building they called a church, I felt no more the spirit of Christmas than if I'd been on another planet.

All afternoon the wind freshened until it shrieked in the rigging and sent waves crashing across *Wa's* bow. By nightfall, barely making way against the sea, I felt us being swept southeastward.

By dawn the wind had dropped to ten knots, and we tacked our way up the east coast of banana-shaped and mountainous

New Britain, the largest island in New Guinea.

At dusk the twin lights of Cape Gazelle, the southeastern tip of Blanche Bay—Rabaul's outer harbor—winked on and off. To our left the Duke of York Islands, islets sheltering Blanche Bay, turned to black stubble like a dark man's beard. And rising from eastern New Britain were three mountains—the Mother, the North Daughter, and the South Daughter—which, black against a bloody sky, towered over us.

The next morning we crossed from Blanche Bay into Simpson Harbor and began dodging the debris of civilization. Empty beer and soft drink cans floated by, along with brush, logs, seaweed, and plastic and paper wrappers. Rabaul had picnicked and dumped its garbage. At the tip of Simpson Harbor sat a sprinkling of buildings.

"Let's show them who the real sailors are," said Pete, grinning. I thought only fleetingly of our inglorious entrances to Tongareva, where Saua had to rescue us, Tarawa, where Mike had to rescue us, and Honiara, where Jacques Sapir had to rescue us, as we heaved ourselves into the work and tacked smartly up the bay.

Pete spotted *Destiny* and brought *Wa* alongside. "Anchor over there," called Mike, who came running from a rambling, ranch-style house twenty feet from the shore. He jumped in his dinghy and rowed to *Wa*.

"How did you do?" asked Pete, searching Mike's face to see if his reunion with his father had been bittersweet.

"It's a bit of all right," said Mike. I knew he feared slipping under Jack Thurston's thumb. The thought depressed me, for soon we'd trade our freedom for the yoke of convention too.

"Lunch is ready and my parents are waiting to meet you."

Mike helped Pete put *Wa's* dinghy into the water, then Pete stepped in. There was a crunch, and he was calf-deep in water. He yelped, grabbed an oar, and paddled furiously. He made it behind the Thurstons' breakwall just before the dinghy sank. Mike roared with laughter.

I was horrified that we'd lost our shore boat. We couldn't afford a replacement.

"I guess that's the end," said Pete, scratching his head.

"We'll patch her up with a bit of Fiberglass. Come on, come in," Mike said.

Mike's mother, a pale, delicate woman, presided over the table with the coolness and dignity of one long accustomed to giving orders. As I drank my first and then my second glass of ice water, I marveled at how she could look as if she never had set foot in the tropics. My body oozed a permanent sheen of sweat, but hers was as dry as if she lived in a bottle of deliquescent.

Mike's father, whose white hair shone in the pale light, was immaculately dressed in starched white shorts, shirt, and knee socks that smelled as if they'd just been laundered. I felt shabby in my salt-soaked, blue-flowered dress and flip-flops.

"Michael told us you met at Tarawa," Mrs. Thurston said. "Did you like it there?"

"Not as well as its sister island, Abaiang," Pete said. "It's a commercial port—noisy and dirty." Mrs. Thurston was busy talking to a tall, gangly black servant dressed in a white shirt, shorts, and flip-flops and probably didn't hear a word of Pete's answer.

"I hear the British are ready to give those islands their independence," Jack Thurston said. "That'll be the end of them. Those natives won't have a clue as to how to run a government—or anything else. Britain will wind up supporting them anyway."

Pete and I threw each other a look that said, *I don't want to go there.*

Conversation for the rest of the meal was strained, and Mrs. Thurston disappeared as soon as we'd eaten.

After lunch, Jack Thurston led us into the living room, where we had coffee. Mike and I drew him out to talk about the 1930s, when he prospected for gold on Bougainville Island. But once Mike had drained his cup, he began glancing at his watch, then at his father, who'd dropped his forced smile.

"We'd best get you taken care of with the customs and pick up your mail," Mike told us. It was clear that, as gracious as the Thurstons appeared, they wanted to be rid of their American guests as soon as possible. I was uncomfortable being where I wasn't wanted and relieved to go.

Rabaul
or
Hurry Up Please, It's Time

under way 11 months

The whites were afraid. They likened themselves to the Kenyan settlers during the time of the Mau-Mau. They surrounded their houses and yards with "boy wire," and they screened the glass-faced windows of their offices with it. They kept guard dogs.

The outcome of the upcoming murder trial would be dangerous for them either way. If the fourteen Tolais were sentenced to hang, the Melanesians would take revenge with more murders. If it were a pittance punishment, the Tolais would laugh and mock the white man's justice. There were some among the Australians who said mass hanging was the only solution. As time went on, their numbers grew.

At the yacht club, Pete and I got into arguments with the Australian sailors. "I wouldn't mind if they hadn't sent those blokes up from Sydney," said slender, dark-haired Karyn Lincoln, referring to the barristers for the defense.

"But who would you get to defend them?" I asked. "Would Lefevre take the case?" Lefevre was one of Rabaul's two lawyers.

"Of course not. Don't be absurd," said Karyn with alarm. She worked as a secretary for Lefevre.

"Why not?" I tried to sound puzzled. She didn't realize I was baiting her. I wanted Karyn to abandon her prejudices, or at least realize they were prejudices. Rabaul in some ways was like 1960s Mississippi. Although the black natives of East New Britain numbered 80,000 people and the white expatriates in the entire country numbered only 50,000, the Australians acted as if the blacks counted for nothing.

"But you're right," I added. "Those city people from Down South don't know anything about New Guinea. With the knowledge they have of the case, Rabaul's two barristers are the best qualified."

Karyn was impatient. "They've got to make a living here in Rabaul. If they know what's good for them and they want to stay on, they won't touch that case."

"You mean their clients would object to their taking a big murder case? But if the defense won, that could make their reputations and their fortunes, couldn't it, and wouldn't the local people be pleased to have winning barristers?"

"Lefevre has enough work without mucking about in trouble that's not his affair. His clients want him to go on writing wills and contracts, minding his business."

There was a pause. I'd pressed the matter enough.

"Why didn't they bring in a barrister from Lae or Madang?" asked lean, blond Alan Jamison. Though he was Australian by birth, he hadn't lived at home for years and considered himself a citizen of the world.

"I don't think anyone from Lae would've taken the case, either. I don't know about Madang," Karyn said.

"What about the judge—he's from Port Moresby, isn't he?" Alan asked. The judge had decreed that the barristers for the defense couldn't come from his community so as to avoid any hint of a conflict of interest. That left very few places from which to choose. "They've got to have some kind of defense," Alan argued, "otherwise you couldn't convince the Matungans that the accused had gotten a fair trial."

Karyn realized she'd been trapped. "I don't object to where the barristers come from. It's who they are. They're long-haired hippies," she sneered. "And staying in the Travelodge? You know whose taxes are paying for the plushest hotel in town, don't you?" There was no argument on that score. Most whites in Rabaul were angry that the fourteen lawyers, one per defendant, were housed at twenty dollars a day plus meals.

The barristers were everything the white New Guineans were not. They came from Sydney and Melbourne and looked down on Rabaul's provincialism. They were educated; few whites in Rabaul had gone beyond secondary school. Worst of all, the men of the defense looked like liberals to Karyn and those like her.

Karyn and others feared the white people of the south had come to oust the white people of the north and "give the black man his rights," meaning give him back New Guinea. The white New Guineans were bitter about this. It was their land, too, and some, like the Thurstons, had lived there for generations.

For weeks the issue flamed. Then the interest of the white New Guineans began to burn out, for they learned that each of the fourteen defendants was to be tried separately and that court procedure was interminably dull. The trials were still going on when we left Rabaul, and we never did learn the outcome!

After Christmas, Mike prepared to leave for Kimbe, on New Britain's west coast, to oversee the Thurstons' timber holdings. He also planned to plant ten thousand acres of oil palms, which produced an orange fruit the size of a Brazil nut.

Mike's excitement—his ambition and sense of command, was electric. He caught me in the current until I realized with a jolt that this no longer was the Mike I knew. Sadly, I said goodbye to this good friend and hoped he wouldn't forget the footloose times that were slipping away.

Would it be any different for us? I didn't want to think about becoming an anonymous part of the great American financial juggernaut.

Trapped in Rabaul by cyclone season, Pete and I got jobs. He signed on as a marine claims clerk with Burns Philp (New Guinea) Ltd., a supermarket chain headquartered in Australia that served New Guinea's hundreds of outlying islands with a fleet of workboats. He was paid three hundred dollars Australian a month. We'd both earned more than three times that in the States.

I worked as a Burns Philp (BPs) clerk-typist for two hundred dollars a month, which would support us. Pete's salary we'd devote to boat repairs and savings.

I served as secretary to the accountant and assistant to accounts keeper Gloria Smith, a short, stocky, no-nonsense woman. If everyone had paid their bills on time, Gloria and I wouldn't have had jobs. Unfortunately—and this came as a revelation—most people did *not* pay on time. Always when I'd gotten a notice in the mail—a deep, threatening pink to match my flush of shame—it seemed worded as if I were the very first person ever to have merited (or de-merited) one.

Most of the black office workers didn't sit with the whites but in a windowless file room that had no air conditioning and no fans. There they waited to be called to errands, to serve tea morning and afternoon, to do the filing, and to handle the mail.

"Eli!" or "Gurian!" or "Boy!" the Australians yelled in a tone that made me shudder. Even the lowliest, most recently employed among the whites could make the boys in the back come running. The cruder Australians called the blacks "rock apes" and "coons," not with malice but matter-of-factly. And everyone called them boys, no matter how aged or venerable they were, for "boy" was the word for man in Pidgin, just as "mary" was the word for woman. I tried to keep myself busy and not dwell on a situation I couldn't change.

It cost $200 a month to live in port when we ate fresh food and drank beer. Pete ordered a dinghy and rigging wire from Australia and a mainsail from Hong Kong, and more equipment and repairs to the boat in dry dock took another $300. The plan to devote at least part of Pete's salary to savings gurgled out *Wa's* cockpit drain into Simpson Harbor.

In early March I wrote to my father, telling him we'd spent $600 in two months on the boat. If we spent nothing more on *Wa*, I said, we'd have the $600 Pete earned in March and April to see us home.

My frustrated father wrote back, "Stop playing, and start acting like adults." Our planning had consisted of hoping we could make it around the world on a thousand dollars! Now I was kicking myself—way too late—for not building more of a nest egg before we left.

His letter continued:

Pete's going to lose his place in law school. You need to get on with the business of establishing your career and having children.

Do you remember my 31-unit apartment complex on Modoc Road? It's getting too much for me to handle, what with weekly plumbing problems, tenants moving out, and having to repaint and re-carpet. I'd rather put my money in the stock market. So here's my offer: I'll sell you the apartment complex for $350,000, no money down. You'll assume the first mortgage, and I'll take a second mortgage for the balance of the $350,000, payable at $700 a month, interest and principal.

He could have hit me over the head with a baseball bat, and I wouldn't have been more stunned. I set the letter aside and stared into space. Dad's offer would change our lives. The hard part would be to convince Pete to accept.

The letter ended, "Here's the kicker: the offer's good only until the end of August, 1973, when Pete will return to law school. I'll lend you the money to get home, and you'll pay me back by selling *Wa* and giving me the proceeds."

Dad had just solved our money problems, almost. It was March, 1972, and we couldn't leave Rabaul until May. The wave of relief met a wall of panic. Could we make it three quarters of the way around the world in fifteen months?

That evening, I handed Pete the letter and said, "I'll get you a beer while you read this."

My stomach churning, I brought two bottles of brown ale back to the table. Pete was frowning. Without thanking me, he grabbed a bottle and took a big gulp. I sat beside him, sipped my beer, and waited.

He finished the letter and looked at me. Pain wrinkled the corners of his eyes and mouth. "We can't take money from him."

"I don't want to feel obligated to him, either," I said, "but your mom barely makes enough to support herself, let alone anyone else."

"Can't ask my father," he whispered. "He'd tell me to go fly a kite."

"I guess that's what we're doing anyway."

He glared at me. "That isn't funny," he said, and angrily pulled on his beer again. "And how do you think we're going to sail twenty thousand miles in fifteen months? That's fifteen hundred miles a month at a hundred miles a day going downwind."

"We can do it," I said with more hope than candor. "We were averaging half sailing and half time in port until we got to Tarawa." I blocked from my mind the hundreds of hours of maintenance we'd put into *Wa*.

"And what about the last thirty-five hundred miles from the Panama Canal to Santa Barbara, all upwind?" There was a raspy tone to his voice, as if he were repressing a scream. "Last time we tried to go upwind it took us four days to go a hundred miles."

I nodded my head, sighed, and took a big slug of beer. "You want to stop in Darwin and work a year? Maybe work another year in Durban or Cape Town?" It was a dangerous question. The sooner we got home, the sooner I could have a baby.

He stroked his beard. "No."

"The *News-Press* hasn't paid me in weeks." I paused. "Think of Dad's offer as a challenge. Besides, what other choice do we have?"

As the weeks bled into months, Pete got more bored and discouraged with his work. On top of that, accepting my father's offer had stripped him of his power: Dad now was in charge. What he'd said without saying it was, "You can't take care of your wife. I will."

Pete's sense of autonomy always had been a tenuous thing. He based it on bluster and creativity, like the Great Adventure, or memorizing pages and pages of the "Faerie Queen," or trying to build a formula for getting both longitude and latitude from a single sunline. His mind flew at warp speed to places I couldn't even imagine. This didn't impress my pragmatic father.

As Pete's spirit decayed, he spent Saturday mornings and sometimes all day Saturday in bed.

"You've got to get up. There's work to do," I said.

"I'm sick," he answered.

"What's wrong?" I asked.

One weekend it was diarrhea, the next a headache, the next stomach cramps. He was unkempt, and his skin took on a pasty look. He pulled the blanket over his head and buried himself. The blanket shook, and I heard him sobbing.

Worried and depressed, often on the verge of tears, I longed for the time we could leave Rabaul for the clean sea. But there was the cyclone season to wait out, and we'd promised BPs four months, until the end of April. I'd never felt so marooned.

Frightened as I was that he might turn suicidal or drink so much he couldn't function, I had to buck Pete up. We had thousands of miles to sail. It never would've occurred to me to abandon *Wa* in Rabaul and fly home. I don't think it ever occurred to Pete either. There was no question: we would go on. Though I lacked his knowledge, I was going to have to lead.

The Keystone Kops
or
Where's the Sheet, Dude?

under way 16 months

One afternoon I picked up the mail to discover a letter from Pete's father postmarked Surakarta, Java. On the back of the envelope Pete's step-mother, Betty, had written "See you soon!" ☺ So like Betty, I thought, who painted portraits, mostly sunny, and once kept a Capuchin monkey loose in her house.

But what did she mean, "See you soon"? Those three words made me uneasy. I studied the postmark, trying to decipher the date. I knew Dr. Peter Eastman had taken a CARE medical mission in Java for the month of April. Did this letter mean they intended to visit us in Rabaul afterwards?

Dr. Eastman had come back from service during World War II a stranger to his son. The little boy had been the center of his mother's and grandmother's universe for two years. Suddenly he was shoved to the periphery and treated with spankings instead of kisses.

Then Dr. Eastman had pushed hard for his only son to go to medical school—Pete would have been a third-generation doctor—but my husband had applied to one medical school, been rejected, and abandoned the project. This was a great disappointment to his father and proof that he, Pete, in some ways would never measure up.

So Pete had always been afraid of his father. Although he was nearly thirty years old, he had not been able to meet his father man-to-man and say, "You were a bastard a lot of the time when I was growing up, especially when you cheated on Mom."

I thought of tearing the letter into pieces and throwing it in the trash. The timing for a visit couldn't have been worse. Pete was in a major depression, which his father could only make worse. Perhaps if they didn't hear back from us they wouldn't come. But honesty got the better of me.

At the yacht club after work, I handed Pete the envelope. He opened it and scowled as he read.

"Well," he said, "I don't suppose they'd want to stay on the boat, so at least we'll have the use of a hot shower in their hotel. That's a plus."

I gave him a weak smile. "When are they coming?"

"May first." His eyes suddenly looked startled. "That gives us just two weeks to finish Fiberglassing the cabin trunk, sanding and painting the deck, and moving the galley to the head. We've got to get cracking."

The best thing I could say about the senior Eastmans' prospective visit was that it jolted Pete out of his lethargy.

On a gloomy day in late April, a friend invited us to a supper of curry, which took a long time to cook. We went through the wine we had brought, so Pete rowed ashore to replenish. When he returned, a long time later, he gave a holler to warn Dave and me that he was approaching.

Ignoring him, we continued talking.

I heard the sounds of Pete's climbing aboard, then a female voice. Startled, I stared up the companionway just as Betty stepped into the cockpit and Dr. Eastman hefted himself over the lifelines.

"Oh my God!" I said, scurrying up the companionway to hug my in-laws. Dr. Eastman's gray hair was cut in a buzz so short I could see his pink scalp. He looked more jowly than before, as if he'd put on some weight. Betty's brown hair framed her thin face and aquiline nose. "How did you manage to find each other?" I asked. It was the only thing I could think of to say.

"Went to the yacht club, of course," Dr. Eastman said.

Crap, I thought, *Wa's not ready for company—she's a mess.*

Foolishly, Pete and I wanted to take Peter and Betty somewhere. They would've been happier in Rabaul relaxing, but we pushed for something more interesting—an expedition.

We wanted very much to see Jock and Louise Lee again before we left New Guinea. I telegraphed. Cameron, their second son, thought we'd fly and replied, "Bring frozen peas." Instead, we set out to sail the approximately two hundred miles back to Madehas Plantation.

We began with cold beer and good cheer in a lazy breeze. It took us all afternoon to tack out of Simpson Harbor and into Blanche Bay. Idling on a gray-silver sea, we watched the sunset bathe in shimmering red and gold the three volcanos—the Mother and the Two Daughters—which had greeted Pete and me months before. Unfortunately, we'd forgotten about the heavy winds and nasty currents in the St. George's Channel.

At dusk we floated past the Cape Gazelle light, and I felt the first wrinkling of the wind. It flecked the gray water white and filled *Wa's* sails. Although we'd eaten a late lunch, I started dinner while there still was light and the wind was gentle. Betty came below to help. Pete lit the kerosene lantern and set it in its rack. He tried to turn on the binnacle (compass) light and remembered he hadn't recharged *Wa's* batteries. He set his father, grumbling at our lack of preparedness, to steering by flashlight.

Suddenly several things happened at once. The wind, which had been blowing fifteen knots, increased to twenty-five knots and caught *Wa* with full sail up. She heeled sharply, plowing the port rail into the sea. The force of the lurch shook the unlashed lantern from its stand, and it crashed in pieces on the floor at Betty's feet, plunging us into darkness. Water slopped over the floorboards and into the port lockers: I'd forgotten to pump the bilge. Betty crouched in a corner of the weather berth, holding on with her legs tucked under her, avoiding the broken glass, exuding terror.

I raced to pump the bilge, then picked up the broken glass. After turning off the stove, I started topside to help.

"Don't you think you'd better get that sail down, Pete?" his father shouted. The wind tore the words from his mouth. Pete, who'd been studying the rising wind trying to decide whether to reef—shorten—the mainsail first or replace the genny with the jib, agreed. As he did and I climbed into the cockpit, the wind gusted again. "Now!" Dr. Eastman screamed.

Pete scrambled forward. I winced at my husband's knee-jerk reaction to his father's command. Pete was *Wa's* captain. But here he was, acting as if he were ten years old and taking commands from his father on his *father's* boat.

Pete yelled for me to release the genny sheet so he could lower the sail. I did, but too soon. A blanket of sail swathed him like a great white wing flapping. *Boy, are we ever out of practice*, I thought.

"Sonofabitch, what're you doing?" Pete yelled. "Get the sheet."

"Get that sail down!" Dr. Eastman shouted. "We're in the middle of a damn gale."

"This isn't a gale—just a squall," I said quietly, hoping my calm would assert my leadership. His assumption of command on my boat—my home—made me hot with anger, but I clenched my teeth and tried to remain reasonable.

"Squall nothing—it's a gale. Look at the size of those waves, and they're growing." His hand clutched the tiller until the muscles in his forearm bulged. His face was drawn and tight.

"Let me steer for a while," I said.

He shook his head and clenched tighter, as if he thought I would wrest the tiller from him. "We had no business coming out here. No binnacle light, no running lights, no lights below."

He glared at me. "Even the most inexperienced Sunday sailor in Southern California wouldn't be this stupid."

I had to agree with him about our lack of preparedness, and I felt like a fool.

Pete lowered the main. *Wa* began to hobbyhorse violently, for she had little stability without sail up. Pete returned to the cockpit. Just then we saw a moving light. My father-in-law was steering an erratic course, so the light was bobbing all across the ocean on the boat's port side.

"Turn on the engine, quick!" Dr. Eastman yelled.

"It's all right—they're not headed for us. They'll be going down the coast," I said.

"We need that engine. We've got to get out of here." His face, gray and worried in the pale glow of the flashlight, told me that my seamanship, which got us across the largest ocean in the world and would get us home whether his son rallied or not, meant not a tinker's damn to him. *You sonofabitch,* I thought, but kept my mouth shut.

Pete cranked the flywheel, but something was caught around the prop. I peered into the darkness on the port side and saw the sheet I'd loosed too soon trailing beneath the keel.

"You!" Pete pointed an accusing finger at me. Anger rose in my stomach like undigested meat, but I swallowed it back down. He was taking out his frustration on me because he feared his father.

"We're going back," I said. Pete wasn't about to argue. He set the jib, took the tiller, and steered toward the Cape Gazelle light.

When we got into Blanche Bay, the wind eased to a whisper, and Betty came topside. "I'm glad I don't do *that* every day," she joked. We all pretended her joke had broken the tension.

I went below to finish preparing supper. We had drinks and something hot to fill our bellies, and my father-in-law's dark fear faded.

The wind, in puffs, died; we were becalmed.

"If you spent more time on deck handling sheets instead of below cooking, I wouldn't have to go overboard," Pete snarled at me.

Shove it, I wanted to tell him, but again I kept my mouth shut as he donned diving mask and flippers. He wasn't my adversary;

his father was.

He grabbed the flashlight and jumped off the stern. After several dives, he cleared the prop, and the sheet floated free like some white snake in the moonlit water. Back aboard, Pete started the engine. The faithful "puk puk" took us at four knots back to Rabaul. It was past one a.m. when we anchored.

Betty, exhausted, slipped into the forepeak and slept. The rest of us stayed up for a nightcap that turned into three or four.

"I remember some nasty sailing on Lake Erie and a squall off San Pedro," Dr. Eastman said, "but I never thought I'd be part of a Chinese fire drill in New Guinea."

Pete attempted a smile but said nothing, as if ashamed that he'd lost his cool and become indecisive. We had both been unnerved by a scared, middle-aged sailor who thought he knew more than we did because he was older.

Then all of a sudden his father said quietly, "You did well."

"*You* did well," Pete replied.

"No. You were in charge, and you kept your cool."

I was furious. Whom did they think they were fooling except themselves?

"Only because I didn't know what was going on." Pete grinned, and I flinched. He was belittling himself, trying to smooth over his father's panic. "I'm sorry," my husband said soberly. "We never should have gone, especially unprepared as we were. I'd forgotten about the St. George's Channel."

"We were in a gale, you know. You can't go upwind in a gale. That's senseless, and foolish. Why beat your head against a wall?"

"It wasn't a gale," I said softly.

"I know," said Pete, ignoring me. "We shouldn't have tried to go upwind. It's a long bloody way to Madehas. We couldn't have gotten you there and back in time for your flight. And we would've made ourselves miserable in the process. I'm sorry, Dad. I should have done better by you." Pete didn't mention that his mother and Father Fletcher had sailed a similar distance in *Wa* and found the experience mostly exhilarating.

"You're quite a sailor, you know. I was proud of you."

"I learned from you."
"No, not all of it. You've learned a lot since then."
They grew silent. Neither of them knew what else to say.

Hetau
or
Why Is the Wind Blowing So Damn Hard?

276 miles and 6 days Rabaul to Hetau
under way 16 1/2 months

The runway was a lake and the gray-white downpour so thick it looked like streaking hail when we saw Peter and Betty off on the morning plane bound for Port Moresby and Sydney. As they hurried from the terminal, my heart went out to Betty, for she hated to fly even in good weather. As we watched the burdened little craft lift slowly, slowly into the shroud, little did I know that I, too, would soon feel Betty's fear.

After taking down the mast once again to paint it and re-rig it with the new wire ordered from Australia, we were finally ready to leave Rabaul on the afternoon of May 25. I was eager to go. Rabaul had offered me nothing but a $200-a-month job and some people I never cared to see again.

Pete was morose. "I feel I've made a lot of emotional commitments," he said.

"To whom?" I asked.

He scowled. "Our friends. Who else?"

"They were drinking buddies, not friends. Will you ever write to them? Will they ever write to you?"

"Sometimes I think you have ice in your veins." He retreated below like a bear going into hibernation, pulled a blanket over his head, and let me run the boat.

I remembered my resolve of months before to lead and thought, with some satisfaction, *It's my job now.*

I grabbed myself some bread and cheese, took the tiller, and gloried as *Wa's* sails filled. I'd forgotten how good it was to feel the tiller hum in my hand, to listen to the shush of water falling away from the boat, to smell the sea. It was clean and uncomplicated. The sea and wind were my friends, as was *Wa*. With the comfort of this companionship, I did not feel abandoned or alone.

The night carried *Wa* on a breeze that made her sails stiff. She glided through the water like a swan, and a nearly full moon lent her magic. The peace after hectic days on end sang inside my soul.

We were headed for the Trobriand Islands about two hundred forty miles south and sixty miles west of us. In the morning the wind hauled from the prevailing southeast to the south, so we decided to sail east while we had the chance. We left the coast of New Britain and made a dash for Cape St. George on New Ireland.

Then the wind began to increase, and *Wa* bashed into heavy seas.

"Let's sneak in behind Cape St. George, get a good night's sleep, and wait for the wind to die down," I said in late afternoon.

Pete agreed. But when we got into the lee of New Ireland, the wind no longer had teeth, and he said, "We're just soft after five months in port. Let's get outta here."

"It's blowing like hell out there," I argued. "Let's anchor." Ignoring me, he brought *Wa* around and headed back into the St. George's Channel.

Out of the lee, the wind was fierce. Sailing under the jib alone, we slogged on.

"We're going nowhere," I screamed. "The jib's not strong enough to carry us. We'll be swept back and lose all that precious way to windward."

He glared but said nothing.

"Let's go back to New Ireland. If we anchor, we can hold our ground."

"We don't have a chart," he barked. "I'm not going anywhere

near that reef-strewn coast at dusk."

I was angry. He had usurped my plan to get us out of the St. George's Channel, then I'd let him make a very stupid choice. As dark approached, we hove to. I curled up on the port berth under a wet blanket and hoped his watch was nasty.

I awoke to a yelp from Pete, who apparently had fallen asleep on watch. He screamed something about the Cape Gazelle light. Despite being hove to to windward, *Wa* had been driven straight across the St. George's Channel at about seven knots. On her present course, she would run smack into the Duke of York Islands.

He rushed topside and unlashed the helm. I climbed into my foul-weather jumpsuit, buckled on my safety harness, and climbed the companionway. Spray like hail hit my face, and I had to grip the cabin top to keep from being bounced into the cockpit.

"This is a drag," I yelled. The noise of the wind in the rigging drowned me out. "I'll take her." I put my hand on the tiller.

"Are you sure?"

"At least I won't fall asleep on watch."

He slunk below and said nothing.

I sailed *Wa* into Blanche Bay. In the lee of Cape Gazelle, there was little sea. Still, we were being driven downwind toward Rabaul, under the jib alone, at seven knots. Despite the blessedness of being sheltered from heavy seas, we had the new danger of the land. There was very little room to maneuver in Blanche Bay. Besides, after our triumphant leave-taking three nights before, when we'd boasted at our farewell party that we were the first cruisers that year to set sail, we didn't dare show our faces in Rabaul.

In five hours *Wa* was driven thirty-five miles downwind, losing what it had taken her twenty-four hours of tough sailing to gain.

At sunrise, despite having wind, Pete turned on the power. We sneaked out of Blanche Bay, hoping no one from Rabaul would see us. By 8:15 we were off Cape Gazelle with seven knots of wind, but Pete said grimly, "Let's keep the power on and get the hell out of this channel. I don't want to get caught with our pants down again."

But the wind rose, again. So did the sea—into short, choppy waves in the shelving land close to the coast. By noon we weren't making headway. As *Wa* struggled, Pete spotted a tiny harbor tucked into the land. "It's Rugen," he said. "We're going in."

We surfed through a fifty-foot wide channel. Our chart showed a Catholic mission on a knoll to the right. On the left was Put Put Plantation, where we anchored. Bone tired, I fell into a dead sleep.

I was badly bruised in the ego. *You call yourself a sailor?* I asked myself the next morning. We'd set out four days before and had made little more than thirty miles! We were battered and exhausted. I was taking penicillin for an infection on my left foot. We both had saltwater sores on our butts from constant exposure, and I had them all over my face. I felt as if we'd grown unmanageably soft in Rabaul. *You call yourself a sailor?* I asked myself again.

It was hard to judge wind speed beyond the safety of Rugen Harbor, although from the weather side of the mission knoll, the sea was an egg-white froth. That should have been warning enough. Still, I was eager to leave.

"We have a thousand miles of sailing upwind to Thursday Island," I said, "and we've got to be there by early July."

"I want to mend the jib," Pete argued, "and it's blowing like hell out there." He pointed to the gray sky and the trees shaking in the wind. He didn't have to mention the moaning as the branches shook, or the clanking of *Wa's* rigging. I could hear.

"We can't count on making a hundred miles a day upwind. It could take us four days to go a hundred miles," I reminded him.

He rubbed his beard, then said, "OK."

Something was driving me, and we heeded it despite the warning of the wind. Maybe it was the fiasco with my in-laws. I wanted to show them we could handle the wind, even if they couldn't. And perhaps it *was* the wind driving us, for there was something compelling in the way it curled itself around that snug harbor, unfurling the trees as its banners, then streaking away seaward into the heavy sky.

After a full day's rest, we tried to up anchor and follow a workboat out. The anchor, however, caught on a submerged wagon. Pete had to dive three times to free it, each time taking us closer to the rocks. Three women and some children ashore helped him pull while I took the tiller and manned the engine.

Outside Rugen Harbor, there was no mistaking what we'd sheltered from. The seas were steeper than when we'd entered. The reefs on either side of the pass were breaking with twelve to fifteen-foot waves. Fear choked me, but with teeth clenched I guided *Wa* through the pass into the open sea as the waves tried to throw her against the rocks. With a shock of recognition, I realized how good a sailor I had become after all.

Why didn't we return to our anchorage at Put Put Plantation? I didn't ask myself then—only later. The wind was sucking me into a kind of madness.

We headed once more for Cape St. George. Under power we made way upwind, which was heartening. But we still had to tack, for the sail—the jib alone—pushed us forward as much as the engine.

"If we were real sailors," Pete said ruefully, "we'd turn that thing off and slug it out." Unwilling to look me in the eye, he turned away. We prided ourselves on being "real" sailors, not power boaters. And we'd sailed a good way across the Pacific Ocean without an engine.

The wind shrieked and whacked the rigging against the mast, drowning out the "puk puk" of the Yanmar. The jib whirred like a small airplane engine. Waves crashed across *Wa's* bow, driving water along the decks, filling the air with spray.

By late morning, when the wind speed had risen from thirty to forty-five knots, I managed to make a last cup of coffee by holding the kettle so it wouldn't jump off the stove. With the porthole closed, the alcohol and kerosene fumes, combined with the motion of the boat, nauseated me. The stove spattered flaming kerosene on the bunk below. I put out the fire and abandoned the galley.

A clothes shelf fell from its bracket, so the forepeak became a tangle of wet sailbags and wet clothing. The books began leaping off their shelf. With each wave over the foredeck, a pint to several gallons of water made it below.

Twice the force of the seas knocked the forehatch open, the second time wrenching the hatch's lock from the wood. Pete, clutching nails between his teeth, crawled forward along the deck and nailed it shut while I steered.

We had to pump water from the bilge a hundred strokes every half hour.

The only dry places were the hanging locker and the aft ends of the quarterberths. Coco wedged himself between the typewriter and the ribs on the port side and glowered at me with red eyes. *At least you're dry, cat, and you don't have to steer,* I thought.

Pete and I took turns of one to two hours steering. Tiring after that, we'd start taking one breaking wave after another into the cockpit.

Fresh to the watch, I was able to shield myself from breaking waves for perhaps ten minutes. I steered carefully, glancing from the seas to the sail to the compass. Much to my surprise, I realized the constant spray bothered me only in that it blurred my glasses, but as the ordeal wore on I was finding this storm exhilarating. I was Ahab challenging the sea and wind, challenging Moby Dick. "Who says you can't go upwind in a gale?" I jeered at my father-in-law. As the tiller quivered in my hand, I became part of *Wa* and she of me. "Yes, Ishmael," I yelled, "this is my Great Adventure too."

"Are you *really* having a good time?" Pete called from below.

"Yes! I've realized how good a sailor I am."

He poked his head out the companionway and withdrew immediately. "If you're having fun, you can take her as long as you want to."

When the first wave broke over me, it drove under my hood, Float Coat, and foul-weather gear, and trickled icily down my skin. Even when I shut my eyes the saltwater managed to find them, and after a while the worst part of steering was stinging eyes. When I could keep only one eye open, I yelled to Pete to change the watch.

Below, I huddled under a wet blanket, getting as warm as I could. I was reading Nicholas Monsarrat's *The Cruel Sea,* about the Battle of the Atlantic during World War II, which gave me strange comfort, perhaps the knowledge that misery at sea sometimes knew no bounds. I was grateful that we were in the tropics.

All through the afternoon *Wa* bashed her way to windward. She *was* making progress, which was enough to keep us going.

At dusk, with the light on New Ireland's Cape St. George just ahead, I knew we had the terrible channel licked. As I clutched the tiller, I saw another light—probably a workboat—off *Wa's* port bow. Then a squall swirled around us, and blackness blocked out everything.

"There's a boat between us and the cape," I called. Pete stuck his head out the companionway and stared. "Put up a light," I ordered.

He raised his eyebrows and licked his lips. He looked warm and somewhat dry. I knew he had no desire to buckle on his harness, light the kerosene lantern, and battle breaking waves to raise the light. "I don't feel like it. If you think we're in danger, *you* do it," he said, and went below.

I feared a collision but was unwilling to crawl forward to the mast myself, carrying a glass lantern, which I then would have to attach to the main halyard while keeping my balance on a bucking boat. *Wa's* red and green electric running lights were so low to the water they would've been invisible until another vessel was right on top of us. Her masthead light was weaker than a lantern.

I kept on course and stared as the light approached. It was a ghoulish yellow. My heart began to pound. Just as I was about to leave the tiller and leap below for the flashlight, which I would shine on the jib, the other boat veered off to port.

After my next watch, I was exhausted. "I won't be able to make it through all day tomorrow without a good sleep," I told Pete.

"You know, we can get to Madehas—a hundred and ten miles—tomorrow if we keep on going."

"Madehas? We've been to Madehas!"

"Sure. Since we've made it past the cape, we might as well go a little farther east. That way we can get in our easting, which will make it a lot easier to go south."

Stupefied, I just stared at him.

"Besides, maybe by the time we get to Madehas the wind'll be back in the southeast where it belongs instead of the Goddamned southwest." He didn't mention his real reason for wanting to go to Madehas, which was to shelter under Jock's and Louise's hospitality.

"It's a hundred and fifty miles to Madehas, not a hundred and ten," I finally had the wits to say (although I was wrong), "so we can't make it tomorrow." A pinpoint in my brain said, *You need to sleep. Nothing else matters.*

"OK," he gave in, and hove to.

"But we can make it by day after tomorrow," I said, willing to go as long as I could sleep first.

He smiled gratefully.

I fixed oatmeal—our first meal in more than twelve hours. I was so tired that I'd lost track of time and thought it was ten p.m. Pete told me it was two a.m.

It was wonderful for us to get warm and somewhat dry at the same time, to turn off the perpetual "puk puk" of the engine, to stop *Wa* from bucking. We had a nightcap and then wrapped ourselves around each other. The violence of the wind shrieking in the rigging flamed our passion; we made love as water crashed against the hull.

Afterwards, Pete was a great sleepy cat. He gave me the blanket and the port bunk, taking the upwind starboard bunk until, sound asleep, he was dumped onto the cabin floor by a wave.

At noon the next day I wedged myself in the companionway with the sextant and watch, waiting for a sun that never showed its face. In late afternoon Pete got a sunline, but the longitude did us no good—what we needed was latitude, which we could get only from the noon sight or star sights. We never saw stars.

We hove to at dusk with Buka Island, north of Madehas, about twenty miles upwind. We'd get our sleep early and be away before dawn came.

Pete got up at 02:30 and set the course to Madehas. *Wa*, under reefed main and jib, plunged across the waves at seven knots. Below, it felt as if we were in a whirlwind. I asked several times if he wanted me to take over, but he looked like he was enjoying himself. After a while I joined him in the cockpit.

Suddenly Pete couldn't move the tiller. He tried to waggle it up and down and sideways but could get no more than an inch of play. His face blankly stoic, he took down the sails. It was five a.m. and still dark, but he had to go into that roiling sea to unjam the tiller.

He tied the mainsheet around his waist, and I held it so that he wouldn't be dragged far behind the boat, which was making three knots under bare poles. In mask and flippers, with a flashlight, he took in a mighty lungful of air and jumped off *Wa's* stern.

I tightened my grip on the mainsheet and prayed that my hands were strong enough. With a jammed tiller, *Wa* was helpless. If the mainsheet broke and cast Pete loose, he would drown.

When he surfaced, he yelled, "It's the shaft," took in another lungful of air, and disappeared into the black again. Shaking all over, I waited three anxious minutes. Then Pete heaved himself onto the fantail with a thumb's up sign. I was so grateful and proud I could've hugged him. His strengths came flooding back to me. My hero had returned.

"That sonofabitch from BPs Marine. I'd like to shoot the fucker," Pete shouted. The mechanic who'd worked on *Wa's* engine in Rabaul hadn't tightened the shaft, which had worked loose, causing the shaft to jam into the rudder. If the rudder hadn't been there, we would've lost the shaft. Of course, if Pete had checked the mechanic's work, we wouldn't have had this emergency, but I said nothing.

Under a gray sky, the outline of Buka etched itself into the horizon. We tacked toward it until about 8:30, when we came around the point that I thought would show us Buka Passage between the islands of Bougainville and Buka. Yes, there were those small islands. But I was puzzled. The reef at the northern entrance was out of position according to the chart, and it was too big.

As Pete steered for what he thought was Madehas, the *Leilani*, a BPs workboat from Rabaul, putted down the channel. Pete changed course to intercept it. "Is that Madehas?" he shouted.

"No. Madehas is twenty miles that way," yelled *Leilani's* skipper, pointing straight upwind.

"Holy crap," I said, "we're twenty miles off course? I rushed to take the tiller, and Pete leapt below to get the chart.

"We're in Queen Carola Harbor," he said. All the misplaced islands began to make sense as we studied the chart.

"Let's see if there's an anchorage at Hetau Island," I suggested. It was closest.

"The island's small and low," he argued. "There won't be any protection if the storm returns."

"There's no harm in looking. We can always back away."

Minutes later, I snugged *Wa* into a thumbprint in the land while Pete set the anchor. We learned later that *Wa* was the first yacht ever to visit Hetau.

I heaved a big sigh and grinned at him. Although I was tired, I was filled with joy. We had worked as a team and brought *Wa* through the storm. I felt closer to Pete than I had in months. But I also felt his anxiety at what the battering of the last few days had done to our little boat: both jibs and the newer genny ripped, and *Wa* leaking badly from some unknown source.

Never had *Wa* been in such a shambles. Water slopped over the floorboards, littered with pieces of chart, potatoes, soggy flour, a jar of jam. The stoves had long since fallen out of their rack. The forepeak was piled with sodden sails, clothes, and books. Neither of us had a dry thing to wear. But we were at anchor, safe, and the sun was shining. When a man and two boys paddled alongside in a canoe, Pete beckoned them aboard.

I put the stoves back in their rack, primed one with alcohol, and set a kettle of coffee water on the kerosene burner.

"*Storm cam long boat make liklik mess,*" Pete told our guests and pointed to the disaster in the cabin.

The man craned his neck through the companionway and turned with a solemn look. "*Cyclone stap long Solomon Islands,*" he said, cocking his head at Pete.

"Oh?" we both said, stunned. Suddenly our struggle took on meaning—we'd been braving the fringes of a cyclone?

"You didn't hear?" the villager asked in Pidgin. "Don't you have a radio?"

"*Have despela radio*," admitted Pete, looking foolish. "*No listen despela radio longtam.*"

We'd been too busy surviving the storm and, more importantly, hadn't thought before we left Rabaul to find the radio weather schedule. Hadn't cyclone season ended thirty days before, on May 1? Then I realized: we didn't need to listen to the radio. In Rugen Harbor we needed to listen to the wind.

The villager shook his head and clicked his teeth. He wasn't sure whether we were crazy or brave.

I served the five of us coffee; we basked in the warmth of the tropical sun like turtles coming out of our shells.

The man invited us ashore, and we promised to go later. "*Yupela want samting long Hetau?*"

"*Have tobacco long trade*," I replied. I told him we'd like fresh fruit and vegetables and, I added, glancing at the rock-strewn reef all around *Wa*, clams.

Word went out swiftly. By late afternoon we were laden with more bananas than we could eat, a fruit-nut I'd never seen, and enough clams for a dozen people.

Because I was still cold from the storm and the thought of putting on wet clothes chilled me anew, I left my foul-weather jumpsuit on. Soon the sun's heat penetrated the nylon, and my skin steamed beneath the cloth.

We worked tirelessly all afternoon, I making the forepeak livable and drying things and Pete repairing the bilge pump and searching for the source of the leaks. He suspected water was coming in along the garboard strake, between *Wa's* iron keel and her wooden keel, the only seam in the boat.

Wa's lifelines carried so many clothes-pinned garments she looked like a laundry. Weary as we were, I'm not sure how we managed to keep going.

At dusk we stopped work and sat in the cockpit drinking gin with onions. It was the first time we'd seen the stars in days.

I fixed a great, gorgeous dinner of clams, making a bitter chowder out of them. We sat in the dark in the cockpit eating and drinking, watching the few slender lights of the village snuff out.

I was at peace and felt a great joy to be alive and safe. We had also encountered the first Melanesians to extend us the hand of friendship.

Next morning, some children took us on a walk around the island. Wading in water up to my calves, I found fist-sized cowries, helmet shells, conches, oysters, clams. The girls told us what each was called in their language.

Pete wrote our names in the sand, with a heart in between, there for all the village to see. I knew the tide would wash away that sign of love but hoped what lay beneath it would endure. We strolled arm in arm after the jabbering children. My sense of well-being reassured me: now everything would be all right.

In the afternoon I took the old jib ashore so that I could spread it out for repair. Joseph Raston, a tribal elder and a man who'd been a sail-maker during World War II, sent one of the girls for the village sewing machine and a table. Soon we were gathered around it, Joseph feeding the cotton cloth through, Regina guiding it from the other side, Mary turning the shuttle. After an hour's work, the jib was patched with quadruple stitching. I gave the villagers our *lava-lava* material from Tarawa to say thank you.

"*Tenk yu too mas,*" Joseph said. There were tears in his eyes. I wanted to hug this man, to tell him that after nine months in Melanesia, I at last had a feeling of affinity.

In the evening we took our cassette deck to Joseph's house for a *singsing*. For a time the children were shy, and there was a lot of passing the guitar about, as if no one knew how to play. But finally the girls ranged themselves on the ground and sang. From the harmonies and tonal quality, we might've been back in Polynesia.

The next day, the wind backed to the southeast. Still recuperating from the storm, we lazed until eleven before setting out. We couldn't have had a more beautiful day for sailing nor a prettier spot. I didn't mind that we were going upwind and had to tack.

At dusk we came up to Madehas and saw the light. The Lees' son, Cameron, came out in the speedboat to take us ashore. "Come and have some steak," he said. It was the nicest thing I'd heard in days.

Jock was surprised to see us. "You must have had a rough time of it in the cyclone," he said.

"On Hetau they said the cyclone was in the Solomons," I said.

"Don't you listen to the radio?" asked Jock, incredulous. "The cyclone was here—at Bougainville. It did terrific damage to Panguna. The eye was at Buin. All the radio broadcasts warned ships to stay away from Bougainville."

"Oh," said Pete, looking sheepish. Cyclone Ida was the first Bougainville had ever had, and besides that, it was a month out of season. How were we to know?

"Bloody, stupid Americans," said Jock, putting his arms around us as we walked into the yellow warmth of the kitchen. Louise instructed her new boy, Betsi, a strapping lad with an ill-fitting name, to put on more steaks.

"What happened to Sepe?" I asked.

Louise turned from her work and smiled. "I don't like boys who chew betel in the kitchen. I don't like betel anyway, but betel in the kitchen is too much."

"But he was with you for seventeen years. He must've chewed betel before."

"Well, yes he did, and he was a good cook and knew what he was doing without my having to stand over him. That's hard to find." She sighed. "Harder than I realized." She paused. "There were other problems. Jock caught him stealing beer—selling it."

Given the way the laborers lived, in cramped quarters with no plumbing, I wasn't surprised. Sepe probably felt he was evening out life's inequities. But that's not something you say to your hostess.

The week passed uneventfully until Saturday afternoon, when a young fellow rushed to the back door with dire news. A bunch of men from the labor quarters had taken the tractor, gone joyriding, and gotten stuck.

Louise's eyes blazed with anger, and she asked where. The lad admitted the joyriders had left the track to careen through the bush and swamplands and along the beach, where they'd gotten stuck on the edge of a reef. In a tone of voice I'd never heard her use, Louise ordered the lad to fetch shovels, crowbars, and whatever other tools he might need and get "quick time" back to that tractor. Then Louise set out to walk there.

The culprits knew she'd come. When she got there the tractor was gone. Only a bit of uprooted coral showed that people had disturbed the spot. She headed for the labor quarters, where the tractor sat, still wet from salt spray. Again her anger flared. She told the men to wash the tractor thoroughly with fresh water, dry it, and oil it.

When Jock returned that night from the Buka Council meeting, she told him what had happened. Jock turned about face and marched to the labor quarters. I never learned what he did, but things were very quiet the next day.

That they treated their men like children bothered me, even though they had acted like kids. Beneath her velvet sternness and his smooth steeliness lurked the need to remain in control.

Samarai
or
Marching to the Betel of a Different Drummer

432 miles and 6 days Madehas to Samarai
under way 17 1/2 months

Samarai was a forgotten place. When naval power had been vital in the southwest Pacific, the little island had controlled the channel between itself and the mainland of Papua. With the end of World War II and the emergence of Port Moresby as the commercial center of New Guinea, Samarai faded. Its somnolent main street was thick with dust and its gutters with fallen leaves.

Yet the mood, after Rabaul, surprised me. The night we arrived, we visited The Club, where whites and blacks drank together and watched the movie. Many government jobs, and office positions in companies like Burns Philp, already were filled by Papuans. Because the whites were pulling back, there was a better feeling between the races.

Our first morning there, I awoke and reached for Coco, who usually slept next to me. No cat. "Coco," I called, and hauled myself out of bed. I padded naked through the cabin and stuck my head out the companionway. "Coco?" I scanned the deck fore and aft.

Pete scrambled into shorts and went topside to look. I searched from the chain locker to the engine compartment, hoping Coco had gotten trapped somewhere. No cat.

I threw on a dress, and we rowed ashore. Pete went one way and I the other, calling "Coco, Coco," each call more frantic than the last. I scanned the shoreline, praying I wouldn't see a lump of fur. *Wa* was anchored more than a hundred yards from shore. *Could he swim that far?* I didn't think so.

Coco's disappearance gouged a huge hole in my heart. I kept seeing him leaping for flying fish, rubbing against my legs, and curling in my lap. How could I bear to lose him? Tears came to my eyes. There never would be another cat like him.

Anchored near us were the workboats of the out-islanders who came to Samarai bearing *copra* and left with cargoes for the villages. These men were a hardy lot, sailing their gaff-rigged craft in and out of the anchorage in all weathers, sleeping in the open when the hold was full of *copra*, cooking over a wood-burning fire in an old kerosene can. On days between sailings they lazed on deck under the canvas awning, chewing betel and talking. As we rowed past the boat from Wari Island, Pete stopped to ask, "*Yupela stap long mipela boat for coffee, singsing tonight?*" inviting them to visit *Wa*.

Pete didn't know whether anyone had understood the invitation, but later an old man named Sila stopped by in his skiff and asked if he could have a look at our boat. He brought a piece of kingfish, a white-fleshed steak of two pounds or more. I made coffee, and we sat in *Wa's* cockpit watching the sun die in a puddle of blood behind the mountains of Papua.

Sila was small and wiry and the color of milky coffee, with graying hair crinkling his head and his teeth red-black from chewing betel. He'd been a U.S. Marine sergeant, worked as a scout during World War II, and spoke good English.

"Have you seen a brown and white cat with blue eyes?" I asked.

He shook his head. "Not very many cats here," he said. "People eat them."

I shuddered and wished I hadn't asked.

"What was it like working as a scout?" asked Pete, changing the subject.

Sila shook his head again. "War is very bad, but I like the Americans. The Australians don't invite Melanesians on their boats." He said it without rancor, but my gut tightened as it had for months whenever racial prejudice smacked me in the face.

"Can you do us a favor?" Pete asked after a while. "I've wanted for a long time to chew betel nut. Can you teach us?"

Sila grinned, scampered into his skiff, and grabbed his *tobo,* a flat, woven coconut frond basket the size of a small purse which both men and women had carried in Rabaul. It was as much a part of the Melanesian costume as the *lap-lap.*

From his *tobo* Sila took areca nuts. "These are *sarda,*" he said. They were green and about the size of Brazil nuts. Next came *harigu,* or powdered lime, spooned from its gourd onto an *ennari,* or fish rib. I'd seen the lime, ground from coral, sold in packets of betel leaf in the Melanesian markets. Last came the *lugu,* or pepper, which was green and knobby and looked a bit like okra.

"It makes the red," Sila said. He took a bite of his *sarda* and began to chew. When he'd worked the nut into a pulp he dipped lime onto the *ennari* and licked it from the stick. Then he added pepper.

Pete and I followed suit. Before I'd worked the nut into a pulp, my mouth filled with saliva; I had an irresistible desire to spit. So I spat, and kept doing so every few seconds, over *Wa's* starboard rail. So did Pete. Sila chuckled.

The nut was bitter. Adding lime reduced the bitterness, and the powder dried my mouth. Adding pepper brought back the saliva along with a slight burning sensation, which prompted me to chew another nut and more lime. It was like juggling with salt, lime, and tequila.

My mouth and tongue grew numb, as if I'd had a shot of Novocain, and my throat constricted. "My head is a bit funny," I said, holding it in both hands. Sila laughed.

"After three or four days," he said, "it is just like chewing gum." Why would anyone go to that much trouble to chew gum?

In a few minutes we spat out the *sarda*. For me the numbness wore off, leaving me relaxed with a pleasant sense of well-being—until I thought about Coco.

"Feels like I'm about four beers gone," Pete said.

Shortly later Sila left, bidding us *agutoi*, or thank you, for sharing betel with him and promising to return. Pete went below, took one look in the mirror at his pink teeth, and brushed them.

After chewing betel, I found the fish dinner delicious, but then the memory flashed that there was no Coco to devour the scraps.

On Monday afternoon, a canoe filled with kids paddled alongside *Wa*. One of the boys clutched something in a blanket. He thrust it at me.

"*Despela blong yu?*" he asked.

Underneath the blanket was a red, blue, green, and yellow creature with white whiskers and brown ears. "Meooww!" he wailed as he struggled to free himself.

Between laughter and tears, I hugged him. "Meooww!" he wailed again. The kids giggled, and Pete let out a sigh.

"*Yupela stap long boat,*" said Pete, inviting the children aboard.

"*Tenku tumas,*" I said, and grabbed their hands.

After feeding Coco, I mixed glasses of Funny Face for all of them and gave them hard candy, which they crunched in mouths red from chewing betel.

"*How yu find despela?*" Pete asked.

"*Despela stap long school,*" one of the boys said, and then looked at the others.

"In a cupboard," said another boy, in English, "with colored paper." They all nodded vigorously. "We make things with the paper."

Pete began to laugh. "Construction paper." He turned to me. "He must've been wet from swimming ashore, and now he's wearing Joseph's coat." Coco, who glanced up from his food, glared, as if it were our fault he looked like a clown.

We were down to our last hundred dollars. In Samarai, however, we were caught in a foreign exchange crisis, and the bank manager would give us only twenty dollars Australian for our one hundred American dollars. That wouldn't buy enough fuel and fresh produce to get us to Thursday Island.

We waited two weeks to get a fair exchange, then left Samarai on July 6, my spirits high at getting under way. We still had sailed only a quarter of the way around the world, but we were moving again. I didn't dwell upon the fact that it had taken us almost a year and a half so far and that we'd promised my father we'd return in two and a half years. That left fourteen months to complete the trip.

Pete was subdued and remarked during the afternoon, "I have an irrational desire to go back to Rabaul."

"Why?" I was horrified that he'd even think such a thing.

"Every place we go, I make friends, and then I leave them."

He sounded like a broken record. How many more times would he focus on where we'd been rather than on where we were going?

Thursday Island and Cocos (Keeling) Island
or
Things That Go Bump in the Daytime

549 miles and 10 days Samarai to Thursday Island
2761 miles and 25 days Thursday Island to Cocos Island
under way 20 months

Rising in golden hills, Thursday Island looked so much like Southern California it made me homesick. Below the hills clustered houses as old as the weather-beaten clapboards of the sun cities along California's coast.

Three wharfs jutted from the island. Beyond the third were the small boats—the pearl luggers and yachts.

Pete strode forward to the anchor, and I sailed *Wa* in a twenty-five-knot wind under double-reefed main and jib. The *Sailing Directions* warned of strong currents, fueled by the wind and funneled through Torres Strait, flowing past the island.

Pete picked a spot between a South African trimaran, *Audacious*, and a British sloop, *She*, then dropped the anchor. He wasn't fast enough. The current caught *Wa* and carried her backwards at four knots, with her anchor dragging, straight for the trimaran.

Luckily, the South Africans had been watching. A nimble man leapt to his port rail just as *Wa* scraped alongside. He broke her force, and Pete pushed her off after she'd given the trimaran a glancing blow.

"Don't you have an engine?" the South African yelled.

"Yes," admitted Pete, chagrined. He turned it on and lowered the sails, and we crept to a new spot well to lee of the South Africans and the British.

Another embarrassing arrival brought to you by Addie and Pete.

We were running out of time. We still had to sail three thousand miles across the top of Australia before we could enter the Indian Ocean, and that would take at least a month. The only safe months for crossing the Indian Ocean were September-November. The rest of the year it was ravaged by cyclones. We were cutting it way too close. But *Wa* was leaking badly, and Pete had to stop the leaks. He pulled one of *Wa*'s seven ¾-inch keelbolts (connecting the iron keel to the boat), and it broke two-thirds of the way down, eaten away by electrolysis. If those eleven-year-old bolts gave way at sea, we would lose *Wa*'s keel—and the boat. They had to be replaced.

He enlisted the help of New Zealander Bob Ballantyne, who cast seven new bolts for us. Pete tried to do the work in the anchorage but didn't have power-driven tools, and four of the old bolts remained stubbornly stuck. He fretted over the project for ten days. We waited for nearly another week for a spot in the boatyard.

Once *Wa* was out of the water, Pete approached the bolts through the keel, searching for the concrete "pockets" cemented in after the nuts were attached. Even using power tools, drilling for that first pocket took him an hour. Then he struck concrete. In his joy, he might as well have struck gold. The job took shape as something manageable. Fellow sailor Karl Warchot came to help.

In the meanwhile, I worried about Coco. Immigration had required us to post a hundred-dollar bond to ensure that Coco wouldn't go ashore. If he did, we'd been warned, we would forfeit the bond and the cat would be euthanized. We were in Australia, which had no rabies and wanted to keep it that way. Now, because

Wa was ashore and he was on *Wa*, he was ashore; an inflexible immigration officer could have him killed. And if he leapt from the cradle twenty feet to the ground and escaped, we'd never see him again. So I talked to him as I worked and spent a lot of time petting and fussing over him. In the end, Coco was so used to being aboard, and so glad for my attention, that he stayed put.

My job was to paint. During the first two days out of the water, I prepared the surfaces, and on the third and fourth days, I painted—white on the topsides and copper bottom below the waterline.

The last evening I felt feverish and shaky and begged off our nightly walk to the Grand Hotel for showers. The next day I had a fever of 103° and a throat so sore I couldn't swallow. Karl said it was "T.I. Disease." He took me to the hospital in his car twice a day for four days for penicillin shots.

Nauseated, head pounding, I drifted in and out of a surreal world. Even with the forehatch open, the forepeak felt like a tropical cocoon. I sweated my way through uneasy sleep and awakened damp and disoriented. Sand blasters whined against the hull of the steel boat upwind of us, and bits of steel grit blew through the forehatch when the wind came up. Pete and Karl drilled and hammered, making *Wa's* hull vibrate and my skull throb. While I lay plastered to the bunk in the heat of the day, Coco, my nurse cat, curled around my feet.

Pete, upset that I'd gotten sick, was frantic to finish the work and leave Thursday Island. I, too, worried and tried to will myself back to good health. It was August 11, which meant we would have to sail for a month, take virtually no break in the next port, and sail for another three weeks across the Indian Ocean, where the winds blow harder than in the Atlantic or the Pacific. It would be a grueling journey ahead.

Twenty-five days after leaving Thursday Island, we had to stop because we needed water. To our dismay, however, we found we had no *Sailing Directions* for nearby Cocos (Keeling) Island, an Australian protectorate. Our only chart was small-scale.

On a cloudy, gloomy day we skirted the atoll's southern edge, and Pete stood on the bow looking for a pass into the lagoon. He waved me past the reef but then signaled that there were coral heads in the way. I couldn't get *Wa* around them, so I let her drift back out to sea.

On the second try we made it into the lagoon. Pete rushed back to the cockpit to check the chart.

"The airport's to the left," he said, "on the *motu* West Island. That must mean customs and immigration are there too."

As I turned left, the sky opened in a downpour so heavy it blotted out all sight of land. Pete raced back to the bow. I could barely see his hand signals as he guided me around coral heads that jutted from the lagoon. I couldn't have heard him above the roar of the rain. Occasionally he scurried below to pump water from the bilge.

The lagoon got shallower and shallower, and still we were nowhere near West Island. As a barge passed close to us, I changed course to intercept it.

"What're you doing here?" the barge skipper called.

"We're looking for West Island," Pete yelled.

"This area dries at low water," the bargeman shouted. "It's a wonder you haven't run aground. Go over there," he yelled, gesturing to the north, "to where the other yachts are anchored. The customs will come to you."

We went "over there," to Direction Island, an uninhabited *motu* populated by coconuts and chickens. When we got to the anchorage, two dinghies powered to meet us as soon as Pete had tossed the hook overboard.

John, *Ulwhilna's* skipper, a tall American whose dark hair was speckled with silver, killed his outboard, nudged his inflatable dinghy alongside *Wa*, and called up to us, "Welcome to Cocos. How in the world did you get here from the south?"

"We didn't have a chart," Pete said as he stuffed the jib into its sailbag.

"We guessed—wrong," I said.

"There's no way to get to Direction Island from the south," John said. "The lagoon, which is a minefield of coral, dries at low tide."

Round-faced, crew-cut, 14-year-old Philippe Jourdan bobbed up and down in the other dinghy and shook his head. It was clear they both were incredulous.

Short, sturdy Maxine, John's wife, said, "You come over for coffee with us when you're ready. We'll come get you so you don't have to row."

"How about a little brandy in your coffee?" Maxine asked as Pete and I settled into *Ulwhilna's* spacious saloon. I nodded enthusiastically, for we'd been dry for more than a week. Maxine brought out fresh-baked pastries, which tasted even better than the coffee. It felt so civilized to sit curled into the corner of a dry settee, wearing a dress, with my hair combed.

Philippe's parents, François and Janine, and his 19-year-old sister, Katherine, sailing on *Arita,* joined us, along with John and Maxine's adult son, Russ. Both couples were middle-aged and affluent. Unlike Pete and me, they had started their families, made their money, and *then* gone cruising in 48-foot craft. Our brash courting of disaster amused but also appalled them.

We all dreaded crossing the Indian Ocean, although none of us would admit it. In all other months but September through November, the red storm tracks of cyclones spattered our pilot charts like blood. I was grateful to be with these fellow sailors, who felt like family. The sense of a common bond was as strong as it had been with the Polynesians and Micronesians.

At dusk another yacht, *Hummingbird II*, arrived at the pass. John and Philippe powered out to guide her in, for the buoys marking the channel were unlit. Harolde and Kwai La Borde and their seven-year-old son, Pierre, were from Trinidad and old friends of the others. Janine Jourdan hastily expanded *Arita's* dinner to serve seven.

Next morning, six of us set out to sail to West Island. Pete had volunteered *Wa* as a carrier of fresh provisions and a taxi for the outing because our boat was the only one in the anchorage shallow-drafted enough to cross the lagoon in safety.

Kwai, Russ, Katherine, and Philippe came along. Thus we had aboard the most experienced yachting crew we'd ever have. The young Jourdans had sailed the farthest, from France, and had been under way for seven years. Katherine, dark-haired with liquid, laughing eyes, was a university student on a long holiday. Russ was a tall, lean, quiet young man with a blond beard. Every time he looked at Katherine, his face lit up. She smiled back and sometimes took his hand.

Kwai was vivacious and talkative, with smiles crinkling at the corners of her dark eyes, which had an Asian look. I judged her to be about my age. *Hummingbird II* was the first boat from Trinidad to circumnavigate, she told me proudly.

Then her eyes clouded. "I'm worried about South Africa. We have to stop for food and water, but I don't know if they'll let us ashore." Harolde and Pierre both were dark-skinned. Kwai, too, the Afrikaners probably would classify as "colored."

"Of course they will," I said. "You're world-class sailors. Durban should be honored to welcome you. Besides, they know under international law they're required to allow you food and water."

"I guess."

"Write to the yacht club asking for a temporary membership and tell them you're the first yacht from Trinidad to circumnavigate. The rest of us will raise holy hell if they give you any guff."

That evening at dusk we gathered on the beach at Direction Island for a barbeque, each of us bringing our own meat and vegetables, with some to spare for sharing. The men built a bonfire out of dead coconut branches, Harolde opened a bottle of rum, and we sat in the sand around the fire watching the embers cast red shadows over the darkness. Russ and Katherine powered out to fetch ice cream from *Arita's* freezer. It was a long time before they returned.

The vanilla ice cream caught in the curl of my tongue. I pushed it, cold and sweet, into the roof of my mouth. Such a simple thing—sitting on that beach, living in the moment, managing to put off thoughts of the arduous journey ahead.

On Sunday after our work was done, Pete and I rowed to the beach next to the pier and walked about a mile to the island's end to go snorkeling. An overcast sky threatened rain, and a chilly wind roiled the water in the white-flecked, murky lagoon. If we hadn't come all that way lugging our gear, we probably wouldn't have gone in, but it seemed a shame to waste the day.

Pete swam into deep water. "A two-knot current's setting toward the pass," he called. "Stay close." I needed no warning; I was already ill at ease. I was used to floating in sunshine, kicking my flippers through clear water, not fighting current in a dark sea.

Our snorkeling revealed some kinds of coral new to us, but the growth was brown and poor. There were few fish.

I was ready to quit when Pete yelled. I raised my head from the water to see panic and pain contort his face. Then I saw the puffy translucent sacs ridged with purple crests bobbing on the waves. I began dodging them.

Deep into the water below each one dangled a purple tendril and several white, shorter ones—stingers. They had wrapped themselves around Pete's right shoulder. He was trying frantically to scrape them away with his left hand.

"Head for the beach," he bellowed.

He struck out in his powerful crawl and soon left me far behind. Every once in a while he stopped, looked back, then treaded water. "Hurry, babe, I don't know how long I can last. I'm having trouble breathing."

Swallowing panic, I made little progress against the current as it swept past the beach toward the sea.

Pete reached the shore and pitched over onto the rocks. I

struggled, peering over the wave caps like a paddling dog, fighting to make land. Finally, my toes brushed the bottom, which gave me a second wind. A dozen more strokes brought me ashore. When I got there, Pete was lying on his side doubled over in pain. I helped him up, and we began the long, long walk back to the dinghy.

Every few yards, clasping his arms around his waist, he stumbled and fell. He breathed in rasping, pain-stricken gasps. Red welts stood out on his back, arm, and hand.

As his breathing grew more labored, he threw himself on his back on the sand. "Do mouth-to-mouth on me," he croaked. "I may pass out."

I straddled him, inhaled a great lungful of air, pressed my mouth against his teeth, and blew with all my might. So different from kissing.

I was trembling. *Was he stung by the deadly seawasp? Is he going to die?*

After way too long he got up and, half staggering, half loping, with a great cry like a wounded beast, crashed through the undergrowth. Clutching our skindiving gear, I stumbled as fast as I could behind him, praying he could make it. I couldn't hope to carry him, and I couldn't drag him over that rough terrain without pounding his body to pieces. I dared not leave him: he might lose consciousness.

By sheer effort of will, he made it to the dinghy. He fell into it as I dragged it into the water and rowed as hard as I could back to *Wa*.

There he crawled into the cockpit. "Get the metho," he gasped, hunched over.

As I ran below, Pete began calling out for John. With my voice added to the clamor, we raised *Ulwhilna*, anchored some two hundred feet away, and John and Maxine climbed into their dinghy and headed for *Wa*.

As I poured the purple alcohol over Pete, he shrieked.

"The metho will wash away the stingers," I said.

"It just hurts." The liquid dribbled down his back and arm and puddled in the cockpit cushion. The smell of it washed over me. It was like some nightmare in a bar.

"Where does it hurt? What can I do?"

He clenched his teeth. "The pain's deep in the muscles. I need Phenaphen." I rushed below, pawed through our medical kit, grabbed our strongest pain killer, and pumped him a glass of water.

"You want something for the rash?" I asked as he gulped the pill.

"I don't feel it." He studied his arm as if it weren't a part of his body. The welts formed strings of raised red circles that made his skin fiery. His back looked as if he'd been flogged. I returned to dousing him with alcohol.

John and Maxine sat with Pete while I searched for advice in our first-aid book, written by Pete's father. Nothing in it helped, but fortunately I'd picked up a brochure on marine stingers in the hospital at Thursday Island. Reading this brochure had taught Pete to treat the wounds with methylated spirits. I decided he'd been stung by Portuguese men o' war.

When the Phenaphen began to take effect, Pete was able to lie down. He stretched out his cramped muscles and, for the first time, felt his skin burn.

By this time I believed that we needn't rush for the doctor on West Island. If Pete had been stung by seawasps, he would have died before we'd gotten there.

My stomach clenched at the thought, and I felt thankful for the presence of John and Maxine.

Pete had survived, but what after-effects should we expect? How should I continue treating him? How long would he be sick? We faced some of the hardest sailing of our trip crossing the Indian Ocean. Would he be up to it? Uncertainty and dread seeped through me.

As a small way of saying thank you, I baked brownies for the crews of *Ulwhilna* and *Arita*. When I rowed over, they were deep in conference. They were preparing to sail too, but there was a problem: Russ and Katherine didn't want to leave Cocos. The two young people had fallen in love and just now revealed their romance. They had gone off daily at Cocos to swim, dive, and picnic on the beach. I'd watched them frisk together like young dolphins, reminded of my own joyous surrender to love ten years before.

"Why don't you let Russ trade places with Philippe on the next passage," I suggested. "Or Katherine could sail on *Ulwhilna*."

"No!" Janine exclaimed. "She is an unmarried girl. That's not appropriate."

Rebuffed, I decided to stop meddling, and we talked of other things. What we *didn't* discuss was the heavy weather sailing facing us in the Indian Ocean.

The Seychelles
or
Pete Finds His Butterfly

*2562 miles and 22 days Cocos Island to the Seychelles
under way 21 months*

We couldn't wait any longer to leave Cocos with cyclone season approaching, so we followed *Ulwhilna* and *Hummingbird* out the pass. While I worried about Pete's stamina, Coco feasted on the flying fish that jumped aboard.

This bounty was a good thing, because Coco refused to eat canned sausages, and I had nothing else to serve him, having bought two cases of them because they were cheap. For the same reason, I'd bought two cases of sheep's tongue and wound up disguising it with curry powder until I traded the remainder for fruit in the Solomon Islands. Lesson learned: canned tongue and sausages were cheap for a reason.

In late afternoon as Pete and I relaxed in the cockpit, I happened to be looking at the self-steering vane when the metal bracket holding it in place cracked in two pieces. The vane began to wobble wildly.

I yelled and grabbed the tiller while Pete scrambled to the fantail. He worked until dark trying to fix it.

"We'll take turns steering all night," he said. "I'll try again tomorrow."

Ignoring the chant in my ears—*Here we go again*—I said, "I can manage two steering watches tonight, but I'm not strong enough to do that *and* steer all day tomorrow. Why don't you rig twin lines to the tiller?"

"I'll rig twin lines to the tiller for you, but *I'll* steer," he said stoutly, as if he had more endurance than I. "The lines don't keep *Wa* closer than fifty degrees to her course."

"Two days ago you were so sick I thought you might die. I have more stamina." He hung his head and let it go.

Pete spliced new starboard and port bracket pieces using bits of copper with turnbuckles in between. The labor took all the next day.

It was miserable and gloomy, so overcast I couldn't get sun sights. I had no idea where the erratic steering during the night had taken us. The wind increased to thirty knots, and *Wa* careened over the waves as if she were on a roller coaster.

Pete was in a funk. He hated working on the self-steering, particularly when *Wa* bounced all over the ocean. He had no power tools, of course. I watched him pound his anger into the metal, leaving a residual despair. I thought of Christian, in *Pilgrim's Progress*, as he sank into the Slough of Despond. I baked bread to cheer him.

By noon the following day Pete had bolted brass plates onto the bearing and reassembled the vane. At 4:30, I watched the vane again slump in its bracket. This time one of the turnbuckles had sheered. Pete replaced it with copper tubing.

The following morning, as we cuddled and tried to find comfort in an inhospitable ocean, a rushing wave and a jibe shook us alert. Pete bounded out the forehatch, and I scrambled through the cabin to the main hatch, which we were keeping boarded because of the heavy seas. The vane was limp in its bracket again—no telling how long it'd been that way. This time the problem was a loose bolt. Pete fixed it.

The next morning, Pete checked the vane and noticed a crack in the bracket, which he replaced with galvanized pipe. He was very discouraged, as was I.

He'd built the bracket in Rabaul during cyclone season, when *Wa* was out of the water and he had access to power tools. He'd prided himself on his workmanship. The bracket *was* a thing of beauty, and it was better than the one he'd built in Santa Barbara. Still, as ingenious as he might be in finding solutions to problems, his workmanship was always flawed. And we hadn't the money to buy equipment that wouldn't fail.

What troubled me was that, when he wasn't working, he retreated to the forepeak and pulled a blanket over his head.

Nearly halfway around the world, my attitude had changed. I remembered the first time we'd lost the self-steering, two weeks out from Los Angeles, and how I'd thought that first instance of broken equipment was an anomaly. Now I realized that what broke and Pete fixed most likely would break again. Added to that, he was emotionally fragile. I had to bolster his ego, not tear it down, for the sake of our survival.

In the past I had thought of myself as moth to his butterfly. Brilliantly colored, he flitted from flower to flower, hatching grand ideas. I, the drab one, followed along, seeking his brightness, making his grand ideas come to fruition. It was his idea to sail around the world, but without my help, he couldn't have made it happen. It was his idea to enter law school; I would work for four more years to make that happen. How I would juggle a full-time job, a 31-unit apartment building, a husband, and, hopefully, a baby, I didn't know. I would make it happen.

Because I was the organizer, the woman who got things done, I didn't worry about my future. I worried about his.

Things really went sour when Pete began work on the engine and discovered he'd done something wrong in repairing the starting mechanism.

"We're going to have to sail into Port Victoria," he announced.

"So? We always sail into anchorages."

He glared at me. "Don't be stupid. We don't have a fucking engine. It'll take me all day to fix it." His tone suggested the whole world was conspiring against him. I raised my eyebrows, clamped my mouth shut, and returned to my typewriter in the forepeak to write another story for the *News-Press*.

Sometime later, I felt the motion of the boat change. I stuck my head out the forehatch and saw *Wa* was going around in circles and had wrapped the fishing line, which we always dragged off the stern, around the prop. I was amazed. He always felt the boat's motion change before I did. "What are you doing?" I called.

He was so engrossed in the engine, he hadn't noticed. He popped his head, smudged with oil, out the companionway. "Son of a bitch! Can't you help? I'm working on the engine. Can't you steer?" He scrambled to the tiller and set *Wa* back on course.

"What's the matter with the self-steering?" I asked.

"Jesus Christ."

I climbed the companionway and took the tiller while he reset the self-steering. "You'd better pull in the fishing line," I said.

"Why don't *you* pull in the fishing line?"

"I have to cook our halfway-around-the-world dinner."

"I'm not hungry."

Ignoring him, I went below, primed the stove with alcohol, turned on the kerosene burner, and set the rice to cooking.

Feeling as if he'd slapped me in the face, I was a jumble of sorrow and anger. I knew he hated working on the engine even more than he did on the self-steering, but it had to be done. I glanced at the canned ham and string beans—our best meal in days—and wondered whether I'd eat alone.

While the rice cooked, I grabbed the sextant and telescope and climbed back topside to take star sights. We were less than three hundred miles from Port Victoria, Mahe, capital of the Seychelles, and needed to know our precise position. A sunline, because it tracked only one celestial body, could give us only a line—not a position.

"I need some help here with the steering and the fishing line. And what are you doing—cooking, taking star sights," he said.

"Goddamnit, we need a fixed position. We'll be there in less than three days. Besides, you just reset the self-steering and pulled in the fishing line. Go back to your Goddamned engine and fix it!"

Trembling with anger, I took my star sights and returned below to heat the ham and string beans.

The galley smelled pretty good. Shortly later, Pete crawled out of the engine compartment. "I guess I'm hungry after all," he said. "Is there some of that for me?"

"If you wash off the oil. I don't want to have dinner with the Tar-Baby."

He scowled at the comparison.

"Just kidding," I said, but we couldn't get to the Seychelles fast enough.

During Pete's second watch, he saw the loom of Mahe's lights, and at dawn I saw a gray-blue shadow of island fifteen miles north. After forty-seven days of hard sailing with only a five-day rest in the middle at Cocos Island, we were ready for a long break. It was early October. We agreed we could stay in the Seychelles for a month.

One rainy morning after shopping, we returned to the yacht club and decided to have coffee while waiting for the sun. A young blonde woman, braless under her Mexican peasant blouse and wearing patched cutoffs, sat alone. We asked if we could join her and learned her name was Cynthia Bouman. Her outfit set her apart from me and the other yachting women, who always wore dresses ashore, not to mention underwear, and she seemed down-at-heel, as if she'd been poor for a long time. Was that why she ignored the club's unwritten dress code?

Cynthia had come to the Seychelles from Indonesia on a 40-foot ketch with the boat's owners, two young Americans, Ross and Gatlin. "It sounded like an adventure," she said. "They needed crew, and I wanted to get from one place to another."

I laughed. "What a way to learn to sail! Crossing the Indian Ocean on your maiden voyage? Did you like it?"

"Not particularly. There's no self-steering, so someone always was on the tiller. And the guys are really different. Ross is a vegetarian and Gatlin's a carnivore, so they prepared and ate their meals separately. They didn't have much to do with me, either."

I raised my eyebrows. "Didn't you feel the magic of being at sea?"

"Not really. I lived in Southeast Asia awhile, but I wanted to move on and see some other places. Now I want to go back to Southeast Asia. Oh, wow, yes. To Laos."

"Laos?" I asked. The Vietnam War still raged, and the Pathet Lao, clients of the North Vietnamese, waged war on their countrymen, the Hmong.

Cynthia's face broke into a grin, and the skin at the corners of her eyes crinkled. She began waving her arms, as if to will us all to Laos. "The Laos are the grooviest people," she said. "They're happy, and their hearts are full of love, and yet they're fatalists. If some terrible accident happens and a bunch of people die, they just shrug and say it's God's will. They're not cruel and unfeeling. Just the reverse. They're prepared, they accept, so they can be happy. It's hard for Westerners to understand."

She'd touched the culture in Laos, and I'd touched the cultures in Polynesia and Micronesia. I decided we had a kinship. Many of the "yachties" we'd met had no interest in other ways of life.

"The hippies are into that stuff," Pete said.

"It's not part of them. They put it on from the outside, and it doesn't really fit."

"At least they're breaking away from the old patterns," Pete persisted.

"That's what we need," she conceded. "A new cosmic view."

"You're talking like a philosophy major," I said.

"No, English lit. Behold Cynthia—former scholar, doctoral candidate, world traveler, bum." She smiled. "When I was an undergraduate, the professors and graduate students seemed beyond the reaches of mere mortal men. Then I graduated—joined the club—and was invited to the parties. The professors got drunk and made asses of themselves with other professors' wives. They didn't talk about great art or earth-shattering events. They were just like other men."

Cynthia sighed, and Pete grinned. "Disillusioned, were you?"

"I didn't know where to turn. If professors were not the stuff of philosopher-kings, then who was? If no one was, where was the hope of the world?" She sipped her coffee and stared into space.

"I turned to the practical side of life, to the Civil Rights Movement. Then that turned to ashes. My marriage broke up. I fled the country. I've been traveling ever since, usually alone. Started in Europe, then worked my way through Turkey, teaching English. From there I went through the Middle East and India to Southeast Asia."

"Arab men don't respect Western women, do they," I asked, "especially those alone and wearing pants?"

"Oh, I would never wear this in the Arab countries or India," she said hastily, gesturing to her cutoffs and thin blouse, which showed her nipples. "I wore long pants, baggy ones—very circumspect—and sandals. I also wore a button-down blouse and carried a shawl to put over my head. I was as covered as their women except for my face. They never bothered me. In fact, the Arab men were very kind to me and went out of their way to help."

She paused and sipped her coffee. "I did see them get a Swedish girl though. She was stupid. She'd been warned but paid no attention. She came with her boyfriend, and I guess she thought that would keep her safe. She was wearing short shorts, very tight, and a blouse tied at the midriff with no bra. They gang-banged her. There was nothing her boyfriend could do to stop them."

I sucked in my breath. The horror of what she'd described didn't seem to affect her.

Pete looked her up and down. "You know, some of the guys in the club are making remarks about you," he said.

"What kind of remarks?"

"They're saying you must be willing to hop into the sack with anyone and are wondering how to approach you."

"Why would they be saying that? I haven't done anything except run off to town to do my piddling errands and sit here drinking coffee."

"Isn't it obvious?" I cut in. She raised her eyebrows but didn't say anything.

"You're unmarried," Pete added. "You arrive here on a yacht with two young, unmarried guys. The men are saying you must be sleeping with both of them."

"Oh come now, really." She giggled. "You're putting me on."

"You come now," I said. "Has it been so long that you've forgotten what middle class morality is like?"

"No, it hasn't been that long," she replied thoughtfully. "Now that you mention it, some of the men have been ogling me. I haven't paid much attention." Her blue eyes flashed, and she drummed the table with her fingers. "Haven't they got anything better to do? What right have they to impose their moral standards on me?"

"This is their bailiwick," I said. "Remember: in the Arab countries you put on long pants and wore a shawl."

Pete studied her, trying to decide whether she was a genuine crusader for freedom or just foolish. I could tell he was leaning toward the "crusader for freedom" label.

Cynthia sighed. "I guess I expect more from my own society—more understanding and more tolerance."

"I don't think Western society has more understanding and tolerance than any other," I remarked.

"I'll have to think about that," she said.

Cynthia's freedom unsettled but also intrigued me. While Pete was an Army officer in Vietnam, I'd lived in Japan. When I returned to the States, my skirts were six inches too long, and Pete's hair was six inches too short. The cultural change of the Sixties that had bypassed us had puts its stamp all over Cynthia.

A few days later, impatient with the rain, we decided to sail to the outer Seychelles and invited Cynthia to come along.

Our destination was La Digue, about thirty miles northeast of Mahe. When we sailed into the anchorage, the trimaran *Mahina* was there. Morgan and Rachel Carter, a couple we'd met at Thursday Island, had recently arrived in the Seychelles.

When I learned it was their anniversary, I invited them to dinner.

Morgan—lean, energetic, and middle-aged—found it hard to sit still. While he talked he gestured with both hands at once and sometimes threw in his whole torso for emphasis.

Rachel, who was slender, dark-haired, and about ten years younger than Morgan, seemed shy at first until Cynthia began to draw her out. They sat with Pete in *Wa's* cockpit under the awning drinking wine while I prepared shrimp chow mein and rice and iced a chocolate cake.

"What was your favorite place—where would you go back?" Cynthia asked.

"Oh, Polynesia," Rachel said. Her voice seemed to sparkle at the thought. "The Polynesians are wonderful people."

"The Laos are mine," Cynthia said. "They are so groovy. And the opium dens. Wow! I never should have left."

That got my attention. Cynthia hadn't talked about opium dens with Pete and me. Were we that square? I remembered thinking of my mother-in-law as unsophisticated, unlike myself. Was that just wishful thinking on my part? What had Cynthia sensed about Morgan and Rachel that was different?

Morgan waved his hand dismissively. "Opium's good for getting into a sacred space," he claimed, "but it deadens you."

"Not in small amounts," Rachel countered, "and not at first."

"What kind of sacred space?" I asked from my place at the stove.

"ESP, astral traveling," Rachel said as she peered down the companionway at me.

"What's astral traveling?" Pete asked.

"It's when your astral body leaves your physical body and travels freely in space," Morgan explained.

"You mean like the spirit leaving the body at death?" Pete asked.

"Same idea. Except we do it through meditation," Rachel said.

When I served dinner, it felt as if I were interrupting a convocation. Pete gave me a wry smile of complicity as I handed him his plate and scrunched next to him by the tiller. I had nothing to contribute to this conversation; I just listened, as did Pete. It was like being in a classroom lectured by someone who thought I was dense.

"We started with séances," Morgan explained. "My sister died unexpectedly, and I wanted to find out what had happened to her. She told us she'd had a congenital heart problem—nobody ever knew."

"But the important thing was the people we met," Rachel said. "Through séances and some coaching, we began to go out-of-body."

Morgan turned to Pete and me. "You probably won't understand this—it took me a long time to get to this stage myself—but maybe you can grasp a little."

What I grasped was that I was being patronized by guests I'd invited to dinner, and I didn't know what to do. I got up to serve the cake, and Cynthia, Pete, and I sang "Happy Anniversary." Then the Carters and Cynthia babbled on, ignoring Pete and me. As uncomfortable as the Carters made me, at least the evening drew me closer to Pete.

The next day Cynthia, Pete, and I went ashore, crossed a coconut plantation and into the hills. The houses were set back from the road and scattered. In their yards, women and children turned to stare at us. From one house the loud, cheerful noise of pop music flooded from the open window, where an old man's face was framed between the shutters. Above him loomed a poster of Jomo Kenyatta, accused of being a leader of the radical, anti-colonial Mau Mau movement in Kenya; he later became Kenya's first president.

"Let's go have a talk with him," I suggested, needing to connect with something beyond the crazy cult that had produced Cynthia, Rachel, and Morgan. "*Bon jour*," I called, closing the space between us, "*comment allez-vous?*" The old man, who had kinky white hair and leathery brown skin, nodded.

At Victoria's native market I'd become acquainted with the Seychellois, who were a strange mixture of French and African governed by the British and hosting an American satellite tracking station. The parts didn't blend well. The Seychellois resented the British and Americans, who, with their high salaries and hardship assignment allowances, had driven up prices and made life harder for the local laborers. The old man's poster of Jomo Kenyatta marked him as a supporter of the Seychelles People's United Party, the opposition, which was expected to carry the next election. I thought I'd let him know I was of his mind.

"Does the music come from Mahe?" Pete asked.

Silence.

"Is it a favorite program of yours?"

The old man remained stony. He didn't turn down the radio.

"*C'est bon*," I faltered, then lapsed into silence.

After standing about awkwardly for a moment or two, Pete and I started to dance. All the old bop steps from high school we pounded out with our bare feet on the hard earth. Cynthia laughed and clapped her hands. The old man came out and sat on his porch, and Pete offered him a cigarette. Silence.

With a look that said, "By God, if we have to entertain him, we'll entertain him," Pete grabbed me by the arm, and we really put on a show to the fast, wild music. Pete then nudged me. "Go ask him to dance."

"He limps, dummy," I whispered. "It would embarrass him."

Discouraged by the coolness of our audience, we sat on the porch steps. No one said a word. In desperation, Pete asked for a glass of water. The old man seemed to come alive. He hobbled indoors and came back with water for all of us, mentioning that he had a coconut if we would like it. Pete said yes. Cordial now but businesslike, the old man called and a younger Seychellois came around the side of the house with a machete and a coconut. After Pete gave him money and the three of us finished the drinking nut, we left.

"You shouldn't have paid him," Cynthia said.

Pete shrugged. "He expected it. We struck out on that one, anyway."

"He seemed almost hostile, or at least indifferent—as if he didn't give a damn. You'd think he'd be curious about us," she mused. "If he'd been a Lao, he would have invited us in, called all his relatives, and gotten together a feast for us by now."

I was silent, frustrated, and feeling silly. I'd wanted to meet islanders ever since we'd left the central Pacific, but why should they necessarily want the friendship I was trying to thrust upon them?

We crossed another coconut plantation and came upon sandy scrub. I heard breakers, and the smell of the sea overlaid the sweet, musky scent of coconuts. Without searching for a path, Cynthia crashed through the chest-high bushes like a stampeding bull, and Pete and I followed.

The waves mounded in turquoise, curved like blown glass, their lips thinned to transparency and edged with white, and hovered, as if unwilling to break the gathering momentum. Then they crashed straight down. White foam hissed along the coral sand.

My breath caught. I hadn't seen surf like that since we'd left California. With a shout Cynthia tore off her clothes as she ran toward the water. I looked around to see if anyone was watching, took off my clothes, laid them in the sand, and raced to the sea. Pete took off his shirt and plunged in in shorts and glasses.

I'd forgotten how it was to fight surf. I leapt over the waves when I could and shouldered them when I couldn't, until I reached the surf line where the waves mounded before breaking. Pete already had ridden to the beach in a froth of foam. Cynthia paddled, her nose stuck out of the water like a dog's. I caught a wave to the beach and climbed out, my eyes stinging so badly it hurt to open them.

I raced back to my clothes and decided, wet or not, I'd better put them on. Sun and wind would dry me soon enough. Cynthia stretched out on her back, her head resting on her cutoffs and blouse. Pete sat nearby, water flattening his blond hair to his head and streaming off him, and kept sneaking glances at her.

It wasn't until she got up and dusted the sand from her skin that he saw the scorpion tattoo. "Wow!" Pete said. "When's your birthday?"

Cynthia giggled. "Oh, that. Do you like it?"

"Oh my, yes." Cleaning his glasses on his shirt, he edged closer to get a better look. The scorpion was tattooed in blue on Cynthia's right buttock. I had never seen a tattoo on a white woman.

"I was tripping one night and decided to do it."

"Didn't it hurt?" He looked as if he wanted to stroke the scorpion.

"I suppose so. I don't really remember."

A deep disquiet, like rancid butter, flowed through me. Cynthia made me feel stodgy and dull. I'd had enough of her Sixties stuff and wished I could take my husband away.

That night, Cynthia brought out her hash pipe. She filled it from a tin labeled "Pastillines, assorted bonbon drops" and flicked her lighter across the bowl. A sweet, smoky odor drifted across *Wa's* cockpit as she inhaled.

She passed the pipe and lighter to Pete. I stared at him, wondering if he'd shake his head and pass it back. When I'd smoked with his sister in a pad in Hermosa Beach, he'd been furious and accused me of being degenerate. Now he was under Cynthia's powerful influence.

Pete hesitated. "Try it," Cynthia said. "It's good stuff." I saw the conflict in his eyes as she seemed to beckon to him. He lit the pipe, inhaled, and handed it to me.

The weed powered through my head on the first puff. "This *is* good stuff," I said, daring him to criticize me.

As we passed the pipe, Cynthia studied Pete, who was silent. It hadn't hit him yet.

Then he felt it. "Wooo," he crooned. "The top of my head's come off. My head's exploding concrete." He licked his lips and took another hit. His eyes were as wide as a child's who has just discovered chocolate. "I'm in an open bunker. The wind is taking me there." He waved his arm toward the stars.

How had this woman cast a spell over my husband? Was it the lure of something unpredictable and therefore exciting? Was sailing now old hat for him, and what Cynthia Bouman represented his new Great Adventure?

Mozambique Island
or
You Cannot Make Humbug

1213 miles and 15 days the Seychelles to Mozambique Island under way 22 1/2 months

Cyclone season struck the eastern Indian Ocean and marched west day by day, week by week, drawing closer to us. On November 9 we left the Seychelles and headed for the Mozambique Channel, between Madagascar and East Africa, where the storms would not hit until December.

In the Seychelles, Cynthia Bouman had catalyzed a period of questioning for us. I felt something between Pete and me, and it was Cynthia, or what she stood for.

As we sailed south, Pete thought a lot and slept when he wasn't on watch. When he spoke, it was to criticize me. "You have a mindset you're not willing to examine, let alone change," he said.

"That's my strength," I said.

"No. It's your weakness. Look at how free Cynthia is. She supports each person's right to do his own thing so long as it doesn't hurt anyone else."

"I can't live in a world without rules."

"You make your own rules. Only the weak live by other people's rules."

He doesn't really believe that, I thought. *He's just infatuated with the idea that there are no boundaries except those he creates.*

"How can you say that? You're training to be a lawyer. You're going to base your professional life on rules." He just shrugged.

I felt him recede like an outgoing tide. I stood on the shore, watched him go, and wondered whether I could follow. I was determined to put Cynthia behind us and mend the tatters in our marriage. The bright side was, after facing heavy winds all the way from Cocos to the Seychelles, the twelve hundred miles of sailing from the Seychelles to Mozambique Island were totally uneventful.

The two-story houses of the Arabs, with adjoining walls, had heavy wooden doors one or two steps above the street and no porches. Their faces were flat, unadorned by trees, shrubbery, or flower pots. They grew together as if they were one unit. Mud on mud, stucco on stucco, tile on tile—pink and yellow and sandstone, on an island three kilometers off the coast of Mozambique proper. An estimated seven thousand people lived on that tiny bit of land little more than a mile long and about a third as wide, making for a greater population density than Betio on Tarawa. I expected to see the streets crowded as they were in Betio, but even the center of town was deserted.

Although the sun beat down mercilessly, no doors stood open to let the sea breeze in, and the windows were shuttered. Some were barred. How different from the open, inviting houses of the Polynesians and Micronesians. I felt as if a hundred eyes stared at us from behind those shutters as we passed.

In the shopping district, though, traffic was brisk. Dark-haired Europeans, I presumed Portuguese, drove automobiles and sat in sidewalk cafés. Most of them were young men in uniform.

There were men in clean khakis and men in fatigues with dusty boots and stubbly beards. The paratroopers, in camouflage, were jaunty and boisterous. The Liberation Front of Mozambique (Frelimo), with seven thousand troops fighting sixty thousand Portuguese soldiers, controlled the north of the country through guerrilla war. The Africans had risen against their Portuguese colonizers. Now the people of Mozambique Island hosted the occupation forces.

We sat at a sidewalk café, and Pete studied the soldiers. "They look like men who've never had a gun fired at them," he said. "That sounds smug, but I think it's true."

"The bravado, the swaggering—they do seem awfully young," I said, thinking, *I must be getting old.*

Their hair was closely cropped and clean off the backs of their necks. Their skin was tanned, taut with youth and health and exercise. I felt flabby and thought back to all the soft, beer-drinking young men we'd seen in so many other ports, young men with doughy flesh, so that a finger jabbed in would come out sticky. These soldiers exuded the confidence that they would dare and beat anything—probably what made Pete say they'd never faced combat.

We explored the native quarter, where a gray-haired African wearing a fez had set up a barber shop under what must have been the biggest and most beautiful tree on the island. Its branches, spreading from a great gnarled trunk, produced leaves so thick they blocked the sky. The barber's customers sat on a bench beneath it, waiting.

We took seats with them. The old man's face was impassive, but he looked at us out of the corner of his eye, and I could tell that he was frightened.

With long, deft fingers, he skimmed his scissors over his customer's black hair, cutting it close, then shaved the man's neck with clippers. Curls drifted like black snowflakes onto the white bib around the man's neck. The only sound was the click, click of the scissors.

Some children playing nearby, curious about the blond man and woman, inched in for a closer look. When a vendor passed, Pete bought candy to give to the kids, but he didn't know how much to pay for the sweets. The children thought it funny that an adult didn't understand such a simple thing and proceeded to teach him to count in Portuguese. Pete added to their delight by pretending the lesson was difficult and he couldn't catch on.

What a good father he'd make, I thought.

The barber's other customers, meanwhile, looked askance. It was plain we'd upset them. When it became obvious to the barber that we weren't just resting but that Pete was waiting for a haircut, the old man's hands fluttered, and he worked faster, all the while glancing at us sidelong.

When Pete's turn came, he told the barber with gestures how long he wanted his hair. The old man, working probably for the first time in his life with straight, blond hair, did a creditable job. When he'd finished, Pete asked him how much, and the barber said "three" in Portuguese. Pete pulled out three *escudos*, the equivalent of about eighty cents. Shock flickered in the old man's eyes. He glanced at us. Then suddenly, as if he'd spent a lifetime practicing facial immobility, he turned impassive again.

"I think you paid him too much," I said as we walked away.

After drinking beer at a sidewalk café, we wandered through the dusk back to the wharf. As Pete untied the dinghy, a man came up behind us, coughed, and said, "Excuse me, but good evening. You are on that small boat?"

We said we were.

"My name is . . ." Just then a wave crashed on the landing and drowned him out. He stuck out his hand—the round, soft hand of a man who didn't do manual labor. Pete grasped it with his calloused one. Then I shook hands with the man. He wore a suit, white shirt, and conservative tie. His face was round and clean-shaven. His black eyebrows bristled and his black hair was plastered to his head with oil. He was Indian.

"You were in my shop earlier today. I was helping another customer and didn't have a chance to talk to you."

"You have wonderful things at good prices," I said. I'd bought canned pigeon—something I'd never heard of.

The shopkeeper beamed. "Will you come to my house? My

wife would like to cook dinner for you, and I will take you on a tour of the mainland."

"That would be very nice," said Pete, glancing at me. He knew I'd never turn down an introduction to another culture. "Thank you so much."

"You will come at eight o'clock on Sunday morning? We will go on our tour before the day turns hot, then have our meal." He explained how to get to his neighborhood and promised to meet us beside the bank on the corner.

Because we hadn't caught his name, we called him Mr. Um-um. Only later, when Pete asked him to write his name and address, did we learn that he was Joao (John) Padamshi Mavsi. His wife was Taramati.

We arrived at the appointed place at 8:03 to find Joao, with a worried expression on his face, which vanished when he saw us. He led us to a two-story stucco building indistinguishable from the rest.

The house inside mirrored the outside's sandstone colors in its walls, dining table, and folding chairs, the only furniture in the living room. Even at eight in the morning the sun was hot, but the room remained cool because it was high-ceilinged and open to a breeze from the courtyard behind the house, where a young African man washed dishes at a faucet. The scent of orange blossoms drifted in.

Tara, a slender woman with creamy skin and kind, dark eyes, came from the kitchen. I thought she must've been strikingly beautiful when she was young. She wore a red and gold sari, which made my faded blue-print dress seem drab. Her hair hung in a black plait nearly long enough to sit on.

When Tara returned to the kitchen, Joao picked up a perfume atomizer and sprayed around our heads and shoulders. The choking odor of one of Paris's heavier scents filled the room.

Joao leaned back, gazing happily at us. "It is a Vaishya custom—that of my caste—to greet visitors," he said.

We'd been talking about why Hindus are vegetarians and to

what extent this makes them different from other people. I wondered whether his Vaishya custom really was a means of masking the odor of meat Pete and I might have been exuding.

"Vegetarianism is necessary in such a hot country as India," Joao said. "Meat makes you heavy. It clogs the blood. When you keep your body liquids light and clear, you do not feel the heat so much."

Joao led us to the home of his friend, who owned a car and would drive us on our tour of the mainland.

"My friend also is Vaishya, but he is a government worker, not a merchant," Joao said as he knocked on the door.

Joao's friend, Anand Gupta, was fortyish, taller, less round, and wore glasses. When his four young daughters came into the room, the littlest, about two and a half, unabashedly claimed the center of attention. Joao gathered the girls around him. "I miss my own daughter," he said as he took the little one on his knee. "She is at school in India. Have you been to India?"

"No," Pete said. "It would be too difficult to sail there—with the storms. But I have been to Vietnam, where I saw the guerrilla war up close." He paused. "I've noticed many Portuguese soldiers here. Your country is at war, too."

The two Indian men exchanged glances.

"We cannot talk about that," Joao said. "We do not know what is going on."

"But it's all around you—the soldiers in the streets, the Jeeps and trucks. Surely you have an opinion," Pete said.

"That is making humbug against the government. You cannot make humbug."

"You can't criticize the government or even talk about it?"

"You can say as you please. You can do as you please," Joao said in singsong, emphasizing the 'you'. "But you cannot make humbug against the government."

Tension filled the room. The Indian men said it was time to leave on our tour.

Packed into the car, we crossed into East Africa on a bridge built in the late 1960s. It was the first time in nearly two years that I had been on a continent. How strange to see land stretching endlessly instead of discrete chunks plopped in the middle of a vast ocean. Islands were manageable—something the eyes could hold. This continent was not.

Its houses were wide apart, and little of the land was cultivated except the areas around the houses. In between was jungle. Then Joao pointed out the cashew trees with their wide-spreading branches and heavy leaves. They grew randomly, for they were "volunteers," the men told us. The seeds—the cashew nuts—had been dropped by monkeys. I had never seen a wild monkey and hoped one would swoop from the branches and chitter at us. But the men said they came around only at night and were a nuisance, destroying crops and bothering livestock.

"Their screeching fills the darkness," Joao said.

Still, I wished I could hear it.

We stopped to buy some mangoes from an African man on a bicycle, then drove back across the causeway to Mozambique Island. At Joao's house, Tara and Indira Gupta waited with Sunday dinner.

Tara squeezed the mangoes through a strainer until all that was left was a thick pulp. This she served each of us in a bowl beside the main course.

I watched Joao, for I hadn't the vaguest notion of Hindu table manners. He scooped the gooey rice with the fingers of his right hand and dipped it into the mango juice, then deftly swallowed it, licking his fingers clean at the same time. He went on to the three different kinds of curry and potatoes, also dipping these in the mango juice. I followed his example but soon found myself wallowing in the food. Before I could lick the juice from my fingers, it dripped down my arm to my elbow. Because we had no napkins, I furtively wiped my arm on the lap of my dress and hoped no one would notice.

I hadn't imagined that a meal made without meat, fowl, fish, eggs, or any alcoholic beverages could be so good. I would have liked to stay at Mozambique Island longer and follow Tara around her kitchen.

But the Portuguese regime, the most repressive we'd encountered, gave me second thoughts. Joao and Tara had to get permission from the police to visit *Wa,* and when Joao went on Sunday to make his request, the police angrily turned him away, saying he shouldn't bother them on the weekend. It was obvious to me that the people were frightened of their government and had no right to speak out. I hoped Frelimo would bring them independence soon.

Durban
or
Addie Catches Fire

*1216 miles and 15 days Mozambique Island to Durban
under way 23 months*

We crossed the Tropic of Capricorn on December 7. It was as far south as either of us had ever been, and still we sailed south. Each day brought us closer to the Cape of Good Hope and what I knew would be the hardest passage of our trip.

For now, to celebrate our return to a temperate zone for the first time in nearly two years and our safe crossing of the cyclone belt, I made Thanksgiving dinner—two weeks late: pumpkin, creamed onions, rice, scone stuffing, and the pigeon that I'd bought at Joao Mavsi's store on Mozambique Island.

On the night of December 13 the loom of Durban's lights stretched huge before us. The next morning, as we sailed into the harbor, I was shocked at the size of the city— millions of people, jagged skyscrapers everywhere.

After we cleared customs, the officials directed us to the Point Yacht Club, where we were to raft alongside four other cruising yachts. Because we were on the outside, we would have to cross the decks and cockpits of the four other boats in order to get ashore.

"Coco's going to have a field day," I said as we stowed *Wa's* sails.

Pete scratched his head. "I hope they don't mind cats." Just to make sure, he ventured aboard the other boats, introduced himself, and mentioned Coco. No one seemed to mind.

When I went to take my shower, the women's locker room would've been the envy of any country club. I stepped out of the cubicle in my clean clothes to see a dark-skinned woman bent over a basin brushing her teeth. *Who in the world?* This was Durban in the days of apartheid. And then I knew. "Kwai, is that you?"

Kwai La Borde, whom I'd last seen at Cocos Island, turned, and her eyes lit up. She shoved the toothbrush in her pocket and gave me a hug. "It's so good to see you!" she said. "Your boat is so small, we were worried about you."

"So the yacht club didn't give you any trouble?"

Kwai grimaced, then scanned the room to see if any other women were listening. "The directors pointed out how magnanimous they were to allow us—the first 'coloreds'—to stay at the Point Yacht Club."

"Bastards. But at least you're here. Did *Arita* and *Ulwhilna* make it in yet?"

Kwai's face sagged. "You haven't heard?"

"No. What?" My stomach tightened. From the look in her eyes I knew it was something bad.

"*Challenge*, a French boat, ran into a cyclone after leaving Mauritius. It pitchpoled." Her voice caught.

"Are they OK?" Turning over in the water stern first is not an "OK" thing to happen to any boat, but a yacht with a full keel will not remain upside down. It rights itself in minutes, for the heavy keel's weight is stable only when it is under the boat. Of course, when a boat flips upside down, it fills with water, turning its interior to a shambles.

"Katherine Jourdan was aboard."

"Katherine from *Arita*?"

Kwai nodded. "She drowned."

"No! Katherine? That beautiful young woman?" My brain refused the news. The Jourdans were like family—all of us circumnavigating that year were family. I felt as if I'd known Katherine all my life.

"Why was she on *Challenge*?"

"You know she had a fight with her parents?"

"I know she wanted Russ to crew on *Arita,* or for her to crew on *Ulwhilna,* so she and Russ could be together. I thought it was overly protective of the Jourdans to say no."

"The fight was only simmering at Cocos. It came on full-blown at Mauritius, where she and Russ demanded to be together and the Jourdans refused. Katherine was furious. The Frenchman, Henri, and his girlfriend on *Challenge,* trying to smooth things over, asked Katherine to crew with them instead. The Jourdans, thinking she would be safe, agreed, and they were to meet in Durban."

Kwai sucked in her breath. I thought she would break down in tears. "Then came the cyclone. It was four o'clock in the morning, and no one was on the helm. *Challenge* was hove to, which Henri thought would be OK. When the boat pitchpoled, Katherine was thrown from her berth onto the cabin floor and knocked unconscious. The cabin filled with water. When Henri found Katherine, she'd drowned. They buried her at sea."

"Where are the Jourdans?" I asked in a whisper.

Tears slid down Kwai's cheeks. "That's the awful thing. They planned to go to the Seychelles after they left Mauritius, but we weren't able to find them there. No one knows where they are."

"Oh my God," I said.

We never saw or heard of the Jourdans again.

Pete and I stopped by *Challenge* to ask if there was anything we could do. Henri's girlfriend seemed dazed. Her speech was slurred, halting.

The boat smelled of wet wood on the verge of decay. Her stumpy mast, looking as if it had been chewed by a beaver, jutted from the cabin top. The clutter of her rigging encircled it like a mock crown. Debris littered the decks, and the boat exuded hopelessness.

Hesitating, I asked, "Do you plan to sail her back to France?"

"Oh, yes, we will go," she said. "I don't know when."

I shrank from the horror of what she had experienced and didn't know how to absorb it into my love of the sea.

Several days before Christmas, I got up as usual to make coffee, planning to return to bed, where Pete and I often cuddled and talked to begin our day. Sunlight streamed across the cockpit, sucking up dew from the cushions, creating wisps of steam. *Wa* rocked gently with the surge. Her fenders creaked as they rubbed against the boat next to us. Water gurgled against her hull.

As I poured priming alcohol onto the kerosene burner, the stench of oil of wintergreen hit my nostrils. The South African government, believing that the blacks would drink untreated denatured alcohol, required that oil of wintergreen be added to it to give it a foul taste. It also made the alcohol oily.

I lit the alcohol, and flames leapt from the stove. Just then *Wa* lurched as a barge chugged by, and burning alcohol jumped from the stove onto my bare torso.

I shrieked and began patting my searing chest, but the oily alcohol kept burning. From shoulders to waist I was aflame. Pete scrambled out of the forepeak, threw a blanket across my chest, and began thumping on me until he had put out the fire.

When the first fear was over, the agony began—the worst pain I'd ever felt. I had second-degree burns across both breasts and down to my waist. Our strongest pain killer, Phenaphen, had gotten wet and congealed into a gluey mass. Pete gave me four aspirin.

"It hurts, babe," I cried out between clenched teeth. "You've gotta do something." I began gasping for breath.

He helped me into the starboard berth and propped pillows behind my back and neck. His forehead wrinkled with worry.

"Will cold help?"

"I don't know. Try."

He pumped fresh water into a bowl, dipped a clean washcloth into it, squeezed out the water, and laid the compress across my breasts. "Is that any better?"

"Some." I panted and clamped my teeth on the exhale.

He dipped another washcloth in water and peeled the old compress away. "This thing's burning from your body heat." It was also red with blood.

"I feel like I'm on fire—still."

He stroked my head. "What else can I do?"

"Keep changing the compresses."

"I've got to get you a better pain killer. If I put the water next to you, can you change them yourself?"

I nodded, and he threw on a pair of shorts, tossed the bloody water down the sink, gave me a fresh bowl, and climbed the companionway. I felt *Wa* lurch, and heard the fenders creak, as he stepped across her lifelines. He knocked on the cabin top of the boat next to us. I heard murmured voices—Pete's and another man's—but couldn't tell what they were saying.

The panting and clenched teeth routine, and changing the washcloths, kept my lungs and hands busy; my mind scrambled out of focus.

He returned with a small bottle and an anxious smile. "This is Talwin. It's a narcotic." He pumped a glass of water and gave me a pill.

In half an hour I was floating in a world where fire came out of the sea and transformed itself into red lilies. I slept.

When I awoke, he said, "I've got to take you to the hospital."

"We don't have the money."

"You need to see a doctor."

He found one of his shirts, which would fit loosely on me, helped me into the sleeves, and carefully buttoned it so as not to touch the wound. I slipped on some baggy pants with an elastic waist. Then he lifted me by the arms and helped me up *Wa's* companionway, across our neighbors' boats, and to a waiting car provided by a yachting acquaintance.

∼∼∼∼∼∼∼∼∼∼∼∼∼∼∼∼∼

At the hospital, the nurses asked if I needed a pain killer. When I told them I'd taken Talwin, they cut away the blistered flesh and treated the burns with Mercurochrome and a spray to dry the skin. The sting of the antiseptic was muted, as if it weren't my body they were treating but someone else's. When I refused to stay in the hospital, they gave me Tetracycline, more Mercurochrome, and more spray.

Pete, probably worried about how much this would cost, trudged to the check-out window while I sat in the lobby waiting. "How much do I owe you?" he asked.

"Nothing," the woman said with a smile.

I was grateful, once again, for the help of generous and caring people.

Although I didn't have to return to the hospital, I treated the wound several times a day with Mercurochrome and spray and was diligent about taking the full course of Tetracycline. I'd had enough infections in the past two years to be scared that a wide swath of open sores could attract enough bacteria to kill me.

The pain lessened every day. Within a week I was functioning as a partner, not a patient.

By early January the wounds had healed.

Pete worried about *Wa's* mast. Its wooden step, which held it to the cabin top, was rotting, and the mast was delaminating, causing the mainsail alternately to jam in, or pull free from, the worn track. Although worried about getting deeper into debt with my father, he ordered an aluminum mast.

Pete also found an Indian craftsman who was willing to replace *Wa's* waterlogged cushions at a reasonable price. The man, who called himself Sam, was dark-skinned, short, and slender, with hands that looked like they could work magic on a piano. He came with a haversack of tools and a measuring tape wrapped around his wrist.

"Do you drink coffee?" I asked.

"Why yes, thank you," he said, surprise in his voice.

I brought him coffee and a mug for myself and sat on the cabin top, hoping to make friends. Getting to know Joao and Tara Mavsi had been a wonderful experience, and I wanted to repeat it. He kept his eyes averted from my face.

"Are you married?" I asked.

"Yes." He glanced at me. Again he sounded surprised.

"Would you and your wife come to dinner on our boat?" I asked.

Frightened, he said, "Oh, no, the government will not allow that. I can only do business with you. I cannot be your friend."

This encounter with apartheid made me sick at heart. I talked with him a while longer, then let him finish his work, for I'd filled him with anxiety, and he was eager to leave. At least the Mavsis had been allowed to socialize with us, although the Mozambique government probably kept a dossier on them. Apartheid was the absolute worst government oppression I had ever encountered, and with the majority blacks and "coloreds" disenfranchised, I didn't see anything changing soon.

Cape Town
or
We Fight for Our Lives

*868 miles and 7 days Durban to Cape Town
under way 25 months*

South Africans like to brag about their bad weather. They have good reason. I knew the passage from Durban to Cape Town would be the biggest challenge of our trip, and I wanted to get it over with. The cyclone off Bougainville had not been life-threatening. I knew the seas off the Cape of Good Hope might well be.

Steeling myself, I convinced Pete to leave Durban on January 31, 1973 into the teeth of a southwester that, according to the weather report, was supposed to return to the northeast by mid-afternoon. It didn't. Tilted at a forty-degree angle, *Wa* bucked and pitched, and a rain of spray covered her decks.

"You're the only person in the world," he said between clenched teeth, "who could have made me face these headwinds." He was seasick, and I was queasy. Apologizing for my bad judgment didn't seem adequate, but I did it anyway.

Coco, in a catatonic ball, curled up on our bedding next to the chain locker which, being at *Wa's* bow, suffered the most violent ups and downs of any part of the boat. Too late the poor cat realized what a terrible mistake he'd made, wobbled out into the main cabin, and barfed. It was the first time he'd been seasick. He didn't cry a word—just threw me a terrible look of betrayal, and huddled on the lee berth.

Pete didn't dare set as much sail as *Wa* needed because we hadn't tested our new aluminum mast. He put up the jib, and *Wa* bobbed like a soggy cork, making not much better than a hundred and eighty degrees between tacks—in other words, going sideways.

After a miserable night, the wind dropped to ten knots, and Pete turned on the engine. When he saw Durban ahead of us, and realized we'd suffered for twenty-four hours for no gain, he grabbed the bottle of rum and finished it, ingloriously ending our worst day's run ever.

Finally, with the wind behind us and blowing with the Agulhas Current, *Wa* danced southwestward. Then, on our third night out, a wave crashed across the self-steering vane, snapping the clutch bar. *Wa* sheered up into the wind and took two breaking waves into the cockpit before Pete reached the tiller and headed her off.

Damage: the self-steering gear broken for the sixth time and the starboard aft stanchion, a piece of steel nearly an inch in diameter used to hold up the lifelines, sheared off at its base. The baseplate, itself a four-inch square of steel, was broken in half. As I looked at the broken metal the next day, I had a whole new appreciation of the power of the sea. I hoped that was the worst we'd face on this passage.

There was nothing to do but steer manually. At seven in the morning I took the watch, sailing under the genoa alone, while Pete slept. Although the wind was blowing between thirty and forty knots, it was behind us, and *Wa* stretched forward like a racehorse headed for the gate. The ten-foot seas heaped up like piles of mounded ice cream flowing from a cone, and the wind blew spindrift off their tops as it laid streaks of foam, in tiny circles, down their curving undersides. The piles crashed against *Wa*'s stern and broke with a hiss.

With the wind on *Wa*'s port quarter, I steered her on a broad reach, turning straight downwind to guide her over the biggest waves. The day was sunny, and I was warm in my foul-weather gear. I sang all the folk songs I knew, then all the Broadway and pop tunes, and sang them again. I was having a wonderful time testing myself and *Wa*, surfing down the waves, speeding toward Cape Town. When Pete asked sleepily if I wanted relief, I said no. I was on the tiller six hours.

When he came topside at one o'clock, he was aghast. "It's blowing Force 8," he yelled. "What are you thinking?"

"We're doing fine!" I shouted. "*Wa's* sailing like a grande dame."

"You're in danger of broaching, this close to capsizing!" He flung his arms up.

He rushed forward, took down the genny, replaced it with the jib, then took that down, too, to run under bare poles. "You are the Terror of the Seas." It was an accusation mixed with admiration.

For the rest of the journey, he called me TOTS, a name I carried proudly. That day, our record best run, *Wa* made a hundred and seventy miles.

The storm continued to build. That night, Pete woke me at ten o'clock to hold the flashlight for him while he put out warps. To these—our two heaviest mooring lines and the mainsheet—he attached four fenders to slow *Wa* down. She stopped surfing, and her speed dropped to about two knots. Pete steered for a while under bare poles, then set the tiller to lee, putting *Wa* to lie ahull, floating with no sail up.

He did this not only because the prolonged heavy winds had built the seas higher than we'd ever seen them, but also to slow us down. The only safe course was to keep the wind behind *Wa*, no matter where it took her. Consequently, we were moving toward Antarctica. On watch at midnight, I saw the lights of Port Elizabeth fade into blackness. The Agulhas Current carried us thirty-five miles farther south before dawn.

At daybreak the gale left us. We sailed back north to return to the coast, then west. With the wind blowing only fifteen knots, Pete raised the twin gennies and was able to fix the clutch on the self-steering gear.

As we neared the coast, we found ourselves entangled in the heaviest shipping we ever had seen. The Suez Canal was closed because of mines left over from Israel's 1967 war, and all supertankers sailing from the Persian Gulf toward Europe or the United States had to go around the Cape of Good Hope. These thousand-foot-long behemoths scared me more than heavy winds and seas, for they were reputed to carry skeleton crews of no more than a dozen sailors and to rely on radar rather than keeping a visual watch. One of them could have crushed *Wa* in its prop wash and not even known we were there. During one watch I saw eight supertankers in three hours. Although the water was rougher, we stayed well to sea of them—avoiding the shipping lanes.

The icy waters of the Benguela Current, streaming north from Antarctica, slammed into the warm Agulhas Current, flowing west toward Cape Town, creating mountainous seas. We had reached a point of no return, and it was time to make a run for it.

We had one more night of gentle breezes, then the wind began to build again. *Wa* went from twin genoas to twin jibs to a single jib, and still she raced over the waves.

When she was in the trough, the ocean was a mighty, overpowering thing, with nothing else visible except mountains of water in front and behind us, and no other sound but the crashing of the sea. As *Wa* climbed the wave in front of her, I feared it would break as she reached its crest, catapulting her in a cascade of foam into the pit of the sea.

But she kept her glide, surfing down its back into the trough again, while the wave behind curled and mounded up, almost breaking over us with a roar.

We didn't mention *Challenge's* pitchpoling, but that terrible image never left my mind. I believed, as did Pete, that Henri's mistake was in not staying on the tiller. If he had, he could've saved Katharine's life.

We steered *Wa* straight downwind under bare poles. Like a

horse with the bit in her teeth, she still surfed, rushing down the fronts of waves and up the backs of the ones ahead of her. Only on the crests could I see the brown land and the supertankers to starboard. As the wind rose, the seas increased to thirty feet, and still the gale blew harder.

"I've got to slow her down," Pete yelled to me from the tiller. "Come and help." His face was ashen with the fear that *Wa* would pitchpole if she moved faster than the speed of the waves.

I took the helm, and again Pete tossed overboard our two heavy mooring lines and the mainsheet, with fenders attached. *Wa* still raced on. He siphoned seawater into our six five-gallon jugs, attached these to the genny and jib sheets, and threw them in the sea. *Wa* now was dragging two hundred and sixty pounds of water plus the weight of the fenders and line. Still she raced on.

In desperation, Pete crawled to the chain locker in the bow. He lugged two hundred feet of quarter-inch chain and the 44-pound Danforth anchor across the pitching deck to *Wa's* stern, lashed them to a cleat, and dumped them in the sea. *Wa*, sailing under bare poles, dragging several hundred pounds of weight, finally slowed to four knots. Pete's ingenuity had again kept us and *Wa* alive.

We took turns on the tiller as we'd done in the cyclone off Bougainville. This was no tropical storm, however. The water was frigid even in mid-summer. Under my foul-weather gear I wore four layers of clothing, all wet, and still was cold.

That night the lights of Simon's Town, the warmth and safety of that port, beckoned off *Wa's* starboard bow, but I didn't dare head up even slightly into the wind to make for it. The danger of capsizing was too great.

Spray pelted my face like hail and coated my glasses with water and salt. *If I make a mistake, or if Pete makes a mistake, we will die.* He said nothing, but I'm sure he was thinking it, too.

When my eyes stung so badly I couldn't see, and fatigue overwhelmed me, I began steering erratically and started taking breaking waves into the cockpit. Pete took the tiller, and I went below to rest. I'd been on the helm only an hour.

I huddled in the forepeak, wrapped in wet sails, trying to get warm. Just about the time I stopped shivering and began to doze, Pete started taking breaking waves into the cockpit. It was time for me to steer.

All night, we fought for our lives.

When the sun came up, the wind died. Pete dragged aboard our warps, filling the cockpit and fantail, and turned on the power. We had no sheets with which to trim the sails, for the lines and chain were so tangled it took him all morning to untie the knots. Patiently, with cold fingers he worked the lines and chain free one by one while I steered for Cape Town.

I had never been so grateful to make a landfall.

Several days later in Cape Town, we met up again with Morgan and Rachel Carter, who invited us to supper on *Mahina*. Remembering how I'd felt patronized during the discussion of astral traveling and séances, I was reluctant to go.

"That was because of Cynthia," Pete said. "They were trying to impress her. It will be different with just the four of us."

How different I never would have dreamed.

Rachel lit candles, turned off the cabin lights, and gave us wine. We went through several bottles before she served dinner. She and Morgan were gracious and attentive, and I found myself wondering whether I'd imagined that earlier condescending dinner.

"Well, you managed to botch another meal," Morgan said as Rachel cleared the dirty dishes from the table. His remark came out of nowhere and was followed by a charged silence.

"It was a lovely dinner. I enjoyed it," I said, trying to break the tension. I'd decided to forget how arrogant Morgan had been in the Seychelles. We were his dinner guests, after all, and fellow sailors and Americans. But this nastiness was something new. I wondered what had put him on edge.

Rachel turned at the sink and smiled at me. When she came back to the table, she refilled our glasses.

We polished off two more bottles of wine.

Then all at once, Rachel began to cry.

"Don't mind her," Morgan said irritably. "She's just temperamental."

"How can you say that?" asked Pete. He moved from the settee next to me to sit by Rachel and draped his arm around her shoulder. "What is it?" he asked. "What's wrong?"

"It's hopeless," she sobbed.

"What's hopeless?" he asked, brushing tears from her cheek.

"She's always maudlin when she drinks, and she's about to have her period."

Pete ignored Morgan and hugged Rachel. She leaned into him with a sigh.

I was confused and anxious. "It's been a lovely evening, but it's time to go home," I announced. Pete ignored me and stroked Rachel's cheek. I got angry. "Pete, are you ready to leave?"

He turned to me with a look that said, *How can you be so heartless?* He cleared his throat and said, "I'll stay for a while."

"We have a lot to do tomorrow."

"Later!" He clipped the word and drew his fingers across his throat as if he were karate chopping me.

"I'll row you back," Morgan offered. "Pete can return in your dinghy." Now I was furious, but I agreed.

Once in the Carters' dinghy, Morgan turned on the charm. "You have a real way about you, Addie, a lot of spunk. I like that." He stopped rowing and grinned, then stroked me on the knee. He raised his eyebrows and cocked his head.

That's when it came to me: this was a set up. Morgan would row me back to *Wa* and take me to bed. Pete, in the process of comforting a very drunk Rachel, would take her to bed. In the morning, we would all be good friends. How many other times had Morgan and Rachel run this scam? It didn't matter that Rachel had to get dead drunk in order to participate. She probably was willing to do that in order to placate Morgan.

I cleared my throat. "I don't want to go back without Pete. He's going home with me."

Morgan leaned forward on the oars and smiled, then stroked my knee again. "You're a feisty little thing. I'll bet you're just as exciting in bed."

"That's inappropriate. We're both married."

"As you wish," he said with an angry jerk of his head, and turned the dinghy around. He didn't say another word.

Morgan made more noise than necessary climbing out of the dinghy and stamping his feet on the trimaran's deck. I waited for him to lead the way below.

Rachel was curled in Pete's arms as if she were a child. "You need to sleep it off," Morgan said. He grabbed her hand, hauled her from the settee, and led her from the main cabin to their stateroom.

Pete stared at me. "What's going on?"

"You tell me."

"I just got her calmed down."

"I don't want to talk here," I said. "Let's go." He looked mystified but followed me up the companionway and into our dinghy. I sat in the stern facing him. As he took the oars, I said, "They had in mind some wife-swapping."

"What?" Pete's jaw dropped, along with the oars.

"Morgan put the make on me, and Rachel was working you. Didn't it occur to you that she might've faked those tears, or brought them on by drinking herself into a stupor?"

"You're out of your cotton-picking mind. Rachel is stuck with an asshole, and she's desperate."

"That's not our problem."

"You, bleeding heart for all mankind, I never thought I'd hear you say something so cold."

"He stroked me on the knee and said I'd be exciting in bed. I don't want to be the next addition to their trophy cabinet."

"You're warped."

Although I knew we were far from done with this conversation, there was nothing else to say. Terrified at having anything more to do with the Carters, all I wanted was to get out of Cape Town as fast as possible.

I knew wife-swapping had taken place in Pete's boyhood

neighborhood. Was that what he wanted? I remembered how Dr. Eastman used to sing, "Hoggamus, higgamus, men are polygamous, Higgamus, hoggamus, women monogamous," and how Pete never said a word, not even "I don't believe that."

Barbados
or
Too Pooped to Pump

*5625 miles and 55 days Cape Town to Barbados
under way 27 months*

The wind of the South African coast wasn't through with us. It came up to gale force our first night out. "Son of a bitch, can't you leave us alone?" I shouted at the storm.

In the morning, with the sun burning across the sea and the wind abating, Pete set the self-steering gear and took the boards out of the companionway to let fresh air blow through the cabin. Shortly later, a freak wave broke over *Wa's* stern, filling the cabin with a foot of water.

"Quick, pump!" Pete yelled as he righted *Wa*, which had yawed off to port with the force of the wave. We'd never been "pooped" before with the cabin exposed to breaking waves.

"I'm sick of bad weather," I yelled back, complying. Once the panic of seeing the cabin fill with water subsided, the pumping became tedious. With each downward stroke, I pushed my frustration out into the sea.

It took me an hour to get rid of the water. When I climbed topside, a Wandering Albatross, its two-foot wings cupped to grab the air, glided past *Wa* straight into the wind. It tipped its black wings, showing the white undersides, as if in greeting, and flew toward South Africa. "Take the bad weather with you, please," I begged.

During those first few days, Pete withdrew. He wouldn't talk about Rachel and Morgan, the future, or anything else troubling him. He drank almost all of our thirteen bottles of wine and liquor in two weeks. I retreated into *The Lord of the Rings*.

As his thirtieth birthday approached, we passed St. Helena. "I really wanted to stop there," Pete said as we sat together in the cockpit in late afternoon. "I'm afraid we're going to run out of water."

"There'll be plenty of rain in the doldrums." We'd discussed the water problem in Cape Town and decided to sail straight through. Why was he bringing it up now? "Dad and Helen will worry themselves silly if we don't beat them to Barbados," I said.

"So we should put ourselves in jeopardy to convenience them?"

"Why are you so angry?"

"You dragged me away from Cape Town because you were afraid."

"Are you still upset about leaving Rachel with Morgan?"

"It's not Rachel, it's you. You and your jealousy."

"You don't think Morgan was coming on to me?"

"So what if he was? He's an asshole. I was trying to help her."

"By doing what? Fucking her?"

"I was *comforting* her."

"So you didn't see Morgan as a threat?"

"Of course not. You wouldn't have gone to bed with him."

"What if I had?"

He glared at me, then turned to stare at the ocean as it rolled away into infinity. Swallowing my anger, I started to go below.

"I feel trapped," Pete said.

"Trapped? Why?" It seemed the most unlikely emotion in that vast sea with nothing around us but water, air, and freedom. Besides, I had taken on his Great Adventure as my own, and now *he* was feeling trapped?

"I've been thinking about Cynthia and how free she is. She goes where her fancy takes her, does what she wants, answers to no one."

"Is that what you want?" A dark thing began beating against my heart. I thought, but didn't ask, *to be alone?* Was his new Great Adventure to be like Cynthia? And where did that leave me? I'd signed on to sail around the world; now it was supposed to be my turn—to have children.

"I don't know." He put his hands over his face. "I don't know what I want."

I went below, dumped my questions into the bilge, and put the floorboards back in place.

Days later, Pete sat naked in the cockpit derusting tools, and I hunched naked over the typewriter in the forepeak. Suddenly a horn blasted like the cry of some prehistoric hunting beast. I rushed into the main cabin. Pete, glancing astern, yelled, "Oh my God! Quick, hand me a towel."

I threw on a dress and climbed the companionway. Crossing *Wa's* stern fifty yards away was a tanker with *Marion* printed on her bow. She looked to be more than seven hundred feet long and towered, like a giant, over us, swallowing *Wa* in shadow and shaking her with prop wash.

Pete waved. The tanker passed well to starboard, then resumed its course.

"Nothing like a jolt of adrenaline to liven up the day." He chuckled and wiped his face with the towel, which came away red with rust. "It probably was trying to warn us we're off course for St. Helena," he said.

I sat next to him and rubbed my hand across his back. "Would you like a cup of coffee?" I asked.

He raised his eyebrows. "If you're offering, I'd like a beer."

I gave him the raspberry.

"You know, I've been thinking," he said. His face had turned serious. He stared at me before speaking again. "You should go off the Pill."

"What?" He'd taken me completely by surprise.

"Yeah. Even if you got pregnant tomorrow, we'd still be home in time for you to have the baby."

"But . . ." I began.

"Why don't we get started."

"Are you sure?" My heart was thumping so hard I thought he might hear it.

"It's what you want, isn't it?" He looked anxious, as if he'd made a mistake and needed to retract.

"Of course it is. You know that."

"Then bring me the pills."

Shaking my head, I went below, returned with the bottle, and handed it to him.

He dumped the contents over the lee rail. Dozens of little white specks bobbed astern. "I cast thee like bread upon the waters. May you bear fruit."

I giggled. "You're mixing your metaphors, and I think you need a lesson in biology. How about I give it to you?"

"Any time." He pulled me onto his lap and kissed me.

With a passage of fifty-six hundred miles ahead of us, and carrying only forty-seven gallons of water, we began rationing ourselves to four cups of coffee/water a day. I was always thirsty. I longed for the doldrums—something I never thought I'd do—where we could count on heavy rain.

When the southeast trade wind sputtered and died and huge, puffy clouds like blackened marshmallows loomed across the horizon, I was delighted. The rain came thick as a waterfall.

Pete raised the boom to make a siphon out of the mainsail, then set a bucket underneath to catch the water. After throwing out the first batch, salty from residue on the main, he filled the bucket again, and I poured its precious contents into one of our empty water jugs while Pete saved more water in the pressure cooker.

We switched back and forth from bucket to pressure cooker until we'd topped off all six of our five-gallon jugs. Working together seemed effortless and filled me with deep satisfaction. It was such a simple thing—gathering water—so basic in the list of human needs. We had pared away the extraneous and concentrated on what was important to our lives.

I talked to the wind as if it were a person; sometimes, I believed it answered me. I reveled in the beauty of a mahi mahi who swam for three days beside *Wa*, as if she were a friend. I no more could have eaten it than I could have eaten Coco. I sheltered a storm petrel, lost at sea, on the folds of the unused mainsail until the bird was strong enough to fly again. Never had I belonged to the wind and sea as much as on that longest passage.

We sailed into the wide bowl of Carlisle Bay, Barbados, in brilliant sunshine on the morning of April 14, having crossed the Atlantic Ocean—fifty-six hundred miles—in fifty-five days. During that time Pete and I had seen no other human beings except the crew of the *Marion*. We'd become so attuned to each other that we didn't need to speak. The sight of other people came as a shock.

After clearing customs, we rowed ashore and had our first beers in two months. My shock turned to horror when I bought a *Time* magazine with Sen. Sam Ervin on the cover and a banner reading "SHOWDOWN OVER SECRECY/Senate v. White House." Washington had imploded during the two months we'd crossed the Atlantic.

I devoured the stories about the Watergate scandal and the possible implication of President Nixon in the burglary at the Democratic National Committee headquarters. What had happened to my country?

Meanwhile, we telegraphed home to tell everyone that we were in the Caribbean. My father and step-mother had yet to fly from Santa Barbara to Barbados. We'd arrived four days ahead of them.

I hadn't seen Dad in more than two years. In the Barbados airport, I grabbed him in a bear hug, smelled the honey aroma of his pipe tobacco, then leaned back to look. Same twinkle in pale blue eyes, same grin, with the laugh lines at the corners of his face. He had a little less hair, and what was left of it was grayer. But with my father, it was the eyes and mouth you noticed because there almost always was a hint there of mischief, and now glee.

This happiness was something I'd hardly ever seen when my mother was alive. He'd been married a second time for only six months when Pete and I set sail, and now it was clear Helen had been good for him. She catered to him (my mother never had), patting him when she passed, grabbing him and whispering in his ear as if they were conspirators. He lapped it up. He, in turn, wrapped her in his protection as her first husband never had.

We spent hours poolside at their hotel, in a courtyard protected from the wind, lazing in the sun and swimming, or playing bridge.

"How about going for a sail tomorrow?" I asked my father the third day.

"Haven't you had enough sailing?" he retorted.

"In a lot of ports, we've taken people day-sailing just for fun."

"That's a long way out in a little dinghy. It doesn't sound like much fun to me," he said. Helen nodded her agreement.

"So you wouldn't even want to visit the boat—see how we've lived for the last two years—and let me cook you a really nice supper?"

"We'll take you out for a really nice supper instead," he said.

The lack of interest hurt, but I tried not to show it.

One afternoon after a couple of drinks, Dad said to Pete, "Addie tells me you're waffling about law school. Whatever for?"

Pete cleared his throat. He was used to his own father's being heavy-handed, but not mine. "Medical school is calling to me again."

"Oh, for God's sake. You're thirty years old. You majored in English lit, not premed. You'd be nearly forty by the time you got your career started."

Pete squirmed. "That's true. But I'd be a third-generation doctor. There's something compelling in that."

"Has your father been filling you with a lot of bull?" Pete glanced at Dad in surprise. No one ever questioned Dr. Eastman. "I was a high school counselor for thirty-seven years," Dad went on. "I know young people—where they're coming from, what they're capable of. You're a writer, but you're also logical and can argue both sides of the fence. Stick with law school. You'll make a great attorney."

Thank you, Dad.

The Panama Canal
or
Hip, Hip, Hippie, Hooray

1317 miles and 10 days Barbados to Colon
58 miles Colon to Balboa
under way 28 1/2 months

It was our last day in the trades and our last ever under twins, because our remaining thirty-five hundred miles up the Central American and Mexican coasts would be upwind. Pete changed *Wa* to the gennies in early evening, and I steered in a beautiful, gray world. The sea was slate-blue and the sky a lighter tone of the same shade streaked with charcoal clouds. I was singing but sad, for I knew I was reaching an ending. I remembered the first time we'd sailed under twins, going from the Marquesas Islands to Tongareva, when the magic of gliding without effort seemed like flying. I wondered whether I ever would know such joy again.

The harbor at Colon, Panama, was filthier with oil than Santa Barbara Harbor ever was, even at the height of the oil spill in 1969. It streaked *Wa's* white topsides and gummed the dinghy. We were eager to get away and through the canal.

Before transiting, Pete, as *Wa's* captain, had to fill out a pile of paperwork and pay twelve dollars, which covered passage through the locks and the services of two pilots. We would go from the

Atlantic, up eighty-five feet through the Gatun Locks, across Gatun Lake, and down eighty-five feet to the Pacific through the Pedro Miguel and Miraflores Locks.

The charge was based on *Wa's* weight, a little less than three tons, probably one of the smallest boats ever to transit the canal. She would have to share space in the locks with another vessel, because the Canal Authority wouldn't waste the electricity and manpower on us alone.

All day Tuesday, May 29, we scurried about scrounging up a crew, for we were required to have two line handlers on the bow and two on the stern to hold the boat steady during the incredible inrush of water in the ascending locks. People at the yacht club described it as being in a whirlwind. In fact, conservative yachtsmen spent days or even weeks at Colon talking about the transit and offering their services as line handlers on other people's boats so they would know what to expect. We didn't want to wait.

At the yacht club we found two young men willing to make the trip the following day for the fun of it. They had two friends of the same spirit, and they would pay for their train fare from Balboa back to Colon. These men were hippies, not sailors, which should've set off alarm bells in my head, but they were strong and available and the price was right.

Pete cobbled together four hundred-foot lines for bow and stern from *Wa's* sheets and anchor line. We would power, of course, not sail.

Unique Fortune, a freighter twenty times as long and ten times as wide as *Wa*, chugged into the first chamber of the Gatun Locks and settled herself in front next to the steel gates. We followed. *Unique Fortune* attached her lines to six motorized "mules" on top of the chamber. *Wa's* lines, attached at the top of the chamber to cleats, were held port and starboard by four strong men.

We found ourselves in a pit a thousand feet long and a hundred and ten feet wide surrounded by concrete walls on the sides and metal locks on the ends. *Unique Fortune's* engine growled and belched smoke, which blotted the canopy of blue above us. The diesel fumes made it hard to breathe.

Our pilot, Jose Fuentes, a small man with slicked black hair, glanced around *Wa* and frowned, making no attempt to disguise his displeasure. He grimaced at the shoulder-length hair, scraggly beards, and unkempt clothing of our crewmen. When I gave him a cup of coffee, he seemed mollified, but when I told him we had no head—that I used a bucket but the men peed over the side—he clicked his teeth with annoyance. He refused all further offers of liquid.

"Twenty-six million gallons of water will pour into each of the three chambers in just seven minutes," Fuentes said. "Hold fast those lines at all times. Never let go," he told the line handlers. "If you do, the boat will smash into the concrete wall, and we all could die."

The men raised their eyebrows. Then they went back to joshing among themselves. Were they taking this seriously? It was too late to ask. I hoped carefree didn't also mean foolish and bonehead ignorant. I was feeling more and more tense.

Pete assigned Carl, built like a football lineman, to the starboard bowline and Paul, just as tall but chunky and vacant-looking, to the port. Richard, short and wiry, took the starboard sternline and Wayne, with a stubble of black beard and bristly eyebrows, handled the port. Besides these men and Fuentes, we had a crew member's girlfriend—Mary, sleek in a red tank top and skin-tight cutoffs—to help out in the cockpit. So anxious his voice rose in a bark, Pete took the tiller, listened to the pilot, and shouted to the four men to keep their lines taut.

The convex gates clanged shut, and water rushed in from the bottom of the chamber. The boat shook and her rigging clattered. We were in a boiling cauldron. The roar of it drowned our voices as the water climbed twenty-eight feet in seven minutes. My stomach tumbled.

As *Wa* rose, her lines slackened. It was the job of the line handlers to keep them taut, so they had to pull constantly, secure the slack around a cleat, and pull again.

I hunkered down next to the engine controls to shove *Wa* from neutral into forward or reverse if the need arose and glanced back and forth from bow to stern, watching the line handlers and Pete's hand signals. Pete looked from bow to stern to the pilot, who signaled directions to the line handlers to keep *Wa* straight. I shivered despite the heat.

After seven minutes, all was good, and we putted into the second chamber. Again the gates clanged shut. Everyone primed nervously for the onrush of water. It boiled in and *Wa*, shuddering, rose. When we'd nearly reached the top, the men on the foredeck relaxed. Paul turned, made a V for victory sign, and yelled, "Piece a cake."

As I craned my neck to keep my eye on Pete's hands, the sky began to revolve. "Forward!" Pete roared. I shoved the Yanmar into forward, and Pete jammed the tiller hard to port. *Wa* slewed drunkenly for the port wall. My heart pounded.

"Port bowline. Where's the port bowline?" yelled Fuentes.

"Sorry, man. I fucked up," shouted Paul, who held the loose bowline in his hands as if it were a piece of spaghetti. He gave it a mighty tug and wrapped it around the cleat.

Pete managed to bring *Wa* around ten feet from the port wall. He chugged us back behind *Unique Fortune* and turned the boat to face forward once again.

"Straighten those lines," Fuentes yelled. "Quick! You!" he said, pointing to Carl.

Richard and Wayne had had the wits to understand what was happening and untangled their lines when Pete turned the boat at the wall and again in the center of the chamber. Carl had let the roiling water rip the starboard bowline from his hands. A hundred feet of ½-inch nylon anchor line slithered to the bottom of the chamber. We had no spare.

Pete shoved the tiller into my hand, grabbed a knife, and raced to the mast. He cut the mainsheet at the jam cleat to create another starboard bowline and hurled one end of it to a worker on top of the chamber. The man stretched to reach it but missed. Pete caught the end of the rope just before it fell under the boat, coiled it, and heaved again. This time the man on top of the chamber caught it and fastened it to a cleat, and Pete handed the other end to Carl. Meanwhile, Paul and the line handlers at the stern strained to hold *Wa* in place as the inrushing water battered her. Fuentes looked as if he wanted to jump overboard.

The gates opened. By a miracle, we'd made it through the second chamber. Shaken, we powered into the last one. "That clown nearly smashed our boat to pieces," I hissed to Pete. He grimaced but didn't reply.

This time the men held fast to their lines. *Wa* completed her ascent of eighty-five feet and floated into Gatun Lake. *Unique Fortune*, motoring at probably fifteen knots, soon left us behind.

It took us seven hours to power nearly thirty miles across the lake, the Chagres River, and the Gaillard Cut. Following the buoys, *Wa* darted in and out among islands, which closed around us in jungle so dense and green I couldn't see beyond. The world was gray sky and water, green land, and deadly quiet. There was no wind; there was no sound except for the "puk puk" of the Yanmar.

I fixed sandwiches and coffee for everyone and set out fruit. Carl and Paul stretched like lizards on *Wa's* cabin top and slept. Wayne ambled forward, clung to the forestay, and stared at the gray water rippling away from the bow. I explained to agile Mary how to use the bucket.

Fuentes hunched in the cockpit, his back braced against the port bulkhead, and closed his eyes as if to shut out a nightmare. Pete and Richard tried to draw him into conversation, but he stayed silent as a rock. Crossing Gatun Lake, he never saw the *Hamburg Express*, a 943-foot container ship aground near buoy #68, listing badly, her deck tilted at a forty-degree angle. I wanted to shake him awake and point out we weren't the only ones who made mistakes.

We let Fuentes off at Gamboa and picked up a second pilot. By early evening we were ready to go down.

After *Wa* had descended through the Pedro Miguel Lock, the Canal Authority held us at Miraflores for three hours while the large commercial vessels passed us, and a ship the size of *Unique Fortune* arrived, so we could transit in tandem.

It began to rain. Soaked and tired, we couldn't rest. I couldn't cook supper, for we had to be ready to leave at any time. We waited. Just after midnight, we got the signal to descend through the Miraflores Locks and into the Pacific Ocean.

It was 2:30 a.m. by the time we reached our reserved spot at the Balboa Yacht Club. We'd been up and working for nearly twenty-four hours when I tumbled into the forepeak to sleep.

Acapulco
or
A Rolling Stone Gathers Moss

*1311 miles and 16 days Panama to Acapulco
under way 29 1/2 months*

I was weary beyond caring. The stress of bad weather, countless hours on the tiller, broken equipment, and no money weighed on me like a stone. The Great Adventure had turned into an endurance test: we still had thirty-four hundred miles to go, all upwind, from Panama to Los Angeles, and we had to push to get to Acapulco by early July, when Pete's mother planned to join us for the trip up the Mexican coast to California. I had envisioned the end of our trip as filled with excitement; instead, it was drudgery.

With hurricane season about to start, our lives turned as erratic as wind and weather. Coco glared at me through slitted eyes. He probably wondered when I was going to turn on the sun to dry his coat. When not on watch, we slept or rested. The engine clamored, so we had to yell to communicate. I might have shrugged off all of this if we were making good time, but for a whole afternoon I watched the island of Montuosa stubbornly stick to *Wa's* starboard beam.

The next afternoon, I wanted to go below out of the rain and let *Wa* drift in the ten-knot breeze. But Pete had sat out all morning in the rain, which shamed me into steering. I took the helm for a couple of hours, until seven, when Pete stepped in, saying he would wake me at midnight if it was raining but at ten if it was clear.

Guilt took the edge off my rest. *He'll steer five hours in the rain? I wouldn't do that for him. Why's he acting like a saint?* I didn't want him bearing the greater load without complaint, as if to demonstrate his love and protection. Because I couldn't feel anything.

The following day the bilge pump broke. After bailing at the rate of forty buckets every three hours on a rocking boat, Pete came up with a solution. He disconnected the saltwater intake that simultaneously fed the pump on the sink and cooled the engine. In its place he rigged a plastic bottle peppered with holes and placed it in the bilge, making sure it was filled with saltwater. He fed a clear plastic hose from this bottle to the pipe that led to the engine cooling system, creating a siphon.

There was one hitch. Water was going out faster than it was coming in, so instead of pumping water out we wound up pouring water into the bilge to make sure the engine cooling system continued to function.

In fact, problems began to multiply: The seacock regulating the flow of water into the bilge came off in my hand. The diesel jugs washed overboard. The genny washed overboard and was torn to shreds. The bushing on the engine's water cooling system wore away.

Then one night, sudden quiet woke me. "You need help?" I called to Pete, who was bending over the silent engine.

"Yeah. The water pump's not working."

Wishing this were just a bad dream, I crawled out of bed and joined him.

The pump was clogged with kitty litter and oily muck. Pete flushed it with water, then kerosene, and cut a new gasket out of a chart corner before reassembling it.

"Running bilge water through the exhaust system wasn't such a good idea," I said.

"Did you have a better one?" he shot back. Then as he turned to complete work on the engine, he dropped a one-inch bolt under it. "Son of a bitch!" He glared at me, as if I had made him drop it.

I peered down at the bolt. "Get another one."

"I don't *have* another one. Hold the flashlight for me."

I crouched in the port berth, holding on with one hand as *Wa* bucked in the swell, and pointed the flashlight down the crevice of the bilge below the engine. The space was just wide enough for his arm. Pete, in his foul-weather jumpsuit, rolled up the right sleeve, lay in the grease next to the engine, and stuck his arm into the bilge.

Wallowing in oil until he was black, he fished for the bolt for fifteen minutes. By then his arm had chafed and swollen so much that he no longer could reach under the engine beds.

"I can't get it, babe," he said. I thought he was going to cry.

"My arm's thinner than yours. Let's hope it's long enough."

I climbed naked into the muck and reached my hand down, stretching from the shoulder as I strained to reach the keel. Without that bolt, we couldn't start the engine. I didn't want to think how long it would take us to get to Acapulco under sail alone.

I stretched harder, and my fingers touched the keel. I groped in the slime, feeling for the bolt. Finally my thumb hit something that squirted away. I took a deep breath, spread my fingers, and shoved the bolt against the keel. I fished it out.

"You're my hero!" he cried. "Let me get you clean."

He scrubbed me down with a towel. Under different circumstances, that gesture would've turned me on, but we were both so grimy the rubbing was simply friendly.

As he put the engine back together, he tightened the nut responsible for the oil leak. The engine started. I dressed in my foul-weather gear, put on my harness, and took the watch in the rain. Pete slept on the starboard berth in his foul-weather gear because he was too dirty to get into bed.

The next day, I steered all morning while Pete scrubbed bilge, lockers, and cockpit of oil and oily footprints. He emptied some diesel from the tank into the ocean to bring the level below the leak point and thus keep fuel out of the bilge.

We powered into Acapulco Harbor a week later as the wind started to build. The next day, Tropical Storm Claudia roared ashore. I was shopping for groceries when it hit, so Pete was alone on *Wa*, anchored in the outer harbor. Her 44-pound Danforth, which had never failed us, fouled in other boats' anchors and chains and began to drag. So he had to cut loose the anchor and two-hundred feet of chain and head for the yacht club's private shelter.

Having hurried back to the harbor, I found Pete fighting to keep *Wa* off the concrete breakwater. As rain pelted and the wind tried to toss me into the sea, with pounding heart and helpless, I watched him struggle.

"Poor bastard. Hope he makes it in," one man said as he put out extra lines to secure his own power boat. Others nodded. No one made a move to help.

Huge combers crashed against the wall. Pete stood at the tiller and used both hands and his thighs to keep *Wa* off the wind. Finally he coaxed her into the inner harbor, headed for the inside of the breakwater, dropped the fifteen-pound Northhill stern anchor, and secured her to the wall with two lines. I stuffed my groceries into the dinghy and rowed out to her.

"What are we going to do about the Danforth?" I asked. "We can't leave here without it."

"I'll have to dive for it, once the storm's passed," he said grimly. "But first we've got to tell the yacht club we're here."

"They know. People on shore were wondering whether you'd make it in."

"Why didn't they help?"

We cleaned up the mess of wet sails and tangled lines on deck, went below to get dry, and waited for the rain to stop. The storm's muggy heat encased us like a cocoon.

When we went ashore, the obese, mustached yacht club manager said, "We expect you to leave as soon as Claudia has traveled on."

"We can't anchor in the outer harbor, on a lee shore, with only a fifteen-pound anchor," Pete argued. "We have to stay here until I've found our Danforth and chain."

"All right," the manager said. "Find it soon. Port fees are $4.64 a day."

Pete borrowed Scuba gear from a fellow yachtsman and found a dive shop outside town, where he filled the tank. I rowed him to the outer harbor, and we set up a grid in the area we'd anchored before the storm. We criss-crossed this grid, I rowing, Pete attached to the dinghy with a rope. I watched for his air bubbles and guided him forward by pulling on the rope, while he walked the ocean floor fifty feet down. Claudia had made the water so dirty that visibility was only six inches: he had to find the Danforth by feel. It was like searching for a dime in a ten-acre field.

Hour after weary hour, my spirits sank to rock bottom, while Pete slogged through mud on the bottom below me.

After two days of hunting and four trips to the dive shop for more air, he yanked on the rope, then splashed to the surface. "Found it!" he yelled, crawling into the dinghy and stripping off the Scuba gear. He began hauling on the rope like a man possessed. Muddy links of chain clanked against the Fiberglass of the dinghy and piled in the bottom. Finally the anchor, encrusted with debris, came clonking over the side.

We scurried to make *Wa* livable, for Susan was to fly in the following day. The worst mess was the kerosene stoves, which had crudded up from watery fuel purchased in Panama. We decided to buy butane replacements with what little money we had left. Pete scraped a quarter inch of soot from the bottoms of my pans when I balked at doing the job. I washed soot off the overhead and cabin walls. By the time *Wa*'s paint shone white again, we looked like chimney sweeps.

There still was enough diesel left in the bilge for it to wash over *Wa*'s floorboards and into the food lockers when the boat heeled.

Pete spent all Sunday morning racing to clean up the mess before Susan arrived.

We hadn't seen her in two years, but she was the same red-headed, freckled, willowy woman, who waved her arms like semaphores as she waited to go through customs at Acapulco International Airport.

Pete clutched her in a bear hug. I grabbed her from the other side. Then I pulled away, tears in my eyes.

"You don't know how glad I am to see you." Her voice caught, and she coughed, as if to choke back tears herself. "I thought I'd never see you again."

While Pete repaired the fuel tank and tightened the shaft log to keep seawater from leaking into the bilge, I took Susan to the native market, a huge building roofed with tin and open to the air. Carcasses of beef and pork, hanging from the rafters, buzzed with flies.

"How'd you like some beef stew?" I grinned, and she blanched.

"You don't really want to eat *that*?" she asked hopefully.

"Actually, I do. I haven't cooked fresh meat for nearly a month." Despite the flies, my mouth watered at the thought of a hearty stew with fresh carrots and potatoes.

She shuddered as the butcher hacked off a kilo of beef and wrapped it in paper. "I'll cook it thoroughly," I promised, "and we'll eat it right away."

When I served her meal, she ate only the bread.

Cabo San Lucas
or
To Doc or Not to Doc

*939 miles and 14 days Acapulco to Cabo San Lucas
under way 30 months*

The temperature in the cabin was more than 100°. Pete left the awning up, and we fled topside to escape the heat. Susan sagged like a wilted sunflower in a corner of the cockpit and slugged down lukewarm sodas. Fortunately, the wind came up. Pete took down the awning and raised main and jib.

The following night I picked up the Roca Negra light off the Mexican town of Zihuatanejo. Pete and Susan awoke to the flutter of wind in the sails and the cries of birds covering the sea like a comforter.

Zihuatanejo was jammed with tourists. We spent the morning running errands, then took a *siesta*. Susan cleaned soot from the stove bracket.

"Bless you," I said, hugging her. It was a task I hated. "You're the best of all possible mothers-in-law."

"I've got to do something to earn my keep." She stood her share of watches despite the drudgery of sailing upwind, and her arms were building those muscles peculiar to steering. She loved the sunsets, wind on her face, porpoises feeding with the little fish jumping just ahead and the birds crying down. She loved coming into strange places where anything might happen. She was sharing our dream.

At last I was getting excited. The worst of the upwind sailing was over, I thought, and we only had about two thousand miles to go.

As we slogged northward, Pete tried to figure out whether he wanted to be a doctor or a lawyer. In truth, he didn't want to be either but felt compelled by family history to be a "professional." His endless *angst* irritated me. He'd been a very good journalist—why not stick with it? But four years of law school seemed the lesser of two evils. The thought of supporting him through more undergraduate work, four years of med school, internship, and residency filled *me* with *angst*.

Just as my father had counseled him in Barbados, his mother advised him while we sailed.

"You got D's in P chem and physics," she said. "They'll average those grades in, even if you retake the courses."

"You sure?"

"I'm positive. I deal with this stuff every year. Even the mid-grade med schools want a 3.5 average or better."

He sighed. "I'm nowhere near that except in the lit classes."

"Medical schools don't care about lit classes. They care only about science."

He sat for a long while, his head bent, as if studying his hands. Finally he said, "OK. I guess that settles it. I'll be a lawyer."

Thank God, I thought.

Because the Baja California coast was unlit, we stayed well off, sailing more than twenty miles north, then running back south to Cabo San Lucas after dawn. The barren land was starkly beautiful and the air blindingly clear. The brown hills, jutting like moonscape, made me homesick for Steinbeck's rugged mountains near Monterey.

Although we were in the tropics, the water was cold. Taking a bath, I dumped a bucket of water over my head and let out a yelp.

Pete laughed. "It must be the California Current," he said.

Almost California, I thought. *Getting close.*

Anchored off San Lucas, we discussed what we *ought* to be doing, then rowed ashore for a swim and lunch, returning to the boat for a *siesta*. It wasn't until eight o'clock that we turned on the radio for a weather forecast. Hurricane Emily, which hadn't existed even as a tropical storm the day before, was at 104° W and 15° N traveling WNW at eleven knots: less than five hundred miles south and three hundred miles east of us.

"Damn! How could that happen so fast?" Pete asked.

"Now what do we do?" I asked. "The wind's blowing straight onshore. We *can't* be caught here in a hurricane. We'll wind up as kindling on the beach."

"But I've got money waiting at the bank," Susan said, "and we're low on food."

"We need diesel and water," Pete said.

We decided to stay anchored off San Lucas until morning, taking our chances with Hurricane Emily, rather than leaving port without food, fuel, money, and water. The only anchorages between Cabo San Lucas and San Diego might not have food and fuel, and we couldn't buy them, anyway, without Susan's money. After dinner, we listened to another weather broadcast and went to bed. I dreaded the morning.

Up at 6:30, we caught the next weather report. Emily was closing in.

The surf broke straight down on the beach in ten to twelve-foot waves that pounded like a rock band. Still, the two of us climbed into the dinghy, Pete rowing, while I counted the wave periods anxiously and watched for the lull. As we got closer to the beach, the dinghy began rolling over the waves, shaking as she went, like a spooked horse. There was only this unstable platform to keep us from being tumbled into the surf.

Pete headed for the far side of the hotel, where there was some protection from the weather. Water thundered to the beach, sucking up yellow sand and churning it like a giant electric mixer.

"How're we going to get in without flipping the dinghy?" I asked.

"Haul ass." He sat on the oars waiting for a lull and then rowed with fury. We dragged the dinghy up the beach just as the next wave broke on its stern.

We hustled first to the gas station for diesel. I went to the market for food while he went to the bank. Fortunately, Susan's money had arrived, and she'd put it in Pete's name. We returned to the dinghy within an hour.

Pete studied the surf. "We can't stand the weight of the water jugs if we fill them. We'll get swamped or pitchpole."

"Let's hope we can get water at Magdalena Bay," I said.

He grunted in assent and left the empty jugs in the dinghy. Neither of us was willing to admit how nervous we were. *We've come this far,* I thought, *and we're less than twelve hundred miles from home. We've got to make it.*

"I'm going to push you out during the next lull," he said. "Row as fast as you can. I'll swim until you're past the surf line. Don't wait for me."

Adrenaline rushed to my fingertips. I helped Pete drag the dinghy to the water and climbed in. "Now!" he shouted, "Row!"

I rammed the dinghy through the surf and rose at a forty-five-degree angle over the next wave. My body shook and my heart pounded. What if we lost the diesel, the food, and the money? Pete dived through that wave, bobbed to the surface, swam to the dinghy, and clambered in. I gave him a thumbs up.

"We're not through yet," he said. "We still have to get *Wa* out of this harbor."

Rowing back was harder because the wind had increased and we were now fighting the incoming waves rather than flowing with them. Pete crawled amidships and took over rowing, and I scooted into the stern. The dinghy was bobbing up and down like a seesaw.

As we approached *Wa,* Pete said, "I'll come up on the lee side to give you some protection, but you'll have to be fast."

When the dinghy rose on the next wave, I clutched the shrouds, hoisted myself aboard, and grabbed the dinghy while Pete climbed aboard.

Susan clung to the cabin top. "I didn't think you'd make it," she croaked as Pete and I lifted the dinghy out of the water and secured it.

"Let's look sharp," Pete said. "We're too close to shore to get off the anchor here. If the engine fails, the wind'll drive us onto the beach before I can get sail up."

Susan started to tremble. "What're you going to do?"

"I'll dive for the anchor and move it offshore."

"What do you mean?" she asked in a whisper.

"I'll pick up the anchor and carry it." He turned away and began putting on his mask and flippers. I knew he didn't want to explain any further. The wind already was blowing thirty knots, and we had to go straight into it to get out of the harbor.

I started the engine.

"I may have to do this more than once," he said. "Watch for my hand signals. Thumbs up means we're ready to go. Thumbs down, I have to move the anchor again."

I stood on the starboard cockpit cushion, backing *Wa* and watching Pete on the ocean floor as he walked toward me with the anchor. He carried the 44-pound Danforth seaward and reset it three times, each time in deeper water, until he was satisfied we could make it out the bay.

Although the morning had seemed like an eternity, we escaped the anchorage by 10:30.

With a Force 6 wind on the nose and the seas building, Pete, on the tiller, was doused with a bucket's worth of water by every wave. He turned west and north up the Mexican coast.

"We shouldn't be sailing in this," Susan shrieked. "We've got to get away from that storm." She held up her hands, pleading, her mouth in an O of panic, as she climbed the companionway to make her point.

"Emily will turn toward Hawaii when she hits San Lucas, Mom," Pete yelled as another bucket's worth of water drenched him. "Not to worry."

Susan, doused with spray, ducked back into the cabin and turned to me. "What if Emily keeps on going up Baja? We'll be trapped." She was terrified.

I climbed the companionway and hung on to the cabin top. "Turn around and head for La Paz," I told Pete. "Susan's scared to death."

He set his jaw and dodged another bucket of water. "We'll lose a day sailing in the wrong direction."

"You want her to have a heart attack? Turn around!" I climbed into the cockpit, grabbed the jib sheet, and started to uncoil it from the cleat.

"Jibe ho! Pete yelled, and headed east for the Sea of Cortez and out of the storm's path.

Magdalena Bay and Turtle Bay
or
Flat as a Pancake

*559 miles and 9 days Cabo San Lucas to Turtle Bay
under way 31 months*

With the wind behind us, Susan cheered up and offered to steer. We sailed toward La Paz until nearly midnight, then hove to until four o'clock. Emily had moved well to the west. Dawn came murky, with an oily swell, as we headed west again.

A day and a half after leaving, we passed San Lucas. Then as we turned once more up the coast of Mexico for Magdalena Bay, fog closed in on us for the first time in two and a half years at sea.

At sunrise the next day, the fog lifted enough that I saw dim outlines of land to the north and east. Susan took the tiller while I cooked breakfast.

When I came topside with her eggs, I checked the compass. "Why are you steering south of west?" I asked.

"I'm heading for land—over there." I cocked my head. She looked puzzled.

"Here's your breakfast. I'll take her while you eat." I took the tiller and brought *Wa* back on course, going north, glad breakfast hadn't taken long to cook. Susan had mistaken clouds for land and steered for them instead of watching the compass. *She must be more tired than I realized,* I thought, and made a mental note to watch her for further signs of fatigue.

Although visibility was poor, the Baja coast gave us an animal show. Porpoises dived, and pelicans and turtles sat on the water. A school of red-orange blobs—prawns—hung lurid in the green-black sea.

In early afternoon we began powering through the serpentine entrance to Rehusa Channel, which was marked sporadically by buoys and sticks.

Pete handed me the tiller, got out the tequila, settled himself in a corner of the cockpit, and began drinking from the bottle. Nervously I peered over the side into the murky water. By the time I'd figured out that light green water meant too shallow, I felt *Wa* jolt to a stop. I'd run aground. Fortunately, the bottom was sand. He handed Susan the bottle, leapt overboard, pushed *Wa* off, and shinnied back aboard.

"Those buoys and sticks are useless," I complained. "Maybe they once marked the channel, but not anymore with the sand moving constantly."

"Not a problem," he said, taking the bottle back. He gulped and belched. "Sand won't hurt *Wa*."

Still, feeling like a screw-up this late in the game hurt my sailor's pride. I turned away and tried to make sense of the buoys, which seemed randomly scattered by some trickster. I hit sand again.

Pete cheerfully leapt over the side, pushed us off, and bellied back aboard. This time he danced around the deck, pirouetting as if he were in "Waltz of the Flowers."

"You've had enough tequila," I said. "I need your help."

"You're doing just fine." He grinned and began flapping his arms like a cock greeting the morning.

Susan smiled as if nothing were wrong. Pete was still the adorable little boy she had once had all to herself.

"That's it," I said. "If you're not going to help out here . . ." I handed the tiller to Susan. "I'm going to climb the mast. From there I'll be able to see the shallow patches and the channel."

"You can't do that," Pete mocked. "You're afraid to climb the mast."

"Just watch me," I told him, then to Susan I demonstrated hand gestures: "If I do this, go left. If I do this, go right."

"Are you sure?" Susan asked. "That's a long way up."

"Susan, this is nothing compared with what I've been through." I was convincing myself as well as her.

Shoving down my fear of heights by taking a deep breath and holding it, I marched to the mast, grabbed the main halyard, and began pulling myself up, clutching the mast with my bare feet and walking my toes up the aluminum like a monkey. The metal was strangely warm. I remembered Pete's doing this two and a half years before on the way to the Marquesas and how afraid I had been for him. Now, I didn't give a damn.

When I got to the spreaders, I used them as a hand-hold and wrapped my legs around the mast. I was surprised at how secure I felt up there. The water was a murky green, but the shallow places were clearly visible as patches of brown. While Pete sucked on the bottle, I guided Susan the last mile or so into Magdalena Bay without running aground again.

In mid-afternoon we anchored off the wharf at Puerto Magdalena. For a change, the estimate of the population in the *Sailing Directions* seemed correct; there couldn't have been more than fifty people in the village. There was no chance of getting water, for the Mexicans brought it in in 44-gallon drums from Puerto San Carlos.

Magdalena was in Baja's *zona seca* (dry zone) and sold no alcohol. Pete bartered some booze for enough manta ray meat to give us a splendid dinner. The Mexican fisherman, who called it a devilfish, cut it into cubes as if scooping balls out of a cantaloupe. Cooked in butter, it looked and tasted like scallops.

The next morning, a school of *langostinas*, or the red-orange prawns we'd seen off the coast, swam by. Susan captured them in a bucket and dumped them in the cockpit. As the water drained away, she popped the *langostinas* into the colander, then she and I shelled them for supper.

Outside the bay, the wind was blowing twenty knots on the nose and kicking up a short, choppy sea in the shoal water. Susan found moving about difficult, and with the violence of *Wa's* motion, she was frightened again. To make matters worse, the air and the sea had turned colder. Each time the spray stung my skin, it was icy. Susan retreated below, and Pete and I took sitting watches, leaving *Wa* to self-steer under double-reefed main and jib.

Still jittery from escaping Hurricane Emily, and tired from having to hang onto something whenever she made a move, Susan studied the chart for anchorages. "How about this—Turtle Bay, or San Bartolome?" she asked, eyes pleading. The freckles seemed to pop off her nose.

Pete glanced at the chart. "I thought we were going to stop at Cedros."

"But this is closer," she wheedled. "It looks to be a pretty good-sized port, with fresh food and water. We're low on water, and we might be able to pick up some scotch." Clever mother.

"I don't know," Pete said. "We need to keep on going. Remember, law school starts at the end of August." It was August 3.

That night, the stove sputtered and died as I cooked dinner. We'd run out of butane. I threw out the watery rice and served lukewarm chicken *cacciatore* as a single course.

"That's it," I announced. "If you want to go all the way to San Diego without coffee, that's up to you. I'd rather swim ashore."

Pete raised his eyebrows. "That's a bit extreme, isn't it?"

"You're grumpy enough even *with* coffee," I said. He stared at me over the tip of his nose. "And I just might bite your head off."

"OK." He shrugged. "We'll go to Turtle Bay."

Susan and I cheered.

I was so cold and tired I spent most of my watch in the cabin, huddling to keep warm, fighting sleep. Pete did the same during his late watch. We let *Wa* self-steer as the wind dropped rather than turning on the power and taking the helm. That cost us ten to fifteen precious miles under easy conditions. Those ten to fifteen miles, it turned out, made the difference between reaching Turtle Bay or sitting out another night.

In the morning, our need for coffee was acute. Pete improvised a cooker out of a bucket, rice, and alcohol, setting the rice on fire to heat water for coffee. We ate cold food during the day, and I heated a large can of beans in the bucket for supper.

Then an engine bushing, which kept two moving parts from rubbing together, fell to pieces. Pete found copper tubing to replace it and laboriously filed the metal by hand to make it fit. Susan and I steered.

"This won't last very long," he said. "If I can't find copper or bronze tubing in Turtle Bay, I'll have to cannibalize metal from the stove bracket."

Because of the failed bushing, the engine leaked black smoke into the cabin, coating the three of us and Coco with a film of greasy gray. Every bit of white paint in the cabin turned gray. We smelled of diesel fuel.

Instead of the joy I'd hoped to feel at completing our trip, I was burnt out, my mind a jumble of resentment. *How much longer will we have to put up with this crap? How much more can we take before everything falls apart, including us?*

At first light, I headed for Turtle Bay and Port San Bartolome. We anchored under sail a little after noon in front of the fishing village's cannery.

We rowed ashore to a harsh, brown, desolate landscape without trees, bushes, or grass. There we met 11-year-old Marisa Gerardo, a slip of a girl, all long black hair and gangly legs. Her older sister, Dolores, had begun to mature into womanhood and was much rounder.

"Come to our house," Marisa invited in Spanish. I felt everything inside me relax, and I gave her a big smile. This was like being back in Polynesia and Micronesia.

We left the white sand beach, Pete and I barefooted as usual, Susan in sneakers, and trekked along the dirt road through town. The houses were mostly adobe clay and needed repair.

At the Gerardos' we met mama—Guadalupe—a dark, flat-cheeked, buxom woman very pregnant and surrounded by children.

"*¿Cuantos niños tiene usted?*" I asked her.

"*Doce.*" She beamed. Twelve children! She didn't look any older than I. The house had two bedrooms, and I could see the entryway/living room doubled as a bedroom at night, for there was a fold-up bed in the corner behind the door.

Trekking through the village, I'd noticed a poster advertising the Tarzan film playing at the local theater. "Do you like the movies?" I asked in Spanish. The girls giggled, and their brother yodeled like Tarzan. I took that as a yes. "So you'll go tonight?"

The girls stopped giggling, and their brother frowned. "I don't have money to send them to the movies," Guadalupe said in Spanish.

Pete pulled a fifty *peso* note from his pocket. "*Por favor,*" he said, handing it to Guadalupe, "enjoy the movie, and give me the change if there is any." The children whooped, and the dark skin of Guadalupe's face reddened as she showed a mouthful of white teeth.

When she asked if we would go with them, I said, "*Gracias*, but we are tired."

The next morning, five of the Gerardo kids hitched a ride on a fishing boat's skiff and climbed aboard *Wa*. "How was the movie?" I asked.

"Terrific!" they bubbled, "*gracias.*" I passed out chewing gum; they went through an entire box. I told them about the boat, although my Spanish didn't stretch to words like "compass," "tiller," and "sextant." I played the guitar. We sang and talked.

Finally I said, "We have to go ashore to get fuel," meaning I'd row them to the beach. Susan and I and the five children crammed into the dinghy with a five-gallon jug. Fortunately, the children were small, and I managed to get us ashore without swamping or sinking the dinghy.

When we stopped by the Gerardos' house to ask where to buy diesel, Guadalupe ushered us into the kitchen and rattled off a torrent of Spanish. Two of the kids vanished and returned with folding chairs. "You sit, please, and I will serve you lunch," she said.

Rolling up her sleeves, Guadalupe mixed flour, pork fat, and water to make tortillas. As Señora Gerardo began patting the dough into rounds, Susan stood and asked, "Please, let me help you."

Guadalupe shrugged. "You have to make them very thin." She took a ball of dough, flattened it between her palms, and patted it back and forth, each time making the round bigger and thinner. When it was the size of a dinner plate and no thicker than a piece of thin cardboard, she tossed it in hot fat. It sizzled, drops of fat jumped from the frying pan, and the kitchen filled with the scent of hot lard. By the time the tortilla was cooked, she had another ready for the pan.

I remembered making bread with Mrs. Saua at Tongareva more than two years before and suddenly felt a deeper connection with Guadalupe, and women the world over. We had this common bond of baking bread, preparing food. Unable to sit and watch, I also volunteered.

Susan's first tortilla was square on one end and oblong at the other and had holes in it. Mine wasn't much better. Dolores, the oldest daughter, laughed.

Guadalupe quickly cleared a place for Susan and me at the table and served us big chunks of fresh fried pork and tortillas. I think she was trying to keep us from helping as much as she was being polite by serving the guests first.

As we ate, the children wandered in and out of the kitchen grabbing hunks of meat and tortillas from the platter of food already cooked. One little fellow, a boy of three or four (his sisters weren't sure), wanted to eat from my plate, so I sat him in my lap and cut small pieces of pork for him. As he snuggled in to me, his small body soft and warm against mine, I imagined that he was my own child.

Guadalupe gave a good third of the meat to Susan and me. She said she used a ten-kilo sack of flour every seven days. I remembered all the Third World countries we'd visited, how poor most of their people had been but how willing to share what little they had, and I was filled with gratitude. Then, with a start, I realized this was my last stop in the Third World. Our next port would be San Diego, California, to clear customs. How long would it be before I had another adventure like this one? Ever? The prospect made me sad.

Completing the Circle
or
Fuming Over Diesel

657 miles and 11 days Turtle Bay to Los Angeles
under way 31 1/2 months

Law school would start in eighteen days. Going upwind, it would take us the better part of two weeks to reach Santa Barbara. We were cutting it close.

Pete and I plotted our course to sail as far north of west as *Wa* could manage, knowing that the farther out to sea we went, the more wind we'd have, and we'd make better time. If we hugged the coast, we'd be at the mercy of fickle land breezes and in constant danger of hitting a reef.

The farther from land and the higher the seas, however, the more apprehensive Susan became. "You're going out to sea. We should be going north," she complained.

"We're going northwest," Pete told her. "Sailing on the starboard tack, we're almost on course for San Diego. If we switched to the port tack, we'd be going almost due east." He pointed a finger at Punta Falsa on the chart and Cedros Island north of it. "I don't want to sail near Cedros after dark. Too many dangers, none of them lit."

She didn't argue, but her jaw was tight, and the knots at her temples worked.

I made a sweet and sour lunch from the Turtle Bay co-op's frozen chicken. The lunch was a success, but afterwards Susan asked again to "head north."

Pete and I glanced at each other. She was as frightened as she'd been off Cabo San Lucas, but for no reason. Well, fear is not logical. I raised my eyebrows and sighed. "We'd better do it," I said.

When Pete came about onto the port tack, we were nearly ninety degrees off our course. He exploded, "We're sailing perpendicular to where we want to go!"

"But we'll be nearer to land and safer," she responded.

Pete handed me the tiller, stripped off his safety harness, threw it in the cockpit, and stomped below.

"I didn't mean to upset him," she said. "It's really the best thing to do." Somehow she was turning her discomfort into a criticism of our seamanship.

"We're nearly ninety degrees off our course," I said. "On the starboard tack, we were fifteen to thirty degrees off." She shrugged.

This anxious, manipulative side to Susan was something new. I had no idea how to deal with it. Sadly, I realized there was no such thing as the perfect mother or mother-in-law. My former ideal parent now was using her lack of experience, and her fear, to take control of *Wa*.

Pete recovered, but I brooded. As the day wore on, I got angrier. Every chance I got I pointed out how much time we were losing and how much longer we'd be at sea.

As we got closer to land, the wind dropped. Pete turned on the engine, and the cabin again filled with diesel stench. He spent most of the next day filing engine bushings from copper tubing. The thin, soft metal didn't last long, and he had to replace the bushing more than a dozen times. Susan steered. I got down on hands and knees on the cabin floor and repaired the bilge pump hose.

Listening to the scritch scritching of the file on copper and "puk puk" of the Yanmar engine and constantly smelling diesel kept me angry at her stubborn fear, especially knowing that we would've been able to sail, not power, if we hadn't been hugging the coast. But I kept my mouth shut. This dreary ending to the Great Adventure couldn't last much longer.

As Pete worked on the copper tubing, he kept dropping the file or the pliers in the bilge. Because I was closer to the bilge and my arms were thinner, I was elected to muck in the grease to retrieve the tools.

"Can't you be more careful?" I screamed. Was he taking out his frustration with Susan on me? Was I screaming at her through him?

Serene now that we were headed toward land, Susan offered to cook supper.

A dozen Styrofoam cups and a pillow, complete with barnacles, floated by. Later on we passed a hunk of Styrofoam, which Pete retrieved to help clean *Wa's* oil-grungy bottom. Now and then she ran through a hunk of kelp; her engine gurgled momentarily but chugged faithfully on.

On August 15, *Wa* sailed proudly into San Diego Harbor. Two customs officers, in immaculate white uniforms, came aboard. Both wrinkled their noses at the smell.

"What's wrong with your engine?" one asked.

"A bad bushing," Pete replied.

He sniffed. "I'm surprised you made it at all. Where'd you say you came from—Turtle Bay? That's a long way."

Susan and I glanced at each other and smiled. If he only knew. Both officers peeked below and spotted Coco.

"You have a cat?" the other asked. "Didn't he try to jump ship to get away from the smell of diesel?"

"No," I said drily. "That was the least of his problems."

The two officers declined to sit on our oily cockpit cushions, sodden with seawater. When I offered to put down towels (also greasy with diesel), they shook their heads.

"I sit all day long," the first officer drawled. "Standing will do me good."

They checked off items on their clipboards and seemed eager to get away. Thanks to their fastidiousness, we could've smuggled in five hundred pounds of cocaine, hidden in greasy sail bags. *That would've solved our money problems,* I thought wryly, *or created a whole new set of problems I don't even want to think about.*

We'd arranged to meet my aunt—my father's sister—and her husband, who'd retired to La Jolla after a career in the U.S. Navy. I looked forward with some trepidation to this meeting. Uncle Joel was a retired admiral. If the customs officers had been offended by *Wa*'s lack of spit and polish, what would Joel think? There was nothing I could do. We were what we were, and we had almost completed a circumnavigation in a yacht smaller than most Navy tenders.

Fortunately, our accomplishment seemed to impress Joel, and he overlooked our failings. "That's a small boat to sail around the world," he said. "Congratulations!"

Aunt Adeline grabbed me in a bear hug, then, sniffing my diesel stench, pulled back. "It's wonderful to see you. Welcome home. Now let's get you to a hot shower," she added. I guess I didn't have to tell her we hadn't showered since we'd left Acapulco nearly six weeks before.

We left the next day for Marina del Rey. Susan slipped away to take the bus to San Pedro.

"It wouldn't be right for me to be on board when you complete your circumnavigation," she'd said. "I didn't make the entire trip with you, and I don't deserve the credit."

This graciousness restored her to her pedestal, even if it was a bit wobbly. Pete and I needed time to gather ourselves together before our lives, once again, changed forever.

The coast teemed with shipping and floating debris, but the

sail north from San Diego to Marina del Rey was otherwise anticlimactic. In the afternoon the northwest wind beat on *Wa* and kicked up a short, choppy sea, forcing us to take long tacks toward Catalina Island, then back toward the mainland.

As the day died, so did the wind. Dusk brought a million lights onshore that glittered in the heavy, cool air. Tankers and freighters, like Christmas trees, passed, and a dozen navigation lights and buoys winked and bellowed mournfully. Even in the depths of the night, when the land breeze came up gently behind *Wa*, giving her a boost forward, there was noise: airplanes taking off and landing, the thump thump of a freighter's diesel engines, the white noise of a million cars on the freeways of Los Angeles. I mourned the loss of quiet and darkness. When again would the world be contained in the whoosh of waves, the fluttering of sails, and the squeak of porpoises?

Pete was silent, buried in himself. I think if we'd had the money, he would've turned *Wa* southwest and headed back for the Pacific islands, where life had been fresh, exciting, and wonderful. I would have. We were about to give up the Great Adventure for the ordinary, the boring. No matter whatever else I'd been at sea, I had *never* been bored. For every hour of being cold and wet, of fighting sea and wind, there had been an hour of delight—a triple rainbow, porpoises chuffing alongside, Coco leaping to catch fish on the fly, and people who opened their homes and their hearts.

I ached at the thought of leaving this behind. Yet we were part of a culture—we'd carried it all the way around the world with us—which demanded that we "settle down," become "good citizens," and live like "normal people."

My father had applied the most pressure. "You're too old to play," he told Pete. "It's way past time for you to start your career and begin supporting Addie." The bottom line for Dad was grandchildren. He believed I couldn't work and have kids too.

Pete called Susan on the ship-to-shore radio the morning of August 17 to say we'd be in Marina del Rey shortly after noon. When we arrived, Pete's family, including Susan, his sister Deb and husband Cliff, sister Susie, and niece Kris jumped up and down on the dock and blew horns to greet us.

Suddenly we were no longer Don Quixote and Sancho Panza but Frodo and Sam throwing the ring into the Cracks of Doom and saving the world from Sauron. Pete and I were heroes—not something I had consciously set out to become, but something I had achieved through courage, hard work, and endurance. And I realized that it wasn't just wind and sea that had challenged me but my own inadequacies, which I had to overcome in order to succeed.

"I thought I'd never see you again," Deb said tearfully. "I thought you'd drown."

"Thanks for the vote of confidence," Pete said.

"Well, it's just that your boat is so small," said Deb, her face now streaming tears. "I had no confidence in *Wa*."

"She was tougher than us both," I said.

The P-28 never was meant to sail around the world. She was a light-weight racing-cruising boat designed to explore the coastal waters of Sweden, not the open oceans of the world, but she never failed us. She had given me strength and the ability to stand on my own and believe in myself. More than once, she saved my life. I wanted to hold her in my arms as I held her in my heart.

My marriage lasted four more years. Addie was born in 1975 and Peter in 1976. Pete left at the end of 1977 to follow his new Great Adventure.

Glossary

Sailing Nouns
backstay: a wire going from the top of the mast to the stern
bare poles: under way with no sail up
beam: middle or width of the boat; wind perpendicular to the boat
below: cabin of the boat
bilge: the lowest compartment in the boat, where the sides meet at the keel
block: disk through which line runs
boom: attached to the mast, the bottom support for the mainsail
boot-topping: a stripe between keel and topsides at the waterline
bosun's chair: legless chair used to support someone ascending a mast
bow: front of the boat (forward or fore)
bulkhead: supporting wall to give the cabin strength
by the lee: too far off the wind
cabin: living area of a boat
cabin sole: the floor of the cabin
chart: nautical map
cleat: bracket to which lines are attached
clew: lower, after edge of a sail
cockpit: area amidships from which the boat is run
companionway: ladder from the cockpit to the cabin
dinghy: a shore boat
dodgers: screens, usually made of canvas, protecting the cockpit
fantail: aft part of the boat between cockpit and stern
fetch: movement of water across an open space
Float Coat: a waterproof jacket with a foam lining for flotation
flying jibe: uncontrolled movement of the boom across the boat
foredeck: the deck forward of the mast
forepeak: the forward V-shaped berth
forestay: a wire going from the top of the mast to the bow
garboard strake: wood separating topsides from ballast keel

genoa (genny): a large foresail, usually fully cut, for lighter winds
gimbals: suspension device to keep a stove level
halyard: rope to raise and lower a sail
hatch: an entry to the cabin, and its cover
head: toilet
helm: a boat's steering mechanism
hull: body of the boat
hull speed: theoretical maximum speed of a long-keeled yacht (square of the boat's waterline length times 1.4)
jib: a small foresail, flatly cut, used in heavier winds
jumpers: upper supports perpendicular to the mast holding out the stays
keel: heavy, underwater part of a single-hulled boat
ketch: a two-masted sailboat with the aft mast forward of the tiller or wheel
knees: supports for a dinghy seat
knot: nautical mile, slightly longer than an English mile
lazarette: a locker aft of the cockpit
leach: after edge of a sail
lifeline: a strip of wire along the railing used for safety
line: a rope
marks: a boat's intended waterline
painter: a rope attaching the dinghy to the boat
pulpit: a metal enclosure around the bow
rigging: stays and shrouds that hold up a boat's mast(s)
rudder: underwater device, attached to the tiller, to steer the boat
scuppers: holes in the railing to allow water to escape
seacock: opening in boat's hull to allow saltwater in or out
sheet: rope controlling the set of a sail; to pull in that rope
shrouds: wires going from the mast to the boat's beam
slack water: change of tide
sole: floor of the cabin
spinnaker: huge sail, in front of the boat, for going downwind
spreaders: lower mast supports holding out the shrouds
stanchion: a pole attached to the deck to secure the lifelines
stays: wires going from the mast to the boat's bow and stern

stem: front of the boat; foundation of a dinghy running the length of the boat

step: an apparatus used to attach the mast to the boat

stern: rear of the boat (aft)

stringers: crosspieces used to support the structure of the boat

taffrail: rail around the stern

tiller: long stick attached to the rudder and used to steer

topping lift: a line from the mast to the end of the boom, securing it

topsides: the sides of a boat from deck to waterline

trimaran: a vessel with three hulls and no heavy keel

turnbuckle: a (usually) metal fastener holding a stay to the deck

vane: a "wing" to catch the wind and steer the boat

whisker pole: used to hold a foresail in front of the boat

Sailing Verbs

broach: to veer into the wind and risk capsizing

come about: switch from one tack upwind to the other

draw: referring to the boat's underwater depth

fall off: head away from the wind

gunkhole: to island hop from day to day

harden up: sail closer to the wind

haul: lift the boat from the water using a crane

heave to: to lash the tiller to leeward with the sails backwinded. This steadies the boat but allows it to make little way.

heel: tilt; angle at which the boat tilts, usually going upwind

jibe: work the boat downwind

kedge: move a boat by resetting its anchor and pulling the boat to the anchor

lay: sail from one point to another without tacking

luff: take the boat too close to the wind, so that her sails shiver

reach: sailing with the wind hitting the middle of the boat

reef: shorten the size of a sail, usually the main, in heavy weather

skull: sweep an oar back and forth, usually from the stern of the boat tack: work the boat upwind; lower, forward corner of a fore-and-aft sail

Miscellaneous Terms
aft: end of the boat

atoll: island composed of islets encircling a lagoon

gaff-rigged: a boat with at least one four-cornered, rather than triangular, sail

lee: side away from the wind; lee shore: wind blowing onto the shore

port: the left side of a vessel

reef: a barrier of rock or coral around an island

starboard: the right side of a vessel

weather: side facing the wind; going toward the wind

wing-and-wing: setting sails, one on each side, perpendicular to the boat

Memoir from Fuze Publishing

The Gift of El Tio
by Larry Buchanan and Karen Gans
When world-renowned geologist discovers an enormous deposit of silver beneath a remote Quechua village in Bolivia, he unknowingly fulfills a 450-year-old prophecy that promised a life of wealth for the villagers.

Nobody Knows the Spanish I Speak
by Mark Saunders
High-tech couple from Portland, Oregon, emigrates with large dog and ornery cat to San Miguel de Allende, in the middle of Mexico. Their well-intentioned cluelessness makes for mayhem and non-stop laughs.

Entering the Blue Stone by Molly Best Tinsley
The General battles Parkinson's; his wife manifests a bizarre dementia. Their grown children embrace what seems a solution--an upscale retirement community. Between laughter and dismay, discover what shines beneath catastrophe: family bonds, the dignity of even an unsound mind, and the endurance of the heart.

Fiction from Fuze Publishing

Satan's Chamber
by Karetta Hubbard and Molly Best Tinsley

Her father was a crack CIA operative who vanished from the streets of Khartoum, Sudan. Victoria Pierce joins the Agency to learn why. From the minute she's posted to this rogue state, nothing is what it seems. Spy thriller.

The Mother Daughter Show by Natalie Wexler

At a D.C. prep school so elite its parent body includes the President and First Lady—three mothers have thrown themselves into organizing the annual musical revue. Will its Machiavellian intrigue somehow enable them to reconnect with their graduating daughters, who are fast spinning out of control?

Black Wings by Kathleen Jabs

Lieutenant Bridget Donovan battles Navy hierarchy to find the truth behind the tragic plane crash of one of the Navy's first female combat pilots, Audrey Richards, Bridget's Academy roommate. Bridget's life is at stake when she uncovers the warped code of honor behind a secret Academy group. Mystery.

Cologne by Sarah Pleydell

London, 1960. Renate von Hasselmann, an au pair escaping postwar Germany, takes charge of precocious Caroline and Maggie Whitaker. The girls' debonair father disarms the young woman with his quicksilver charm, childhood collides with history, and the traumas of war are visited upon the children of the peace.

More Fuze Fiction on the next page.

Fiction from Fuze Publishing

Leaving Tuscaloosa by Walter Bennett
1962. Racial turmoil in the deep South engulfs two estranged boyhood friends, one black and one white. Veering from the heat of erotic passion to the spreading fires of racial violence, their paths converge in a moving, shocking climax.

Pepperoni Palm Tree
by Aidan Patrick Meath and Jason Killian Meath

A story about the only tree of its kind in the world and a boy named Frederick, the story portrays the challenge of being true to oneself and celebrates the uniqueness that enables each of us to shine, and thus enlighten the world. Children's Fiction.

Learn more at www.fuzepublishing.com.